For Evernaissant Christine James Mc Sween's Biography

Author: Christine Mc Sween
Revised and corrected by: Asiatis.ca
ISBN: 978-2-9814450-0-1
Illustrated by: Marcel Mallette

Preface: page 1 to 14
Chapter one
Sacred memories: page 14 to 47
Chapter two
The event: page 47 to 65
Chapter tree
The dream of a royal member's departure :
page 65 to 80
Chapter four
Departure and new encounters: page 80 to 91
Chapter five
Visitors: page 91 to 128
Chapter six
Love destroyed by a war: page 128 to 161
Chapter seven
Murder: page 161 to 192
Chapter eight
Separation and war: page 192 to 259
Chapter nine
Hope of a waking dream destroyed:
page 259 to 275
Chapter then
Pursuit: page 275 to 293

Preface

I decided to start writing this book in hopes of finding some people that had been close to me in a past life. I thought that the book would become a reference and a useful guide to help me during the process of my next life. I also wanted to attract the attention of people who would be able to help me. In the future, this book will serve as an instruction guide that will awaken my soul before it's too late to stop life's misfortunes, if life brings me back. The enthusiasm that results from the hidden plot of my soul's past journey should help me accomplish this. This has always been the strategy; each time, I wonder who I could have been. Thinking about it makes me feel a kind of excitement, during which I am waiting and hoping that the person I will be meeting had already met me and that she or he will also recognize me. I often tell myself that if I do not find a way to remember who I was, I will have to relive the same obstacle that my past life inflicted on me. The future life won't be better, if I am not empowered to change the misfortunes, because the soul is subject to dormant recurrences which often bring back the same hideous obstacles. Therefore, for my next lives, in order to continue where I left off, I need to have the ability to remember so that I can work on better ways of living my life. I have to have some clues if I want to evolve to a process for a better system of living, for me and for those that are with me now and will still be around me in future lives. I know that it's possible to be happy if I am aware of what I should do and where I should go, which means not wasting my precious time running around, looking for something without knowing what. I know that I'm unhappy if I'm not sure that I belong where I find myself, especially since I'm drawn by a force that tells me that I belong somewhere else. Therefore, I want to be fulfilled in order to be able to do things other than looking everywhere for love without knowing where to find it. There are memories from the past that I've shared with others and that are of good use and I won't be able to go over them or remember them if I don't spend time with the person with whom I've shared these events. In conclusion, there, needs to be

Preface

at least two people involved to be able to remember and relive emotions from a past event. But maybe if the two people simply think about it at the same time, this would be sufficient to bring us back to that special place, as if we were still there, just like a déjà vu experience. I am sure that some of these memories are of some help for me; this is why I think that it could probably help family relations. Although these beliefs are often considered extreme and are even rejected, and although reincarnation seems unreal or insane, I could just interpret it otherwise. I could say that a mixture from a union could feel much more comfortable when the familiar emotion of having already been established appears to be present. For this reason alone, i.e., emotion wanting to be reunited, could be a legitimate reason, if the union had resulted in something good, that is. Personally, many memories came to me when I ran into some of those special people. First, there was a friend named Ronald a Spanish Egyptian who I met here in the city through Kurt, another friend from Haiti. The funny thing is that a vision-type memory appeared when I first saw him. I remember it clearly as though it were yesterday. What I saw was myself entering a restaurant with either my husband (or was it just a boyfriend); anyway I could see Ronald sitting on a table with his wife and her father, a Cuban or republican army president. In the restaurant I can see myself giving Ronald a list and the names of psychopaths and photographs of some people in need of protection. I remember not forgetting to give him my fees for my work, with the names of the ones to be pursued and the justification that came with it, because without the justification, no insurance could be claimed. Also if investigators ever discovered any false declarations, Ronald would have lost is life. In this memory, I can see some Chinese or Japanese people sitting at a table waving at me and I can hear other people whispering:

- Look! The Japs are socializing with her, I wonder what they told her!

From that memory, I heard through the clouds that Ronald's name was Henri in that space-time. Still in the past, when I met

Preface

Ronald, he had just gotten his accounting degree and he was working for the P.D.G., an important organization that protected rich people. The legal organization had gathered presidents from all different countries then. Ronald, along with others from a past life, came to help me with some problems caused by criminals. I was trapped in a small apartment when I was attacked and raped and psychopaths where trying to kill me. Of course, this is a memory of the past and did not happened in this life time. Ronald and his friends came with their M16s and fired at those criminals who were breaking the law. Let me tell you that during this lifetime, things don't happen exactly the same way that they did then and let's say that my problems are not yet solved. In this lifetime, Ronald has not yet met the wife he had in the past, but I keep an eye open and put out the word just in case I find her for him. Today, just like yesterday, many people complain and are angry for not receiving the protection they need from the law when they pay taxes for that purpose. I'm only saying this to point out that it should be more important to know not to steal and to stop the killers that are repeatedly committing crimes of murder. In my opinion, the emotional disturbance that causes misunderstanding is what leads to the proliferation of nature's cruel events. Why do I say this? Well, because I often tell myself that we probably could avoid some disenchantment from angels or from nervous unstable clouds! Suppose that we really believe that angels exist, in a context where we are advised of an upcoming angry depressed state of nature! It is sometimes possible to change what's going to happen and save the lives of many innocent human beings. I must mention that my stories derive from real lived events. Some of my stories will seem extreme or impossible, even exaggerated, but I insist on telling you that they do not contain any lies whatsoever. Knowing this, I have come to believe that natural disasters could be diminished and sometimes avoided. I've found odd coincidences between disasters and some situations. I will show you why later on. I am also writing this book in hopes that it could be help me get back

Preface

insurance from my stolen funds. I am hoping to retrieve the strength and the right to live again, because I relied on my funds which I invested, which were legally earned through good luck and inheritance, all my life. I also want to say that a lot of people I have met came and made me endure injustices; they abused me and they still owe me money. I say this because I have the legal rights to claim this money. In addition, I don't feel that I would be abusing people's good will and hard work, because I already gave my private or professional time to friends who will build the things I need. But they are more than willing to start working for me at a good price, a price they deserve. They will work at it because they know what they owe me and because they know they have the right to come visit. And for the special ones, I will help them write their biographies. During the course of my life, I have learned about human domestication and I have been through every possible psychological hardship. The reason they chose me makes me wonder if the gossiping about my father's influence is what made the participants do what they did to me! Thinking further, I also stop and wonder if God was the one that decided to put me on such a difficult road. I suppose I went through this in order to gain the knowledge I need to achieve the task that I have been assigned to do. There are specific ways of achieving what I am able to do. A different way of life is the only way I was programmed to understand in order to work at it. Therefore, it is through the apprenticeship of obstacles and from the understanding of the resulting proof that I have arrived at this state and am what I am. My rights of acquisition have been taken from me.

Those that took what belongs to me have no notion of the position they decided to take. Some criminals took funds they had no right to take and, in my opinion, these people are very dangerous. Corrupt people use legal public funds, as an idea to confuse people about the laws for their private funds; this way they take advantage of them and take their private funds. Some will even make themselves believe they have the right. While this is going on, time goes by and the

Preface

victims suffer. They might never be able to recover, just because someone wants to prove they are better, but better for what and for whom? They had no business to butt in where it did not concern them if their only intention was to take what was not in their name. We know that in the end, the criminals won't be there with the victim to provide help, in the way that they need. Anyway, no one is interested in listening to a criminal who is at fault and accepting his reasons for his bad actions. I did try to call the police and lawyers and none of these organizations wanted to try to bring me my legal right of acquisition. Anyway, even if financial needs are a major reason to create a work of art, my state of mind also needed a more significant reason to achieve it. I hope this non-violent way is the key to the insurance, which never came back to me. Briefly, what encouraged me the most was simply to try to make this book a reference. With enough luck, this book could become a valuable object to help me with this creative act, for my life and for my next life. I think that if I am in possession of the information about what, who and how and why, this is important to know. With this information, I would be able to achieve a better path of life, in my future life. To me, writing this book seems sufficient to solve my memory disorder. Let me add that at first an idea with the strength to destroy my will to write this book appeared, and it was the fear to give the power to others, to make me relive the same misfortunes over again, the ones that had been infringed by repeated life habits. I had to analyze this possibility and I convinced myself of the opposite, because there is no other possible way to become conscious in my next life of the probability of circumstance, which could appear repeatedly if I am not aware. The recurrence comes from memories, which often feed the spirit of our unconscious temple. Since some images come from our past lives, if I could associate these images to the reason for actions, I could become aware of those who risk being afflicted by terror. However, how could I even have a clue if I do not have some sort of a hint about the whereabouts of these images. I believe that the soul exists

Preface

and know that it is the desire of a majority of people; therefore, I am sure that my experiences can give others hope and make some people ask themselves if the soul and angels really exist. I also know that if abstractions stay in someone's mind, the person will end up abandoning his spiritual idea, no matter what it is. On the contrary, if good faith remains as a stronger force, the circumstances for greater ways of life could become better for future lives. I'm hoping that this pursuit will be an interesting study and hope to succeed in bringing a comparison that will also help other people's lives. I am aware that all of my affirmations reveal nothing new, although the ways that I achieved my knowledge might change a person's state of mind even if he has no faith. My soul can also project images of memories; therefore, there is a chance that some might be able to remember themselves. I am sure of this, because it has already happened that my presence made someone's memory reappear. I know that just by suspecting the existence of the soul, memories can be awoken, which are still hidden somewhere behind foggy images. Strangely a second disarming idea almost made me abandon this project, when I told myself: If I reveal all of my secrets, I won't have any place left to hide in my conscience, but it didn't make sense! In my life journey, I have made many voyages, I have also meditated a lot. I have taken the time to analyze all valuable aspects that could be profitable for my way of life in order to pursue my way, because I cannot live by other life styles and the costs exceed my current financial situation. I also was haunted by an agonizingly terrible vision. On the other hand, it could be a vision that was showing me the vivid possibility of achieving my goal. I am on my way back from a visit at my mother's in some tropical islands. I am in the airplane, looking through the window when suddenly I realize that my vision of things have been different since the accident. While we are passing through the city of Atlanta, I see the houses and all of the buildings, and I suddenly realize how many of us there are and how tiny this place is that I am looking at. I always knew that there were

Preface

many of us but I never had visualized it so widely. That is when I started feeling unimportant and so small around so many others. We are infested, I told myself, and that made me feel bad. This bad vision of seeing us as an infinite multitude of existing people awoke the reason and images for the abstract wars. It was not a very good dream, bad enough to make someone sick, and I had to find a way to erase that terrible vision, which brings the idea of a plague. Terrified of the future, I stopped analyzing the predicted amount of people, which will be multiplied outrageously in the future. I wondered if there was a way it could stay about the same, because, the instinctive idea of having to terminate some of the living appears in the mind, when you see what I was imagining. I am human just like everyone, so I want to live well, while being protected, just like all people that want and have to live. There has to be a solution so that we can continue to live eternally while being happy and well at the same time, not having to live running towards our death over and over again. That vision was present in many places and in many people and I was disgusted to see all of that.

I am sometimes scared of not wanting to come back, or I think, what if life doesn't feel good anymore and what if I was not able to make that someone come back if that person is asking me to! With all of these thoughts and knowing that I will come here on earth for eternity, I understood why someone like Hitler deemed it logical to start a war if it was to protect himself! Despite my understanding of that kind of desperate behaviour, I don't agree that this bad way of acting is the solution! I also wonder why I give so much importance to the idea of searching for those with whom I had a connection in past lives. The question is, is it selfish to make someone that has suffered, or made others suffer, come back? This kind of questioning is outnumbered and is distinctly different for each life but complicated enough to get my mind off those bad visions. For me to want to be involved in such matters, I needed to keep an open mind that angels exist. In revelations since the beginning of our time, we can see that

Preface

some laws were attributed by superior forces. They show that God or some kind of force will inflict punishment on us all if it is the only option left to stop criminals from putting victims in such a state of misunderstanding. I say this, because to know if a punishment was imposed by superior forces, we can simply observe how natural disasters manifest themselves. It's easy to know what makes sense because what doesn't make sense is always where an illegality occurred. Humans are not so stupid; they were conceived with laws integrated within themselves and know what is right and what is wrong. A person knows what he is entitled to, because he knows what he is capable of doing; he knows precisely what his tasks in the world are. He knows it because he thinks of it for himself, although sometimes he tries to impose on others what he is supposed to do, and sometimes he wants to make everyone like him. In my mind, there are conditions that make it so we can live well on this earth and that is why there are laws to follow. We are conceived as thinking beings, not to commit, or let others commit, crimes. We know that when laws are violated, many innocent people are often punished, and sometimes also destroyed. I have noticed that ignorance of a bad situation can become a crime. Let's remember that beliefs have proven more than once that when laws are disobeyed, punishment begins, with the consequence being the beginning of a manifestation of disaster on earth. Everyone knows that too often, if justice is served, the storm within us will calm itself, which stops the victim from panicking and the superior substance that derives nourishment from us will also calm down. Even if we have been warned since before the arrival of Christ, many have disagreed with the theory, but was it useful to fight against the idea? Some call these beings clouds, water, earth, or magical objects, and they are sometimes evil, although these things are a species, just like all the rest, and respond to the all-encompassing magnetic emotion of our souls, comparable to a plant thriving when it is fed by two compatible people. In addition, if we believe in angels and eternal life, we have to

Preface

acknowledge that there is an attributed resting time for the soul to be in celestial paradise. All of my thoughts have many questions, which sometimes have a tendency to deviate from their objective. I will stay with the challenge of proving how strong our love is, in order to grow the will to live eternally, with all of the different mixtures. If and since the soul becomes eternal after the first life, isn't there often someone waiting and asking to come back? I have to say that if the desire to bring someone back is present, when I do not retain the concrete information of where and about whom that person arrived, I will end up with a more embarrassing problem, which could create many more beings! I would like to have a clue to guide me; I want to be able to find the necessary link when a person asks me to come back, because here in my story, such a case occurred. I thought that there must be a way to recognize those that are back, because if we have met before, the images will come back in one's memory just like a movie. If we did know each other we will remember all that we had experienced together; it will rewind in our thoughts, as though we had just seen the person. So many replays are projected in lots of places at the same time and it causes major confusion, when we need to identify someone. What can we do when many are considered to be, or might be, the same person, in the same time-space? I suppose that we will have to wait until some kind of proof appears before knowing who is who! Even worse, imagine when someone is mistakenly referred to as being that expected ancestor and yet the person will only be coming in the next generation! In my mind these circumstances give rise to many more. I think we are smart enough to be able to study our situation more closely, in order to evolve with those already existing because they still will be there. The solution to recognize a person is to know who, what, and when, and to be aware of which were the good and bad circumstances around them! I will achieve my goal with this book. I know indeed that the soul has its baggage already and has already been filled with its advance knowledge from its previous

Preface

life. Therefore, to find a way to know should be the solution, but it is rather difficult to conceive. Knowing that it could protect us from vanishing and save us from extreme suffering makes me want to try. The quest to find out how to perfect ourselves is the desire that makes us want to evolve and understand. There continues to be confusion about where and how we can identify the soul! Most of the time, the newly-arriving souls don't understand the ideas of the elderly souls. Moreover, I would say that, when a person is struggling in their mind to obtain memories, such as those of the person you suspect them to be, you could be mistaken about the identity of the person. The person who is mistaken for another would not have the time or would not awaken images from those encountered with the ancestor, nor as they acquire knowledge from that person's life journey. This subject has so many possible ways of being further developed but does not show an example of a concrete situation, so I decided to work on the matter for myself and for those who asked me to. Problems that arise from events that already occurred can sometimes make us aware of our previous life. In addition, if a conflict appears, there has to be a settlement, on the table, placed at the right place, in order to please all of the people involved. For example, when a person has committed bad crimes in a past life, if that person is back and alive, in my opinion they could still be sick, and because of that, she or he should be closely watched. In such situations, when people don't know that the theory is possible, the chances for them to repeat their mistakes are more probable. I have noticed that even after so many warnings shared with many of those concerned, some probably did not watch over the dangerous person as advised. Often people ignore this theory because of their religious beliefs; unfortunately this has not solved these problems. I had personal proof that the soul of a person often repeats its mistake! I have my reasons to believe that we should give special importance to this philosophy, even if we do not believe it to be true. After so many tears, I blame the unbelievers for ignoring that this

Preface

philosophy is true, when they were so wrong. It's a waste of time, which causes the event to happen again when the theory is ignored. For a moment, I wanted to defend this philosophy, after the loss of many people, when they were executed repeatedly too young in this life and in the life of their ancestors. The worst part is that the person who executed them has the same bloodline and the appearance of a murderer from many different past lives. One of the victims, it's not important who she was, made me live many years with emotions as if it was my daughter who was one of the victims. It took me five years to find out if she had really experienced this atrocity. I still today bear the pain. I believe that in order for good people to have the chance and right to live, depends sometimes on the theory at least being considered possible. One must have an eye open to this possibility as the only purpose for changing the course of lives interrupted by others.

There is also the idea that it causes subpopulation, if we don't know where we come from and when the correct time was that was lived by our ancestor, referring to our body from the past life. However, looking on the bright side, we can analyze the phenomenon of a man and a woman who have been linked together in a past life. What would become of the good people if they decided to remake their lives elsewhere? The children of their children from the ancestor are often there when they arrive; the love ones we loved so much and who loved us back! What will they do if they want to come back? Even if I think they will find a way to come back one way or another, I'd say that they will probably try to influence the people concerned by filling them with their love. I believe that a person, if they existed in the past, is able to find himself 4 or 5 generations back, within the great or great-great generation. I know that sometimes couples from the past have the desire to look for each other in order to obtain that stronger emotion, which has been cultivated longer. Also, the images projected from the recalled memories make others feel good by providing those around us with an interior place to live, making us

Preface

humans feel comfortable around those who are together longer. In my mind, the most current and important reason will always be wanting to be together to fulfill the love of those that love us and want to come back. During my stories, I will also talk about parapsychological dreams and memories from the faraway past. Even if I've heard so many times, "Come on, it was in the past and has no meaning now", I know that a person is not the past even if he or she is constituted of more knowledge and has acquired understanding from life's past misfortunes and good fortunes. The memories from the past fill the aura with a taste of déjà vu, giving the person a capacity to project himself to the images of the others, making them see and feel an energy that is the same as in the past. In addition, the past journey is too often a symbol of the upcoming future, showing us how to perfect ourselves. They know that knowledge from the soul of someone that had an ancestor referred to be them will stay important to those that were around them. It is important to become conscious that ideas already acquired can help to locate those we need to recognize. We just mostly do not want to relive the same suffering and for most of us, we want to be able to remember ourselves. The desire and strategy to discover the memories that the ancestral lives bore will bring us to a new discovery or to a state of desire to be in the presence of those we cannot get enough of. In my mind, no one can refer a person to be the past; Rather, I'd say that they already know the result as a consequence of what they have lived. In addition, the knowledge acquired, interpreted in a modern way, will adapt to the time when they arrived. For the critical point is that life's misfortunes are evil, and could incite some human beings to never stop repeating the same mistakes. They do this out of the enjoyment of the feeling of doing something again and again, which is fed by the baggage of the unconscious soul. Therefore, misunderstanding or addition can cause some people to redo evil actions. Unfortunately, it is difficult for the conscience to awaken the soul's memories. Evidently, the soul bears

Preface

images and emotions, but the mind has to realize this before believing it and to be able to awaken the unconscious. As for understanding the misfortunes of the past, they are hiding behind the certainty
that they really did occur. In my mind, the soul did not die in the past; rather, the soul will keep the images it wants to keep from a life within our ancestors. As a result, worms and the understanding of situations that were experienced will be in our souls, engraved for eternity. Although, don't we often avoid ideas that make us anxious!

***

At first, I wanted to wait until I was in possession of all the necessary information before writing this book, but my financial necessities have pressed me. I have to run to see those I need to see and to do what I know how to do, while being able to provide what is needed, which costs more than what a normal job pays. In addition, I am not safe here because I don't have the riches that I had before. I am programmed and am used to living with different paths of life, and considering what happened to me, there are some people to blame. One way or the other, someone will have to pay for the illegal action I have suffered, and it's the law that has promised it. Every day I am confronted with the criminal mind saying, "If we owe her money, let's kill her", and this is from those who did took advantage of it all. At the same time, I hope that with this book, I can find the bloodline and the person considered to be the father of a child from the past, which has asked me to come
back. I want to add that my ideas are fuelled not on
the basis of the phase I am in. I tried it and I know that I do not deserve to die, just because I cannot adapt to a lifestyle where criminals decide for me where I should be. It is certain that the ideas about my conscience being awoken do not change a lot, in terms of a humane way of living. I would blame everything on what I have been inflicted with. Also, what I am used to is not necessarily adaptable to the lifestyle of the majority of people.

Preface

Usually, in such cases of indictment, insurance and lawyers should handle my cause, but in my case, they were afraid to get involved, as I am living without life's conveniences, as I see it normal to be. I hope I have not frightened you off, and that you will enjoy the stories from the path of my life, and I hope they won't worry you too much. It's important to point out that all of the names mentioned in this book are fictional except for mine, and a few from a faraway past. Thank you, and I hope you will enjoy reading the stories of my life.

*****

Chapter 1

Sacred memories

I wonder if I have the right to rebuild my love life before my journey brings me back into the unknown. I started to write this book in 2006 at the age of 33. It is so strange that since an accidental event occurred, some strange paranormal events revealed to me two of the first names of my ancestors and they referred to my having been in two different past lives. One is Sidney and the other Evernaissant. The latter sounds like an impersonator, and it comes from a more distant past and is not the real name which my ancestor bore. Sidney James Krownier Mc Sween was the name from my bloodline and which comes from the closest past. Why they used the name Evernaissant to refer me as well apparently comes from a legend. In the past, some members of the James family started a business writing doctrine biographies they called legends. They offered to make their customers popular in a way that could make their stories immortal for other particular purposes and they did achieve that for some people. I live in a small apartment in the city of Verdun in Canada. My problems restrict my freedom to go out, so I spend a lot of time analyzing memories of my dreams, thinking I probably will find something useful in there,

Sacred memories

which will guide me. Today, I went out to get 6-49-lottery forms, on Saint-Catherine Street. While walking, I saw some faces passing by; some Chinese people smiled at me and one pointed a finger at me, calling me Evernaissant? That made me wonder why is it that other people named the music group that interpreted my stolen songs, just like the echo of that name the Chinese person just called me? I sure want to find out more about this, so I might look into it on the internet when I get back. I would like to know who recorded me, because I've noticed that my inspirational state satisfied the ears of an audience, and I need to find out where my copyright rights are and who took them. I finally arrived home and looked at photos from the albums which contained my songs. I noticed that there are many different ones and it was not the same person on all of them; they also said that the author was deceased. This is odd, because I am not dead. In addition, how is it that they sold and made money with the songs, when it's illegal to sell or make money with a composition whose author is deceased. It is illegal to sell until 50 years after the author dies. I find it to be an odd coincidence that one of the girls on the photos looks like that 16-year-old girl who continues to appear in my dreams upon awaking. Let me explain. In my day dreams, I see images of a girl who tells me: "Mama it's me, Nicky". This image appears to be during the end of the 18th century, and these images are as fresh as if she had just left a few minutes ago. While looking at all of this, I don't know what to do about it. I'm angry because no one came to ask me before they went ahead and recorded me and sold my singing inspirations. One thing is obvious: someone, somewhere is continuing to make money from this. I also find it kind of strange that some visitor from the church came to see me just after my compositions were broadcast. I remember the day they came to knock on my door. I was sitting at my broken desk and someone knocked at my door. I walked to the door, opened it, and decided to invite the two men standing there to come in.

- "Come in," I told them.

Sacred memories

- "Please sit down; what brings you to my home?"

Curiously, one of them had the same family name as the insurance company with which I was insured when I was young. This tall handsome man reminded me of something! I suddenly heard an echo that whispered to me that his name was Alexander in a faraway past. I then had a vision from that faraway past, in which I saw that he was the owner of a fabric factory. I must have been having a hallucination or something, although these dreams seemed to be so real. These two young men probably came to get some information in order to do some research or something. On the other hand, maybe they came out of curiosity, if they heard about the event I suffered. The taller man started speaking to me.

- You look gorgeous, he said.

I thought he was exaggerating, especially since he was the handsome one, but it was still very flattering, and I smiled back at him.

- Do you need anything? he asked.

I tried to answer correctly before he left, just in case he was here on behalf of the insurance company.

- Well, I do have some serious financial problems.
- We don't have much, but... He then slipped his hand into the briefcase to grab something. I wasn't sure, but I thought it was his Mormon Bible.

I don't know why, but I started to worry and I thought I was having these paranoid confusions. What if they were dangerous and he took out a gun or something? I don't know why I was having these thoughts, but it could have been because I was too busy filling out the lottery forms.

I decided to stop him.

- No! No! Not for the moment!

We continued chatting. I shared with them the situation about someone recording me, also about the police attacks and about my ex-boyfriend, Mustafa. They could see that I was very busy so they got up and walked towards the corridor in order to reach the

Sacred memories

door. The tall man looked at me, and before leaving he make a finger drawing on my wall to show me where his home was located in the United States. They finally said good-bye and left. Night came and I was listening to the radio when strangely they were talking about the same young man who had been at my house during the day. The announcer said that the family in question were the owners of an insurance company that made a gross income of seven million dollars a year. That made me wonder why, whenever I have a visitor, the news or police intercepted them and investigated them. I surely started to wonder if they were spying on me. At least a week passed since that visit and I was daydreaming again while working on the papers. I remembered the legend of Evernaissant. I was told that her name was heard being called from the heavens on a war day. She would have lived about two thousand years ago. She was remembered from the dark grey day when the Gods where so angry, continuing to devastate the earth. The crying angels where spreading trauma, which caused many terrestrial disasters. Anyway, suddenly, somewhere near England or Ireland, some people heard the name Evernaissant echoing in the sky, at the location where the event had occurred. The witnesses associated the name to the person who was there, because she was injured by the sky, right there where the name was being called. After the accident, she received a gift, which made her have visions of memories from a faraway past. Her images were the same stories of grandparents about their grandparents. There is another similar dream, which appears to have happened again in the 18th century. Similarly to what was mentioned above, the sky had recognized the soul in the body of an ancestor. I also think the name could have been the given name from God, of all us humans in general! I heard many theories after this event happened to me. I was labeled as either a saint, a majesty or as someone from other religions, which is not nice. The worst that was said was that I was being possessed.

I am going to share the event in detail a little

Sacred memories

further in the story, while sharing the many other events responsible for bringing back my memories.

It might have also happened in the 14th century, still in the same circumstances, the name blowing out of the clouds and the grounding coming from where the angels live. The clouds formed into a circle in the middle of the street, while the thunder manifested itself, then it happened. I suppose the reason they assumed the ancestor to be the same was because they looked alike, they came from the same bloodline, and had had to endure the same events. As for the witnesses, they came to an understanding about eternal life, saying that we came back to life. This theory doesn't have the power to ease some to stop creating wars. Evernaissant was the daughter of a an emperor named by the Japanese. She was trying to ease her sadness from seeing a horrible murder of what she thought to be her own child. After many children were assassinated, a French-British protestant made up a different reason for doing so. In the year 0, she was looking for Jesus; in the 14th century, she was eliminating the offspring of the one she was in love with, and she did it again in the 18th century. The odd thing is that the assassin always had the same appearance and she always came from the same bloodline. When I awoke from these horrifying memories, I started looking in the encyclopedia at Alexander, Jeanne of Arc and Marie Madeleine, but their appearances in the books were different. Nevertheless, if I could be confident about my visions, I would say that the murderer from the year 0, Jeanne of Arc, came to have the same name as her daughter, Marie Madeleine, in the 18th century. I have to admit, it is difficult to associate the images with the right time and space also. It is difficult for me to hear all of the echoes from the conversations. That is why I cannot say that I am sure of all the information from my gifted memories. In addition, I surely wouldn't want to turn my book into research about that female murderer. I mean that I would rather not have any encounters with any person who bears her sick soul.

I should remember for the next life that when I am visited by the

Sacred memories

person who was Alexander, I should be prepared and know what to do, because the child murderer will be just about to commit her crimes. I have to admit that I was curious and while reading, I found it odd that some French have a different definition of what a Saint is, particularly when they identify murderers as being saints! I could not find an answer to that so I presumed that they thought of those chosen by angels to be liars. In conclusion, they were not spiritual believers. I admit it is difficult to believe in stories like the one from my ancestors, saying they were awakened by angels in order to live their lives, with their souls present to be receptive and receive memories of the past. Anyway, I would translate the name Evernaissant, heard from the sky, derived from two languages, and having French and English meaning, as "will be reborn forever". The idea changed many states of mind and has protected some people from not forgetting that if angels get scared of not coming back, it could become a trauma which could cause natural disasters, from angels without hope. I now awake at the age of 12 or 13, to see if there is not a link attaching my memories to a revelation from the beyond. This confusing moment occurred at a young age and is one of those events I still wonder about. Since my soul is still showing me some of the images, there has to be something in there I have to solve. While I did not remember this, I had endured the event before. Since these images came to me at a younger age, I did not understand any of it; in addition, the morning after the signs appeared to me, I had totally forgotten about it because there was no logical reason for me to dwell on this. One of these phenomena was my appearance projected on the T.V. by itself. It was just some images on the television, not something appearing to be real. This is a common situation, which many people must have witnessed and if you have experienced the phenomenon of image caption, which related to you or to people close to you, I would say to you that you can think of it as being signs of real images from the past, which belong to you or to those you saw.

Sacred memories

This happened to me, while I was watching a movie. My father had brought me a film on a cassette that was part of a book from European Universities that someone had lent him. The movie was about real-life events of the past that had been kept secret and involved paranormal activities. The books are about parapsychology, written by a psychiatrist during the end of the 18th century and beginning of the 19th century. I was curious and wondering about what was happening during the time. I was watching the movie, but the scene started to change images by itself. It definitely was a paranormal phenomenon. At the bottom of the screen words appeared which said "past and future". At that time, I was living with my father in a little mansion that made my friends cry when I invited them to spend the night. It was located next to a lake, near an Indian reserve. In the middle of the flower landscaping, in the parking area, my father was hoisting up a flag that has a skull on it. I must say that, because of the flag, most of the children in the neighborhood were forbidden to hang out with me. They even said mean things about us, because of it. There was some hearsay that we were mafia gangsters and that we were dangerous. Honestly, there was no one who was dangerous in that house; it was only my father and me, with our original way of scaring away the curious. Returning to the movie scene, my father was watching football, in the left part of the living room, with respect to where I was sitting. I was watching the weird movie and after just a minute, the cassette started to be defective and I was seeing weird things. I impulsively called to my dad, screaming.

- Hurry! Come see this, we are in the movie, and I can see you and mom in an older time. I also saw you at a very old age and what your murderer looks like. Hurry! Come!

My father finally arrived after what seemed to be a long time after telling him to hurry. Well, of course, the film had to stop right at the moment that he entered the room.

- Oh! No! This cannot be happening!

Sacred memories

- Don't worry; I'll just rewind the cassette.
- Yes, because you need to see this!

I remained calm while trying to find the scenes, but there was no hope, the scene was just not to be found.

- Well, I've had it with this. I'm going back to watch the football game. Just call me if you see it again.

I was left alone, so I carefully watched the movie and saw something weird. I again called to my father for him to come see it, but there was no hope, the screen turned to snow or just paused every time he entered the room.

My Father gave up the idea of seeing what I wanted him to see.

- Well, instead, try to remember what the killer looks like and if you ever see him one day, just let me know.

I couldn't know, who the killer was until the day I met him for real, and today I know who he is. When I first saw the man who looked, like the guy from that scene in the movie, I recognized him right away. The man's soul was carrying images from those memories. I was even able to remember the scene from that movie. It was Arnold, the French ambassador's nephew, also the right-hand man of the Irish King. Arnold was a tall black man, 6'4'', who had a white mother and a father living in Barbados. I remember that, in the movie scene, my father was not the only one to die.

Arnold stood at the door of my dad's room.

- Open the door or I'll force myself in, Franck.

Arnold got into the room.

I watched them argue about a check that Arnold wanted to give my father. My father started screaming.

- Liar, you just want to get close to me and hurt me. Damn you, Arnold, go away.

In that picture my dad looked old and his nails were long and black. In his small room far away from the city he had a view from the top floor. The exterior was round and made of stone.

All of his children were married. As for his last wife, she had been in

Sacred memories

an accident many years before and she was deceased. In the movie scene, Frank, my dad, was sick and he was hiding from those who believed him to be dead.

He had faked his death just before dying to make sure everything went where it was supposed to go and to get rid of the robbers.

In the scene, I suddenly heard a gunshot. The bullets hit the side of Arnold's heart.

In his suffering, Arnold walked towards Frank, pulled out a knife, stuck it into his stomach, and then screamed.

- Franck, you sick bastard. I only wanted to give you a check from the company; it's from your daughter. Why did you do this?

Arnold then fell to the floor and died. My father sat down on a chair, bleeding to death, but

just before he fell unconscious, he looked at the check and realized that it was real. Before falling into the deep sleep of passing into the unknown, he took a pencil and paper and wrote the following:

My daughter, I miss all of you. I also think of you sometimes. Forgive me, but what else could I have done! I was always scared of Arnold and never trusted him because, I knew that Arnold often helped the old and sick to die and I was not ready to go. Give my apologies to his loved ones and tell them I didn't mean him any harm. I only wanted to defend myself. I know, I was sometimes difficult but I never forgot about you. Go visit your brother and sisters. I did not raise them to be as strong as you. Bye, my daughter, this time is for real.

The scene then disappeared. This weird phenomenon of a scene that appeared and disappeared was, in my opinion, only a projection of the soul's past memories, just as if a cloud had filled itself with images of memories and went to project itself onto a television. It is similar to when we intercept neighbors and they appear on the television screen without the use of a camera, or when we capture the voice of people on the radio. It is a common phenomenon, which has occurred many times before. It is the transmission of the unexplained functions of the mind. During the movie, I also saw a

Sacred memories

female muse, one of the imaginary figures from mythology. The women had been seen before in apparitions. She was half-human and half-animal, made of a substance from the clouds and she appeared with a blood stain. Mythology recounted that she lived in between two worlds, at the gates of hell. During the scene, she appeared in a cloud, beside an angel-crying child. The muse carried a star as her crystal ball, which she used to make a path with the child. The muse would be able to get some time out of hell if the child exchanged her time, because it was a sin to see and talk in the dreams using the crystal star. While being given this opportunity, the star would cause there to be an electrical disaster on nature. I think it was the mythology of the muse that helped create the esoteric system. In the images, I was watching the muse having access to the human mind. The muse could listen to the thoughts of those she chose to, with their voices echoing through her star. The evil power of her Crystal ball could hypnotize some people only if they were in the wrong. I must say that she was not so pretty with her hoofed feet and animal body that had a human head with the nose of a mule. That scene was very fast, lasting less than a minute and felt like the ideal movie for a cartoon Disney story. I saw other scenes, such as watching what appeared to be me in my twenties. I could recognize that it was really me because my mother and father were there. We seemed to be in the late 18th century. In the movie, I had just met the person who I think was the father of the two children from my ancestor, Nicky and Jo, though, I am not sure that he was the one for sure. The train was leaving for America. We were boarding the train. Then, in a closed cabin, Flint, a tall, handsome young man, with blue eyes and big hands, was with Sidney, my ancestor. They were lying down on the bed. Flint started the conversation.

- My mother told me that I am to meet with a Swedish-Australian woman. She keeps telling me that I am to have a baby with her because it is I who am the identical bloodline to a generation of an important family.

Sacred memories

Sid was attentive and silent, her ears sticking out listening, her eyes staring at him. She had no reaction and he took advantage of her moment of absence to start caressing her all over, wrapping his arms around her;

- You know, we could just tell my mother to go to hell. At worst, we could run away together!

He then slowly penetrated her, deep into the heart of her vagina. As he was holding her bumper, she suddenly lost her sexual mood. Why was she still thinking about what he would do with this other woman? She realized this could be the last time he made love to her. Tears started running down her cheeks.

- Don't worry, I still love you, he said.

However, there was nothing he could say that would take away the awful idea of having to share Flint with that other women. She just lost the mood, slipped out of the sexual act and got out of bed. She grabbed her red flowered dress, put it on, then took her hat and looked at Flint. Incapable of saying anything, since she had a lump stuck in her throat. She wanted to start screaming, but she turned away and left the room, leaving Flint there by himself. Flint looked disappointed, having failed to make her happy. Arriving in the alley, Sidney stopped to straighten her dress, which had gotten stuck in her panties. Then she hurried to dry her tears, which were still running. Sidney walked towards the dining room table.

I could hear her thoughts echoing in the movie saying: - I guess there are more important things in life than a love based on sex, especially when there are no real important objectives to it. I will forget about Flint. That is what she told herself. She then reached the lounge. The news was playing on the radio, announcing that a boat had just sunk in the ocean. It could have been the Titanic or one of those before that. Many of the people on the train were panicking, especially those who had friends or family on board. The emotional atmosphere, which flowed through the room, made me feel as if I had experienced this before. The people related to those who had

Sacred memories

died make me shake and I can still feel myself absorbing the agony running through that room from the past. Sidney's sadness about Flint seemed to have lessened due to this more tragic event. After that scene, Sidney just stayed near her parents until they had reached their destination. The image of the people in that picture was the same image of my parents. The train finally arrived. Sidney was getting off the train, when she stumbled on a man that she was seeing for the first time. The men stopped and looked into her eyes. I could see that she was still hurt about Flint but she froze there and stared back at him. He was very good looking, with his gold-green-blue eyes and his strong body, standing about five-foot-10. He was very different from her very tall and handsome 6'4" lover.. Sidney was small, about 5 foot 2, being a white Irish girl. She finally passed through the crowd when the man's voice echoed out to her. - Hey, wait! Who are you. What's your name. When can I see you again? Sidney couldn't hear what he was saying; she could only see his arm in the air, waving at her. Unfortunately, they were too far apart. The scene then changed and very quickly 3 or 4 other images appeared. I was able to see the man, leaving the train, asking his friend for some information about Sidney. I then saw him in a room with the same woman that had assassinated children. In that scene, she was his girlfriend, but he was unaware of that woman's illegal activities. They were stoned from sniffing cocaine and were having an argument about wanting to get separated. He heard that she had murdered someone some time ago. I also heard that they had been together for about one year. The images changed and I then saw him with another woman. He was in a room, both were lying in bed in a house they had just bought together. In that scene, he was again getting separated, this time after a 2-year relationship, because she had cheated on him and I heard him say that he had been sober during that relationship.

I also saw him married to a Hindu woman, with whom he had conceived some children but I didn't see what happened with them. I think his name was Jo or Fred but I am really not sure. I then saw him

Sacred memories

in at a hippodrome with Sidney. The accountant, Henri, along with his wife, was also present. As for Sidney's children, I was unable to see for sure which one was the actual father because in the scenes, it seemed that sometime, somewhere, there was a return to Ireland. Many of the people that I will talk about in this book were present and they all came to visit my ancestor. Joe, Frederick, Henry and other Henrys were there. There was definitely one of them, who was to be the father of those children. There was also a man who came to visit. He was the father of the soon-to-be husband of Nicky, my ancestor's daughter. He looked like a good man and helped to pay for Nicky's studies. She also had a guard who followed her all the time, making sure she did not get raped. Of all the things I saw, I couldn't associate these astral projections with my real life because I was not aware that it could have something to do with my past. If I hadn't experienced the event, I would never have awakened any of the memories. Therefore, these memories would still be sleeping in the unconscious side of my soul. I wonder if the image of that man was the one I should remember in order to bring these children back from my past lives. I don't know why these images are there but there is definitely something important that I should remember about these people. What I know for sure is that the man who Sidney ran into appeared to be the nephew in the past of a woman name Janice Kennedy. She was married to a Joe Maxwell in Ireland around the end of the 18th century, before her family started a war with the Irish about her.

Anyway, he was the nephew, but from which side, the woman Janice's or her husband Joe's, that is unknown. As for Flint's whereabouts, I already knew the person who could be considered to be his perfect replica. From what I saw from the small scene that appeared in the movie, it ended with Flint holding his head down, out of the window of his house, right after he had met the Swedish woman. Flint was looking guilty and pitiful, and was talking to Sidney. Probably, because he had fallen in love with the woman, his mother

Sacred memories

had made him marry. Anyway, he started screaming at Sidney while she was leaving.

- No, please don't leave me! We can find a solution; please come back!

In the movie scene, Flint got married and she left him two years later, just after she gave birth to the baby. She left to go and become a model and the baby was adopted by the family. There was another scene which appeared in the movie. It was in another century; it could have been any century up to the year 1000 or 1400 even 1700, I can't say. I was in a coma and my body had a high fever due to an accident caused by a natural event and my mother was taking me to a medical specialist in China or Japan. I know this happened in a far away past because there were no cars or trains, just a horse carrying the wooden box in which I lay. Evernaissant awoke in a bed where a couple of Asian people were observing her. They talked but I couldn't hear the conversation and in the end, Evernaissant left when she awoke from the coma. In front of what seemed to be an old palace, she was hugging the couple, thanking them. Standing at the top of the stairs, with the street full of carols and horses, the man stared at her, that same man from the train in another century. It was about the last of the scenes that was to appear and the movie about the Italian being arrested by the P.D.G. of psychiatrists came back on the screen, as well as discussions among the psychiatrists about supernatural phenomena. That night, I said goodnight to my dad and went to bed. I forgot all about it the next morning and never thought about it again, until the accident happened to me. It's rather strange that on the same day that I was correcting the part about the train in my book, a weird thing happened. I was walking on Wellington Street with my friend Francine, who had to get her nails done for an appointment later that night. I was thinking about that guy and I remembered his image. All of a sudden someone came out of an apartment, a person moving some furniture. He looked exactly like that person. This couldn't be

Sacred memories

happening again. He was right in front of a store named Max.

- Francine, please stop here for a minute.

- Why, I don't want to stop here. We're in a hurry. You said that you were going to curl my hair for tonight and it's getting late.

My voice became more insistent and she finally stopped.

I grabbed her arm and replied.

- Stay here just for a minute.

- Ok, don't panic; I'll stay since you're not giving me a choice. Now that I'm not moving, can you tell me why we're stopping here?

- Sure. Be quiet. Look at that guy right there.

- What's up with him? Don't you have someone already! - Yes, that's not the point. He looks exactly like the person I'm talking about in my book, the one that could be the father of Nicky, my ancestor's daughter.

- Are you crazy or something? That's not him.

- I'm very curious to know what his last name is! I swear to you, he looks very familiar.

I wondered if it was a coincidence or just a hallucination or maybe an angel made someone that looked like him appear! Maybe it wasn't him, but just seeing he brought back a clearer, longer image of that space-time in my memory. I froze, kind of hypnotic, and I stayed like that for a couple of minutes. That is when it happened: a little girl's voice whispered in my ear. - I want to come back.

This was not a hallucination, nor a voice echoing, but a real sound blowing in the wind, entering my ear. Meanwhile, Francine was getting tired of waiting.

- Come on, Christine, let's go. We don't have a lot of time, before my appointment this evening.

In her excitement, Francine didn't give me enough time to talk to him; anyway how could I tell him why I wanted to talk to him? He probably would have labeled me a nut case. It wasn't normal for someone on the street to come up and start asking about personal stuff. In addition, I would need more proof before making any kind of

Sacred memories

allegations. I started thinking about going to Ireland to visit the gravestones or even to ask for any old pictures that I could see myself in, along with the concerned person. This way, I could find out what I needed to know.

However, it can be kind of confusing if you don't know who you are. I have an example that shows just that. Once, I was at a boyfriend's mother's house. She was 80 years old and I am mentioning her age only to be able to see about how many years it takes before a person could reappear. Anyway, she had an old picture of her grandmother and the odd thing was that she looked just like my boyfriend's cousin. During the following week, I started questioning myself about that picture. Coincidentally, on the news, they were talking about a fire in Greece which was close to their origin. The news report showed a woman standing there on the street, watching the fire, and she was the identical twin, look-alike of his cousin. I must say that she looked more like the real person from that picture. She had that sense of taste and images projecting glowing around her. Sometimes, finding the answer is too complicated but the problems often get solved by themselves. Why is it that once in maybe 50 years, there's news on TV about Greece, and the image of a person which at that very moment I was wondering about, appears?

***

Years earlier, actually, during the dawn of this century, I was in my apartment. Outside, many street wars were taking place. I often looked out my window because many crimes were being committed in the neighbourhood, so I had to be alert, just in case they came for me. Maybe, I was becoming a little paranoid, but I still cared about this life. While looking outside, I wondered why I was seeing people I knew going into my downstairs neighbour's apartment. This was really odd. Pépé, an Italian-Spanish man, and Lira, the wife or, I presume, ex-wife of my mother's neighbour from Mexico were visiting my neighbour, here in Verdun, Canada! Seriously, it didn't make any sense. Why was it that they weren't stopping here to say

Sacred memories

hello to me? Pépé followed me every time I came back from visiting my mother. I'd known Pépé for a long time, even if, I hadn't seen him many times. I think he didn't not remember who I was, although it was confusing that he visited my mother, asking if I was coming, but never visited when I was there. Maybe he was just shy. Anyway, I saw him leave with some cassettes in his hands. I knew he worked in big bars in hotels, so he had to know who to ask to add music to a good song. Anyway, 2 or 3 days after they left, the song I had invented while singing was playing on the air. I therefore presumed he had added the music to accompany me. It became a hit song. The only catch is the name of the beneficiary of that song was a Laura Paucini. I think I had met her before in the Daddy Rock Bar in Cancun. It disturbed me to know that I was so much in need of funds and someone made some off my emotions asking for some. I know for sure that it was I who was the person on the recording. The funny thing is that the woman named Laura had so many albums and her songs were all in Italian, except for mine, which was in English. I very clearly remember the morning when I got inspired to create that song. I was still filling in my lottery forms, hopping to get enough money to be able to get away from this arduous life style that I was stuck in, and for other purposes. Cindy Lauper's song, "Girls just want to have fun", was playing on the radio. It was about one in the morning and I was singing the lyrics. I was standing in front of the window and saw my ex-sister-in-law arrive down on the street, accompanied by 2 police cars. I open the window, thinking, no, not again! This woman must have wanted my skin, trying to have me arrested. I start to tremble, scared that they would come and take me again. I had not committed any crimes. How could I defend myself? What if the reason was because I was singing at a late hour! I was curious to know how she could have been able to hear me, since she lived a one-hour drive away from my place. I didn't know what kind of idiotic lies her new accusations were filled with, but the worst thing was that this idiot woman, probably didn't know that she could

Sacred memories

convince these people to end my life. However, that night, for the first time, I saw my ex-sister-in-law become frustrated for not being obeyed. She was there, standing in front of the police car window, and I could see that she was holding her fist real tight, arguing with the police officers. I could see they were hesitating to act in the context, which could be an infraction, if they decided to come and arrest me. I labeled them the police kidnappers. Can you imagine that they drove an hour to arrest me? I knew that it was organized crime but did they know the accusations were nothing but lies, or were they in on it, because every time, I was arrested they asked for money in exchange for my release? It wasn't the first time I was a victim and witness of their unlawful ways. I decided to open my window wider and stuck my head out to scream at them.
- Damn criminal police robbers; go away before I call the embassy. You'll see; they'll come to play your war game with you. After a couple of seconds, a third police car arrived. They seemed to come from this city. I couldn't believe it; they were taking my side. What a relief! This had never happened before. I watched them leave in silence without having to see them come to my door. My ex-sister-in-law was still standing there, this time she was ignoring me and bitching at her silent husband, who was keeping his head down. All of a sudden, they all disappeared and everything was as if nothing had happened. They left me behind, without even saying a word. I wondered why the police had decided to help me. Maybe they needed to repay me for giving them a tip on the whereabouts of some drugs. I remember, my intention was to save the life of a young Italian boy, just a week before. A couple of hours went by and it was very early, 4 or 5 in the morning. I was still working on these papers. Cory Hart's song "Never surrender" started playing on the radio; that's when the inspiration came to me. I started by singing the opposite of what the song was about, I was replying to the message he was sending, trying to entertain myself. It was the emotion coming from my frightened soul that created the goodness of that song.

Sacred memories

In the back of my mind, still asking for money made it good enough for a listener to want to hear it and to sing it. I wondered if, since Pépé and his friend had arrived, from Mexico by plane that morning, it might have helped my nerves sound like this, at that moment of inspiration. That morning, I had seen their images. I wanted to talk a little about his friend, just because there could be someone looking for him somewhere, even though I thought it could be too late. Anyway, this friend of Pépé's, I had seen him before in my memories and in a projection from the past which came to me when I saw him on a trip to Mexico. He had an affair with a Russian girl, which had resulted in the birth of Billy the kid. In the office where, I saw them, there was a meeting and many other Spanish and Italian people were present. This is why I hesitated to identify him, for sure, because of the many look-alikes, although I'd met many people in my life and he was the only one that made me remember and see these memories. About the song, Pépé did try to pay me some money for my composition, but the black intermediary, who was complicit with the bank manager, stole my check. I am patient and in time, I will find the right person to help me with my legal funds before my time is up, and before I get too old and incapable to do anything else but to wait to die, since I am the one who legally should win the prize.

***

I am again seeing these images from the past, knowing that my soul existed at some time and place in the past in an ancestor of mine. My immortal soul is teaching me an understanding of my ancestral lives so that I can regain a state of mind, which will help me confront the reality of my present life. My soul is giving me a taste of the emotions it had experienced, making me want to experience some of them again. In the 1st or 14th century, according to Evernaissant, she was soon going to leave to study parapsychology at her uncle's in the North of Ireland. This paternal uncle had invited her to see if she could find a way to help reduce earthly disasters, which had been extremely prevalent in those years. She believed that their source

Sacred memories

was a poisoned cloud which was absorbing innocent souls that were unable to discover a logical reason as to why they had been given to God as an offering by sick murderers. People had also become sick because the murderers had acquired an evil manipulative strength when they started sucking all the energy from the pure defenseless souls, taking rights that were not theirs to take. During that time, when vegetation was dying and increasing numbers of people were falling sick, great sorcerers came from Ireland, Japan and from everywhere, even from Rome, to pool their knowledge and strength and find the solution to what science had found unrealistic and uncontrollable. They had to restore sanity in the people and de-traumatize the spirit. Too many people still favored black magic and mean cruelties. Her uncle had a strange notion that the magic beings in the clouds were able to hear her. He placed his hopes on the connection she had with the substance, and he thought that she might see the cause and receive the ideal solution which would cure them. Their last hope was becoming aware, which is a natural medical remedy. I could see that her uncle had taken her under his wing, and he was confident about her honesty because the identity of some of the ancestors had been revealed through an echo coming from that angel. He believed there was a chance that the angel cloud could also reveal to her the identity and whereabouts of the criminals guilty of provoking these disasters. The victims' cries for help were causing natural disasters. As for the memories or images on the television, I cannot tell if Evernaissant did find a way to help reduce the disasters, but one thing I can say for sure is that she did make some people find each other. In the castle, I could also see Arnold sitting in the study. It was a wide room with many bookshelves and in the backyard there was a field of potatoes. In that scene, Arnold looked so pitiful as he asked for the hand of Evernaissant in marriage.
- Marry me, Evernaissant! He said.
- Come on now, Arnold. Don't you think you should marry someone who is more like you! Don't you see that we're not made for each

Sacred memories

...-other!
- Don't say that! You're perfect for me; can't you see that I love you! Think about it. I'm a rich man. Please say yes. I'd do anything for you! He kept on insisting.
- You understand me.

Evernaissant listened but couldn't see herself with that strong scary man. She hoped he wouldn't decide to hold her hostage, just to have her be his wife, because she didn't want to marry Arnold, even if she loved him as a friend and as her bodyguard.
- I want you to know, Evernaissant, that if you don't marry me, I won't be your friend anymore. I only have one space available and it's reserved for the person I will share my life with.

He tried as hard as he could to make her change her mind but he wasn't the one for her.

***

I've met people who seem to be old ghosts, or should I say, people with the same soul as some of the friends of my ancestors in past lives. I'm sure that I've met them before because their presence alone illuminates the image of the memories of a time spent with them in a space and time other than the present one. I sometimes think I might have been there in another time-space but the moments I experienced get lost in a deep sleep, saying that we don't always meet those that will make us feel and see these flashbacks from the past. That is why I believe there are different stages in life which allow us to evolve to different states of mind to achieve different accomplishments. It could be that these states are experienced in order to accomplish other life activities or it could just be that I had gone somewhere else, to another dimension of the universe. When I think about all this, it makes me stop and wonder what I could possibly do to gain the advantage of living a better life next time. In the hopes that the next time I could get my information this way before my teenage years, I could ask my parents to set some rules for me in order for me to achieve my goals. Then again, I am not sure

Sacred memories

what kind of rules I could possibly need to get where I want to be. Therefore, I need to ponder this subject a little longer. While waiting for an answer, I am going to request some information about where I came from. I am not allowed to give any of the real names but I heard many stories and I am going to see if they match what's in my memory. I am going to call my mother and my aunt to see what they know about it. Obviously there will be discrepancies between their versions because they themselves are not aware of all the information. I will find a way to resolve all of it. From my mother's side, the distant family names are kept somewhere else because my grandfather's grandmother once said that only those worthy of her name would be able to obtain the information about their origin. Supposedly it was a great-aunt or maybe a distant cousin of my mom's father, and since that is rather distant in time, asking living people if they remember my ancestor could be futile. I know another name was added to change my grandfather's father's original name, which is the one presently used. Now why, somewhere in the life story, were many names changed or added? Well the reasons are numerous and they always did so during wartime to protect the innocent from evil criminals. I have a memory about a long time ago some people orally transmitting the message to my ancestor, saying that my boys were doing fine and that they were still alive. In the story, a cousin Mc.G adopted one of the boys. Some Irish-Italian people coming from the kids of the kids of Nicky adopted the other boy. Anyway, one of the names was often heard and they memories decided to use it as their family name, since the family needed a new name to replace the real one. They thought of using that specific one, and to have a location in time and space in order to keep in memory the many events surrounding those years. They also did so to protect some of the members of the family from I don't know who or what, but I know the priest responsible for the changes was French. Much unfounded gossip followed the Irish, as always. The reality in this country was that they constantly worked

Sacred memories

with Spanish and Japanese people to study situations that caused psychological diseases and that rendered human behaviour extremely uncontrollable. They always did this in order to find a medicine or cure to treat those suffering from this. My point is that the place is renowned for the care of disorders related to psychological behaviour. I think it was in the 18th century, when there were men returning from war. During that time, some wives of these soldiers came to Ireland to ask doctors for help. These women were so frustrated about the behaviour of their husbands that they took control of the bank assets, threatening the Irish, saying they would not get their money if their husbands were not cured of their violent behaviour. The soldiers lost their patience and constantly yelled at and beat on them and their children. They blamed it on the English, saying they directed the embassy. At the end of that war, instead of killing them, the English authorities took advantage of them buts, which insulted them. I'm not sure why I am talking about this; I guess I just somehow found it worth pondering and it was part of what was happening at the time. I mentioned Billy the Kid and I remember that he was adopted in Ireland. He appeared to be present at the same time and space as the children of my ancestor. His mother had come to live in Ireland to study and she left after she got married, when her first love from Russia came to get her. At that time, the situation made it difficult for her to bring Billy with her to the husband's home. During that time, many children were looking for either their mother or father and for a period of time, my ancestor's children were trying to find her. Billy's Spanish-Italian father had lots of influence at that time. In my memories, this man named Eduardo was with those who brought me back to Ireland when I was gone and lost in a place somewhere. I can see this happening in a more distant past, maybe the 14th century or even the first century. Anyway, this man brought along a tiger as his pet and gave my family a baby, who we named Cesar. I can also see his office in another space and time, where he had a collection of human

Sacred memories

scalps he named the Irish Fred. In reality he was on the hunt for an Irish-Franco-Italian man who was abusing girls with crude sex, causing some to die from internal hemorrhaging. The story went that he personally got involved because one of the victims was his sister. I heard that someone else had caught the real murderer after he had caused the death of a black girl. Coincidently, I recognized the black woman in this image as being the same one who sang a song with Sidney, the song that was put on one of Whitney Houston's albums about 100 years later. It was a Russian or German company that was in possession of the recording. You all know the song, Heartbreak Hotel. It's also possible that the same script in a different past came from that same recording. About this black woman, she seemed to be the sister of the woman who had been one of Flint's mistresses during the same time that he was seeing Sidney. I met this woman again in this lifetime on a trip to Jamaica and like the rest, I was unable to connect her to the images of the past before the event had happened. Even if the sought-after Fred was not named Fred for real, he looked like an Irish Fred. A killer's stone head used Fred's name when he was doing his bad deeds. It's difficult for me to know for sure what his name was, and if he was the one who died, because there was also an Italian named Tony that could have been the one who died young because he also looked like them.

***

Out of all of this, I wonder if I could open up memories of what had happened in the lives of the children in the generation following that of my ancestor; this way, I could find them and warn them about the misfortune awaiting them. Unfortunately, I do not recall much about the children's lives. I suppose I had not been there to witness it happening.

The only thing I remember is who was there and I probably could find some information in medical records. At least I know who was from which generation and because of that, I can identify some of them. Haven't we all heard the story of Jesse! He is the distant cousin from

Sacred memories

the generation after my ancestor's generation. He came down from the big mansion to join the party, looking for the love of his life. The one I am referring to was the link to the sister's or brother's line of the children of my grandfather's grandparents. During that time, Jesse was just a little bit younger than Sidney's children were. His mother was one of the richer women of Ireland. What I saw, heard and remember is different from published stories, which could be from bad informants, with bad intentions. I know they went to defend their rights and for others to look for the lost parents during that same time when funds were held by French Protestants. A group of these Protestants had gone nuts and had planned to run away, taking the money in the bank with them. With all that was going on, the idea was to put the blame on the children as their way out. They knew that if there was a problem, the police might start shooting at the banks; therefore, they had replaced the employees with criminals in order to not bother with the threats, and just to ignore the payments due while they organized the robbery. I guess that is when they started to go into private homes. The rich woman's son tried to capture those who were running away in order to bring the money back to the beneficiary. His mother ended up paying a huge ransom for his capture. As for the money hidden in the trains, I do not have to continue and say how confused the people became AND HOW IMPOSSIBLE IT WAS FOR them to make a CLEAR JUDGEMENT. However, much unfortunate legislation occurred in relation to these events. There was confusion about identifying this individual because many names were the same during that and other space-times. Also, the family's partner protected him by hiding him.

***

In 1996, I was still not aware of the images from my past lives. One day I went to visit my father in his small mansion. My daughter was 2 years old and full of energy, running everywhere. My father, trying to be nice, took her to his office upstairs to show her his miniature car collection. After a while, I went upstairs to join them and I noticed a

Sacred memories

frame with a page from an old newspaper with the photograph of my distant maternal cousin, with a ransom for his capture. My father had received this as a gift. I was told that they captured him and since so much was wasted, he became the cause for new insurance laws after death. As for him, they had to falsify his death, because too many women he had impregnated were looking for him. He was finally getting married. Let's not forget that he had to put an end to the problems that his family was having, which had been instigated by the families of the unfortunate people who had died, when he had to defend himself during his journey. Apparently, the truth is that he lived until an old age. Many people wonder why they still talk about these same individuals, making some kind of models out of them. Why is it that we always hear about the same ones? The reason is simple: they are the ones who will be in demand if they come back because they produced many offspring. Obviously, they are important for so many and they have to get whatever they need in order to make it happen again. Anyway, with that newspaper, if he is to come back as a reincarnated version of himself, we will know what generation he was from and what the one from this story looks like. As for my family, my mother's father was a member of a family whose name had been changed. The change occurred at the beginning of the 19th century. George, a fictitious name, was the father of 12 children. He and his wife left Ireland to immigrate to southern Quebec on the Canadian Indian reserves at some time in the late 1950s. I was born in Canada, but my past-life ancestors lived in Ireland. I wonder how I'll be able to find out if it is me, when I can't even write down all of the proper names. I guess that, once again, I'll have to trust the angel to show me the way. The problem with putting my trust in angels is that they don't know how to avoid the problem caused by mankind's system. Otherwise, I risk experiencing many burdensome situations. There must be someone, somewhere, who I can trust - someone that will never play games with me and never, ever rob me. At least I still have some memories of Ireland;

Sacred memories

that will help me find a clue. On my father's side, the name was invented as far back as the first century A.D. and a lot of them have since changed their names, but not us. The images of the day the decision was made to take that name show a house that was kept and still exists; supposedly it's still owned by family on my father's side. It's approximately the first year of the first century A.D., in a big room with columns and cement statues. At that time, my uncle nephew Arnold was not there; he was living somewhere near Egypt. He was a barbarian or something during those years and many had been kidnapped. In that room, Evernaissant, her uncle and a couple of security guards were standing, forming a kind of circle.

The event legislated that day was carried out by a stubborn person wanting to meet me and it had turned into a scene of horror. What I was able to see was a black man making a disgusting gesture, as he presented himself to be the brother of a queen. He looked young, about 25 years old. He was at the door and my uncle decided to let him in, even after the guard had warned him not to. The man was there for Evernaissant. He asked her if she wanted to come with him to meet his queen because she wanted to make contact with Evernaissant due to an event she had experienced.

Evernaissant, thinking the man was some kind of wacko, responded quickly to the man:

- Imbecile, there is no way I will follow you anywhere!

The persistent man said:

- You have to come with me; I order you to do so!

He then started yelling:

- You'd better obey me; my sister is a queen and the queen gets what the queen wants!

My uncle decided to introduce himself:

- My name is Arthur. Let me tell you, sir, that here we don't force those we don't own to go anywhere they don't want to go! I am warning you. I am McSweeng.

The black man then started to move around like a maniac, dancing

Sacred memories

and getting closer to my uncle. Then he slipped a knife out of his boot and thrust it right into his heart. After that, the black man was labeled as the king's wicked man.

Anyway, the scene ended with the man sitting down. That last image was exactly like a painting of a distant family member of my mother's, sister's husband. This painting, worth 250 million dollars, used to be owned by the Queen of England. This business transaction occurred in this lifetime, not too long ago, and was published in the newspapers. Anyway, the man in the painting was exactly the same figure as that man, the king's murderer of these memories. I therefore say that, if that man's soul were alive today, and if he still had those ideas of killing the Irish king, my family on my father's side can at lest know not to get close to anyone who looks like the man in that painting.

***

One day I asked my father if he had any memories of past lives.
He answered me, unsure of himself:
- Maybe at times, I think so, but I'm not sure and I'm not even sure if I was your father then.
He started to giggle.
I didn't understand all of what he meant and for that reason, I will think about it some more. I know that when I'm around him, I get many images, which remind me of a previous life. All of this questioning haunts me. I need to know why he said such a thing. This idea only brings me back to that same question, which psychiatrists still wonder about. Does the transfer of images come from us or did we receive them from another person? After wondering about this, I will need more proof before believing that it was my soul who lived there before because both options are possible. I need to stop and acknowledge that some religions say that reincarnation is a satanic idea. I probably wouldn't believe in it either if I hadn't experienced situations that proved to me that it does. I understand that

Sacred memories

the soul under duress has become lost, without any proof whatsoever and in such situations, our soul becomes overwhelmed with doubts. Therefore, I know that only those who have experienced something that proves to them that life exists after death can believe in eternal life. Fortunately, those who haven't had any such experiences can still hope and have faith. Therefore, I think it's good to keep an open mind, so fights between those who know and those who are skeptical can cease. Getting back to my life, my paternal grandfather told me that he knew what my name was in a past life. I can tell you that it was the only thing I ever heard from him in all of his living days. Although, a paranormal event happened to me on the day he died. It was a cold winter's night in 2003. I forgot to write down the date and in order to retrace the exact time, I'm referring to an event, which had happened the week before. Lindsey, a young girl who was the daughter of my father's friend, got stabbed to death in her apartment across the street from me. They said on the news that it was her boyfriend who killed her. I had been alone for some time in my room. 48 hours had passed since I had awoken from my sleep, I had a very high fever and no one was there to help me. I sometimes opened my eyes. I must have gone to Glasgow where the souls meet or I must have been on an astral voyage. I thought I must have had a heart attack or something. While in bed, I became very thirsty, and I had to get up to get myself something to drink. The kitchen was just a couple of steps away from my room. I felt calm and a little scared. I finally reached the door of the fridge. My throat was so dry I thought I'd die if I didn't have a drink right then. I tried to open the door, and could feel my hand on the handle but I wasn't able to open it. I tried and tried, but it was no use; the door just wouldn't open. I was panicking by then. I needed to drink something and had the urge to run for help somehow. As I again tried to open the damn door, I decided to stop for a moment and look into my room, which I could see from where I was standing. I then noticed that my body was still lying in bed while I was standing in the kitchen. I then started to feel

sacred memories

scared and I wanted to scream:
- No! My life isn't over. Please! No! Tell me this isn't happening so soon!

I thought that I would no longer be able to see those I loved. It made me feel so bad and so disappointed. I thought that the fear I was feeling was going to stay within me forever. Now that my bodily life was over, was this the feeling that would be the fragrance filling my soul? I started to scream again.
- Help! Someone! Please, help!

What was happening that my words made no sound? That was when the shadow of a tall man suddenly stood in the center of my kitchen. I looked at him curiously, and he then started talking to me.
- Christine, your name was once Sidney and please do not be scared. I want you to know that I've known you for a long time. First, I want you to know that you're not the one who is going to die today.

He then stopped to take the time to tell me something that seemed to be hurting him.
- It's just me leaving for the other world.

I wondered what I could possibly ask him before it was too late and he was gone.

Since no sound wanted to come out of me, I just stood there, paralyzed, staring at him.

He then began insisting, and I could see he was about to leave:
- Please, you have to promise that you're not going to follow me. This is really important.

I could see his shadow moving and in a flash, he had gone right through the back door. He disappeared just like that, without even telling me who he was. I was unable to see him because his shadow was in the dark and with no light to help distinguish his features, I had no idea of who he was. Not knowing what to do next, I turned once more to look at my body still lying there on the bed, and I was still not in it.

I wondered what would become of me. I decided to wait and see the

sacred memories

light, as I had heard would happen, but no such thing appeared. It was still the middle of the night. I decided to close my eyes; I was trembling too much and couldn't see properly anymore. Finally, I started feeling myself being sucked back into my body, just like into a tornado that keeps on turning. I stayed awake for a while in the other side of the world. Then it took me a couple of seconds to awaken. Unfortunately, when I thought I was back into myself, only half of my soul was inside and the rest was still on the other side. I could see and feel that I was still being pulled back in. I wanted so badly to repossess my body. My soul was crying and it wasn't water, but a warm feeling of blood running into my stomach. This desire was just like the thirst that I had been unable to quench. I struggled, holding onto the doorframe, shouting.

- Help! Please, someone! Help me, I can't move! Someone! Help!

Sadly, no one could hear me. For a moment, I lost hope of regaining my body and I was terribly scared. Fill with regret, I still wanted to find love, I wanted to stay alive so badly and I wasn't ready to die yet. I didn't want to believe I was dead, and I thought to myself "Not now, I'm still young." I held on to the idea that magic existed and that miracles happened, With that thought in my mind, I fell into a deep sleep but just for a short period of time, until I awoke in my body. I was back but my heart was beating so fast that it was hurting me. Luckily, I was back and alive. I wasn't sure, but I could feel how painful it was for me to breathe. For at least a half an hour, I was paralyzed and couldn't move, but I knew I was saved. I can still remember the feeling at that moment, when my soul made love, sticking like heavy glue when entering my body. I shook just like the relief one feels after giving birth. I understood that a place really existed where we go after death. Yes, a continuity of life existed somewhere, and this eased my worried mind. I also noticed that the phenomenon came with some issues, such as an unshakable thirst. Anyway, the forces of a higher world had come to nourish my soul in need. After all these emotions, I took my phone and called 911

Sacred memories

for an ambulance; it was the only number that worked. When they got to my house, I offered no explanation, but just decided to let them take me to the hospital, where I was able to sleep some more, in the safety of the hospital staff's supervision. Because I was still in shock, I didn't talk much. The next day, I found out my grandfather had died and I realized that the man that came to visit me in the night had to have been him leaving this world. I concluded that he wanted me to know that he knew my name from before because it is the only thing he told me. It took me a while to get back to normal. I was very tired from the intake of information that my soul had ingested. Many memories had sprouted up in my mind when he had called me Sidney, the name I supposedly had gone by in my other life.
I must say that it was not the only paranormal event which brought me the same information.

***

A couple of days before going to the hospital, my friend Steven came to visit and asked me if his friend could stay with me for the night. He thought it could be necessary for my protection until they found out for sure who had murdered Lindsey. Also, he thought the protection would be needed because a black guy who I thought was my friend had left some of his things in my apartment until his mother finished some renovations at his home. There was a rumor going around saying that I might be in danger and the way they said it made it sound serious. Poor Steven; he had not chosen his friend wisely, and I had to make the protector leave after two days with me. He was as dangerous, if not more so, than that murderer, but I will get back to this story later. A couple of days after my visit to the hospital, Lesley, who had left his things at my place, arrived in the middle of the night with three girls he had picked up at a bar in downtown Montreal. They were some American girls here on vacation. I don't know why they decided to come to Montreal when their chalet was a 2-hour drive away. One of the pretty girls looked exactly like an actress. She was blond and very attractive. She had a cut on her finger and asked

sacred memories

me if I had any Band-Aids. I gave her the Band-Aid. The girl was giggling a lot and she and her friend looked either drunk or stoned. Lesley asked me why I had gone to the hospital and I told the entire story about what had happened to me on that night my grandfather died. I was kind of afraid of Lesley, since I had seen him in the window at Lindsey's house the night she got murdered.

For me, he was now a suspect who could be dangerous and I wasn't feeling great being around him.

I wanted to tell the girls not to trust him and to stay as far away from him as possible because even I wanted him to get far away from me. The actress wanted to use the telephone but mine wasn't working, except for 911, so I told her where to find a phone booth nearby. They wanted to visit my apartment and I couldn't let them see my ratty possessions I had, nor did I want them to see the papers I was working on, so I just told them:

- There's nothing to see. Just don't go snoop around for nothing.

While the actress was talking to Lesley on the back porch, I drew near and tried to tell them not to go with him but he was right there. The only words I could say were "Don't disturb the children they're sleeping."

That sure did not make any sense, but if I told them what I thought of him and then they told him what I had just said, he might have become hysterical and might have started to act like a psychopath. The way I was feeling made me look like I was the lunatic, but I still tried to warn them.

I tried to insist:

- Please, if you don't mind, I'll take his car to drive you back, and since there isn't enough space, he can stay here! Anyway, he looks like he's been drinking!

- No, no, it's ok; he'll drive us; it's his car!

- Yes, but I really think it would be better if I went, because I know my way around better than him.

Nothing I said had any effect and they finally left after waking the

Sacred memories
neighbour to use the phone. I never heard from them again.
The odd thing is that some time later, maybe a year or more, that actress played in a movie that showed a scene very similar to the idea of what I had described to them as happening to me on the night my grandfather died. I am implying that they used this idea to make a movie, but forgot about me! What bothered me the most was not that they used my experience to make a movie, but the fact they put more trust in Lesley the robber, who could also be a murderer, to take them home.
Even though I had insisted, I can see how being frightened can make others be mistaken about a person's true character. It was heart-breaking; however, judging only by appearances can often make an innocent person the target of the worst upcoming dangers.

*****

Chapter two
The event

I have often had doubts about the existence of a past life and about whether I am the person I remember being. So many people with similar physical similarity exist and some people that look alike can be thought of as being the same person. I guess I was lucky to remember something that happened in the past and it happened again. Some people were doing research into the families where it occurred, to see if it would reoccur. The event sounds more grandiose than it really is but I found the effect to be somewhat exceptional, as well as confusing. It was a summer day, in the late afternoon; I had just arrived from a 5-month trip to Mexico to visit my mother. I came back to this apartment in Verdun near Montreal, which is on the same corner where my paternal grandmother lived all of her life. Coming in the door, I took off my shoes, slowly unpacked my luggage and went straight to bed. The sun had not set yet. I was very tired

The event

from my long trip but couldn't fall asleep. I felt very anguished, as though death was coming upon me. These ideas must have been the result of my being depressed because I had not been allowed to see my children after separating from my partner after an 8-year relationship. I kept thinking that they just wanted me to die because they didn't want to reason and they kept making up lies about me. I was so hurt and since I was innocent of the accusation, I couldn't hide in the guilt, since none of the actions and none of the ideas of the behaviour existed. I really missed them and the situation was too depressing. I was lying in my bed when suddenly a weird noise caught my attention. It sounded like fireworks. I hardly gave it a second though, which was not my usual habit. I turned my eyes to glance at the upper part of the window, which I had left curtainless so that I could see the sky. I was taken by surprise and had no time to avoid what was coming at me. Time stood still while I watched an unusual cloud trying to move away from the other clouds, which were all being blown by the wind. As the small hurricane passed by faster than the speed of light, everything happened in slow motion so I was paralyzed. The little grey cloud made its way out of the sky, came down in a straight line and stopped right beside my window. It was the first time I had ever seen a cloud so low in the sky. With all the noise, I thought it could be the end of the world. Still paralyzed, I stared at the cloud as it illuminated a muddled shadow of someone's soul. I felt as if it were staring at me. Then, unexpectedly, part of it quickly entered my window. As I tried to avoid the substance, it hit me right in my lower back. This natural event made no sense to me but it hit me hard enough to feel it like a big punch, without even breaking the window! Could this have been scientifically possible? It did happen and I was not stoned or drunk or sick in the head, and I did get a backache. The cloud substance took the shape of an arm and its beating heart was on the outside. After it had disappeared, time resumed its normal speed. I took a moment to try to understand what had just happened to me. I had a weird notion that I had been

The event

struck by a bullet, and that I was in heaven and real life at the same time. Very possibly angels were hiding the truth from me as it was happening to prevent me from seeing or feeling my death. I then placed myself in a foetal position, sweating and soaking wet; I just wanted to fall asleep. I thought I was dead. My curiosity wanted to know what I was going to become and what was disturbing me. I didn't know why, but the thing which I had just had contact with seemed to have magic powers and seemed to be able to make decisions about its actions. After being in contact with this thing, I was a changed person; in fact, many of my spiritual doubts disappeared. Startled to my soul, I could no longer sleep so I decided to run downstairs to tell someone what had just happened to me. The older man at the store was there and I stood in front of him, but he looked right through me as if I wasn't there.

I again wondered if I were dead.

- Sir, can you see me? I'm right here. Can you hear me, sir? I was just hit by a cloud! Hello sir; please say something!

It took a moment before he looked at me and finally responded with a small laugh.

- Of course I can see you! You're standing right in front of me! Did you tell me you were hit by lightning? Just go to the hospital, Christine, there's not much I can do about it.

- No, I don't think I'll do that just yet. They might take me for a nut case. I'm having trouble believing that it really happened myself. On the other hand, what if they decide to do all sorts of weird tests on me. I think I'll just go to bed and see how I feel later. If I really need to go to the hospital, I will, but not now. But I could use your help since I am a bit scared. If I don't come down in the morning, just send an ambulance or someone to check to see if I'm still alive!

- Sure, I can do that; Tell you what, before I open the store tomorrow, I'll come and knock on your door to see if you're okay.

- Great! Thank you, sir; it's very kind of you!

I went back home and in the morning he knocked on my door and I

The event

was still alive. He also sent the delivery boy to check on me from time to time. For about ten months after that, I stayed in bed with a high fever. I didn't go to the hospital out of fear that they wouldn't believe me. But I spent those ten months with someone. I met him one week after the event, when I was in the store. This man was standing next to me and I asked him for a cigarette (I smoked at the time, but I no longer do, thank God). Anyway, the man in the store decided to interrupt me.
- I'd like to introduce you to Christine. I bet you don't know her! I want you to be nice to her.
The man with the pale blue eyes then looked at me in a weird way.
- My name is Gus and I am here working for the owner next door. Could I come up and have a beer and chat with you?
- Sure, why not! The owner next door is my cousin's half brother.
When we reached my place, he sat down on the sofa. As he drank his beer he told me his life story.
- I just split up with my wife after catching her in bed with another woman. She admitted to me that she preferred girls and no longer want to be with me.
I don't know why, but I felt as if I could trust this man, and he got in my pants very easily. Then as quickly as one week later, he moved in with me. He was going to keep an eye on me. I don't know if he believed me or even if he had seen through his window what had happened to me, but he never told me that I was a liar and that comforted me. I slept all the time, my fever was always a bit too high and I was also very dizzy most of the time. I was able to shower, clean, cook and do the shopping but that took up 3 to 4 hours of my day and the rest of time I slept, hoping that I would regain my strength. Gus worked as a plumber almost every day. Unlike me, he only needed one day a week to rest. Then one night, while we were in bed, he told me something which came as a surprise to both of us:
- I'm adopted.
Then he told me where he was given up for adoption, along with his

The event

age. All this fit the information about a son my aunt had given birth to and had given up for adoption. I was sleeping with my cousin; how weird was that! I was not expecting this to happen in my life. We both knew we were going to split up, because this was not healthy. In addition, I couldn't get pregnant, knowing the children would probably be born with disabilities. This situation explained why I was seeing my girl cousins inside, as if I was living with them. The funniest thing was that all this time he was working for his half brother without even knowing that he was his brother, so I thought. Now I know why I felt like I could trust him, he had my own comforting blood running through his veins. Obviously, it was not his charm, which could have captivated me so quickly. Unfortunately, I was not getting much better and he, on the other hand, was becoming rather violent. He made me feel so bad, especially when he started to say stupid things such as "I hate my real family; they abandoned me and they don't love me". I remember telling him my story about how I felt about them at times.

- Gus, don't hate them so much. Just look at me, I didn't even know you existed and sometimes it makes no difference to have family. Once, not long ago, I was without food and without a job and I had no money at all and I called some of my mom's sisters for help and all they could say was "Don't ask me, I can't help you. Call your dad." Imagine! They were going to let me die thinking my dad was going to help, but he didn't want to help me that time! In other words, sometimes having them as family is the same as not having any family at all.

He looked at me confused but continued saying the same thing.

- You should know, Gus, that if your sisters or I had known about you, we would have helped you.

That did not make him change his mind. I guess forgiveness or understanding were not part of him; he was unable to sympathize during moments of despair. Gus and I did not last very long. He lost his sanity once but I'll get back to this later. As for the event, I

The event

wondered if someone saw the cloud hovering next to my window. I told many people about the event and most of them had no reaction. They were mostly mean about it, telling me to stop inventing stories and then they just ignored what I was telling them. For a while I just wanted to know how this attack by the cloud would impact me, if it was dangerous and if I could die. I didn't want to argue with people about whether it was the truth or not. I just wanted to talk about it normally, since I was losing so much water but I wasn't even sure if I was losing water or making it. One thing that had changed after the attack was that I was dreaming a lot more and usually about real people who were hovering between life and death at the time they were dying. Sometimes I was able to hear people thinking after I had just seen them. At times I heard a whisper in the air, revealing the ancestral name of the person I had just met. The worst thing about this event, apart from the fatigue, was being treated as a liar. I had never been able to deal with any kinds of false allegations since the day my ex lied, accusing me of things that I had never done and bringing others to perceive me as someone that I was not. Obviously he made sure I wouldn't have a life after him. My ex took away my friends, my family and my children's rights. As for my wondering about clouds, I came to think it was rather sad that we humans were not able to tame these creatures. There are not many medical studies on the subject; therefore, I was not able to find out what would become of me because of this event. I did meet a young student doctor, a smart guy who came to visit me a couple of times. I suppose he was the only person who considered that I was telling the truth. This person was kind enough to go to China to get me some information on the subject. When he came back, he told me that in China it did happen to some people, but was a lot rarer in this country; in fact, he couldn't find any instances. In China, studies had been carried out about the phenomenon of people who had been hit by clouds. My friend discovered that the victims usually experienced headaches and dehydration, and that some part of their brain that

The event was usually inactive would start functioning. They concluded that it was a small electric shock. I saw a show on television about a man to whom this had happened, although he was hit outdoors, as if by lightning, and the result for him was that he regained his vision after being blind. After a while, my skeptical mother decided to believe me, and she found a book written in England, which talked about a little greyish cloud. The little greyish cloud has struck many people. It is said that this specific immortal cloud escaped and is stuck between two worlds. This book also talks about religion and student's home directions. Anyway, there are about 2,000 books with this same title, the Cloud of the Unknowing. In some religions, if a person is touched by the lightning cloud, he or she is chosen to become a saint. A friend who is an airplane pilot told me his theory, which I found amusing: he thinks that the cloud made love to me because this is how they multiply and grow. Well, I also have my opinion on the subject, because changes came over me after I was struck by the cloud. Let me start by telling you the ideas I had in my mind before it occurred. My life was a mess; I was lonely and very sad and I thought I was going to die from this loneliness. I was wondering why I was alone and I didn't want to die, because I knew life would become very good at times and because I had some things to do before leaving. I needed to find the reasons and remember the places, which anticipated my will to go on. I believed this cloud held a magic power. It was not like the others; it had a dream, a life within it. It seemed to have a traveler aboard, which came from the other world in between the dimension of the afterlife. I will reveal to you that this thing had to be feminine, since the echo of a girl's voice emanated from it. I thought that this echo might be a projection of myself but that was impossible, because I didn't have the answer to these names that she was revealing to me.

Who could claim to have the scientific answer about what that cloud was, when it seemed to be a spiritual being!

***

The event

I felt as if this cloud was an angel carrying the laws of judgment. I felt as if she needed to protect me because when she had come and hit me during that time of slow motion, she spoke to me:

- No, you cannot die just yet. Remember, you still have some tasks to accomplish.

That is when I started thinking that she might be an existing soul waiting to be reborn. I speculated and came to many conclusions. Anyhow, I had another visit from a cloud about a year later. I'm not sure if it was the same one. There was also a gold electrode that kept appearing and disappearing after the event occurred.

It was January, I had just returned home after spending the holidays at my mother's. I was all alone in the living room working on those lottery papers, and I heard a sound coming from the bathroom. I got up and walked as far as the bathroom door. I jumped when I saw a big ball of cloud pass right in front of me. I watched as it flew into my kitchen, but before I could try to grab the substance, it went through the door and disappeared into the sky. It was odd: I hadn't taken any drugs nor had I been sleepwalking. I wish I knew why this always happened to me when I was alone. I went back to what I had been doing. 15 minutes passed and I heard a knock at the door. Who could it be? Not the cloud! I opened the door and saw that it was just Peter, the young man who worked at the store downstairs. All anxious, he said to me:

- The old man at the store is very ill. He keeps treating the customers very disrespectfully!

He's going to get himself killed!

- Calm down, Peter! Come in and let's calmly talk it over.

- Sure, but don't ask me to calm down. Don't you know about the 4 hold-ups last year? They shot at him because of his behaviour. I should know; I was there when it happened! I'm telling you, it's going to happen again if he doesn't start to talk nicely to people. You should try to help him, Christine.

Peter was not my lover. We had never made love, although he would

The event

come to visit me, since the man downstairs had sent him to see if I was ok. Peter was in his early twenties, with red hair and blue eyes. He was fine-looking, but I had no interest in him in terms of intimate relationships. Still, he talked to me about his personal life.
- Christine, I want your advice on what I am about to do to my girlfriend. Since she left me, I decided to go ahead and take the children away from her.
- Peter, come on, don't do such a thing. At least try to make some kind of friendly arrangement with her.
- Why would I even try to do that? She's just a stupid cow and I hate her.
- I can understand why you're so angry, but take my situation as an example! Don't you think it's unfair what they did to me! You should be aware that if you lie to get custody of your kids, you could put their lives in danger. Look at what happened to me. They tried to kill me about 3 times. And don't you think the children would hate you for not letting them see their mom and for hurting their mother! You know, Peter, if you need some ideas about what to tell her instead, or if you want someone to talk to her for you, come to me and I'll help you with that. I owe you that for coming to check on me. Please don't declare war.
At that moment in time, I took Peter's intention to take revenge very seriously. Thankfully, he took my advice and listened to me. I was able to make him reason and remember how to remain a sensible, normal human being before it was too late.
- Okay, Christine. I'll try it your way because I don't want the children, or me, for that matter, to get hurt.
Peter left the room to go to the bathroom.
When he came back, I saw that he was holding my Vogue magazine. It made me remember about the cloud I had seen earlier.
- Hey, you won't believe what happened to me before you arrived.
I told him the story and spontaneously changed the subject.
- Can you believe that I saw Bill when I was in Cancun? It was weird; I

The event

heard him talking on a C.B. radio in a cab. It's funny that we went there at the same time. By the way, do you know who Bill is? I assume you do because most people in this city know him!
- Well, yes, I've heard about him, though I'm not sure I've ever met him.
- Wait, there's a picture in this magazine with a man that looks exactly like him. Let me show you.

I started to leaf through the pages and finally reached the page, which had a picture of two black men sitting on chairs in a Moroccan hotel lobby. However, impossible as it may seem, the image of the two men had disappeared.
- This is very curious. I swear that they were there. I'm 100% sure of this. I've looked at this specific photo many times. I really don't understand it!

I looked at Peter with a smile and continued to turn the pages.
- Peter, you have to look at this. There's something that wasn't here before and it's kind of strange-looking.

I've heard about angels making drawings before and this drawing, with a multiple coloured bird coming out of the neck of a woman, had all the characteristics of what an angel child would draw. It's very unusual that there were crayons on the floor. I had washed my floor on my hands and knees and had cleaned every corner of it many times since the kids had left. From a scientific perspective, I had to exclude the idea that this drawing was drawn with those crayons because it was printed and had a glossy finish. The only thing I have to say is that I had looked through this magazine page by page many times before and that it was the only one I had had in my home for more than a year. I started to wonder if the fact that those two men had disappeared meant something. I had to conclude that the cloud, which I had just seen had done this drawing. Like all normal people, I am skeptical. Maybe someone came and replaced my magazine with another one or the page that had the drawing on it was so stuck with glue that I hadn't seen it before. I asked around to find out if other

The event

issues of this magazine had the two men still sitting in the hotel or if they had the drawing, but no one was able to find any other issues of this magazine. Anyway, maybe someone else has this same magazine and can tell me if it doesn't have the drawing and does have the picture of the men sitting on the chairs and if I'm hallucinating. I found this drawing the very same day I saw a cloud come out of my bathroom! The magazine is a March 2001 issue of Vogue. The drawing is on page 479 and the two men in the hotel lobby are on page 382. That evening ended with Peter kissing me on the cheek then leaving to go home.

The next morning came fast. I had to go downstairs and talk to the owner of the store. When I got there, it came down to a conversation about civility.

- Sir, I need to talk to you and you need to listen.
- Sure; what is it, Christine?
- Well, I was wondering if you're trying to die, given the way you're acting towards the people you're in touch with every day? It looks to me like you're asking to get killed!

He stopped and gazed at me with a very tired look, then replied:
- No that's not what I want. Please wait for me; I'm going to get my keys. This is what I have been trying to do for a while and what you just said to me gives me the courage to finally do something positive. Thank you. Let's close this store.

He turned off the lights, then came out and locked the doors. That was the end of his working days at the store. The next morning he had put up a "store for rent" sign.

Somehow I feel guilty about the fact that right after I was touched by the cloud, I touched the store owner's hands and they became very swollen and filled with water. Was it my fault? In addition, Armand, my father's friend who also lived downstairs, got water-swollen feet and hands after I just touched his hand.

However, the odd thing was that it only happened to those people who I had observed being mean to children! Was it a spell that this

The event

angel had cast on them? I don't know why, but I started wondering if I was a danger for others because of this energy substance thing within me. At that moment, I was scared because if it was true, people were going to want me dead so that they wouldn't get this water-logged swelling sickness. Doctors call this disease dropsy. I am again thinking about the changes that have happened to me since I was in contact with this thing. This thing told me she had the power to bring me people who would be able to help me. I have to admit that she has brought me hope and proof, but can she become dangerous? After thinking that I might have become a danger for others, a miraculous event occurred which made me change my mind. This happened after I met Joy. I met her when she came knocking on my door, looking for Gus just before we got separated. Anyway, she kept coming to visit me. It was a nice, sunny spring day when Joy arrived at my door. She was with the 2-year-old child of her friend or her sister. The poor kid had a disease which had left him mute and deaf.

Joy came in.

- Hello, Christine. How are you today?
- Good, and yourself?
- I'm exhausted. Can you help me change the baby's diaper?
- Sure, no problem; just give him to me.

So I took the child and put him on my bed, caressing his head. He smiled at me.

- Tell me, Joy. What's wrong with this child? I can't move or straighten his legs!
- That's because he's handicapped.

I felt for the poor kid, so I started to rub his feet and legs to try to straighten them. I felt that his nervous system was totally inactive.

- Joy, come look how nice he is, even though he can't function normally. Look at how nicely he's smiling at me!

Joy seemed happy to see her smiling boy, so she decided to invite me

The event

over to her place.
- Do you want to come to my place for a couple of hours?
- Sure, why not! I have nothing else to do today!
- We'll walk there, since it's close to here, about 10 minutes by foot.
- Good. It's such a beautiful day today.

As we walked through the back alley, she showed me where her apartment door was, up on the third floor. We had to go up an old, dangerous-looking metal spiral staircase to get there. While climbing up, I wondered whether I could discover what had caused his nervous system to fail. I refused to believe that at his age there was no way possible to reverse his non-functioning nervous system. Could I project an energy onto him which would enable him to hear my thoughts? I believed I could help activate his nerve system because I still had a strong electrical force all around my body from the touch of the angel cloud.

Joy finally opened the door.
- Christine, just sit on the sofa until I finish giving him his lunch. It's not going to take long. The thing is, I don't have a table and chairs in the kitchen.
- Ok, I'll wait for you in the living room.

The boy didn't take long to have his lunch and before I knew it, they had joined me in the living room. The boy went to play with his toys right near us, where we could see him. Joy sat down very close to me on the sofa. I think Joy had a thing for girls, but maybe I was mistaken. I guess it was Steven's fault, since he tended to exaggerate when he made up sexual stories, which is why I thought that about Joy. The other day, he came to me with a question about my sexual orientation and he said that Joy told him she was going to make me her girlfriend, meaning her sexual friend. Personally I like men. I have always liked men, but I have to admit that Joy was a good-looking girl and I might be curious about experimenting something with her. I

The event

wasn't sure, but I think she was hitting on me, so, I decided to ask her something.
- Joy, can I kiss you?
She smiled, then she nodded yes.
I wasn't sure what to do, although I knew it wasn't going to go further than a kiss, since we had to take care of the boy, who was still awake. I slowly approached her, putting my hand on her breast. I hesitated and then lay my lips on hers. Suddenly there was a noise at the door. I stopped and turned around to see what it was, and the little boy went crawling up to the door. In a fraction of a second, he disappeared. The person who had just came by, probably decided to turn around and leave but hadn't closed the door properly and the little boy slipped out. I got up quickly, adrenaline rushing through my veins. I then pushed the door open and saw him sitting on the edge of the balcony, which had no railing. He was looking down three storeys to the ground below. I jumped out and grabbed him without hesitating. I felt stressed, I was shaking all over and my head was throbbing. It was very weird, because right when my energy moved from my body to the boy's, his nervous system started to regain its normal activity and his body began vibrating for the first time. Joy was right behind me. I turned towards her and stretched my arms out to her.
- Here, Joy. Take him.
She took him in her arms but he fought to get down and play, so she put him down. We started to talk to him even though he was deaf.
- Jay, Jay! Are you all right? Come here; come see us.
He looked at us and nodded, then a miracle happened. While raising his arm to show us his toy, he spoke, saying "Look, it's a toy." It was a miracle, the boy was able to speak. He was no longer either deaf or dumb. He had lost his disabilities instantaneously. The stressful incident had tired me out, so I called it a day.
- Joy, I'm going home. I might see you later.

The event

- Okay. Anyway, I'm going to take a nap with the baby soon.
- Bye, then. Take care of yourself.
- Okay, you too.

I went home, thinking it was odd that we had not discussed the fact that he was cured! I guess we had remained silent, scared that speaking about it would change the miraculous situation. However, I can say that happiness was felt in that room on that day. I wondered if angels had caused this miracle to happen and who had opened the door? I know that the transfer of electricity and nervous energy from me to the little boy had somehow helped to reverse his non-functioning system. It had also made me feel better to know that having contact with people didn't just make them sick, because this time, contact had caused a miracle. I was happy to see that sometimes believing could answer some prayers. That day was the last time I saw Joy except for once when I saw her walking down my street with a black girl. She was pointing towards where I live, for the girl to see. And whatever she might have been saying to her about me, I'll never know. It's very strange that later, when Steven came to see me, he had not seen her anywhere either. He had also tried to find her but couldn't find any indication of where she might be. I did see a girl who looked just like her, sitting at a table in a restaurant, but it was on TV, during a music award. She was sitting with an old lady, that I heard was her grandmother, named Mrs. Joplin, but I could have been mistaken. A little further was this other girl, a singer presented at the awards. I recognized her because she had frequently come to visit the people across the street before they sold. I think she was friends with Gus and the owners next door. This girl was known to pretend to be the author of one of my inspirations back in my singing days. I hadn't found that song to be very good but it had made it to the top 10. It was called "The first cut is the deepest," and I had dedicated it to Gus, because he was the one I had been thinking of when I had sung it. The worst thing about this song was that it was a mix of an older song, which had existed a

The event

long time ago and had been originally sung by a man. Therefore, this specific song was not really composed by me; it was one that I had found. But it was my voice they were playing on the air at the place in the song where a curse was uttered that I sang Gus. I saw that the people who had stolen the song had added a line, then left me like a good-for-nothing. I wanted to say this, but the reality was that I didn't really want to follow them wherever they were going. However, I did worry about Joy and at a certain point,
I even thought she might have told the truth about some of my songs. I worried because the black girl I had seen her with was dangerous. I had seen her before pushing a 12-year-old white girl very hard onto the cement sidewalk. What if the black girl was related to the R.C.A. Music Group's owner or to the owners of the music station that sold the recordings of I?

I wondered if those who were making a profit weren't just hiding the songs under the name of just any artist, while they collected their profits. Those who had made the record could have been collecting the profits while placing the blame on innocent people as they could be asking them to sing it. But no matter who the guilty person was, they hadn't given me any of my legal share of the copyright. Companies making 78 rpm records had made lots of profits. And just look at the number of deejays in bars who buy singles! Sometimes I wish I could have added up all the sales figures and have those people arrested who took my share of the copyright for the songs I had composed, mostly because they had come and murdered many people near my home while trying to kill me. Anyhow, no matter who the girl was, her behaviour was definitely dangerous and animal-like, and that made me wonder if Joy was still alive.

***

At a moment in time, I wondered if hell really existed. One day, someone recorded my singing inspirations and they turned out to be hits. I had been having a hard time trying to find a way to make enough money those days. I needed to scrape together just enough

The event

money to be able to get quality time with the people I loved. That was why I was trying to filled-up all the possible combinations of a lottery that night. Some analysts say that only one person in a million is capable of doing so. I was listening to the radio with the volume set not too loud. It was about one o'clock in the morning. The breeze was blowing in through my slightly open window and Bryan Adams's song "Heaven" was playing. In my mind, I was anguishing about how to get out of this apartment so I could go live in the countryside, while still having the security I needed. I wanted a haven from all the wars. I wanted to live in an enjoyable place, where I could have my kids, the people I loved and my friends over for visits, a place they would enjoy and want to visit to see me. I also wanted to be able to spend time with my children and friends while being able to provide them with their need to get away, without putting them or myself in any kind of danger, which I don't want to talk about. However, I am getting old and soon it will be too late for me. Suddenly, an unusual sound from outdoors caught my attention. It sounded like a combination of a windmill and new age tinkling music. The sound was very loud, as if it came from an amplifier. I was curious, so I got close to the window to see. I was amazed when I saw what was there. I couldn't believe my eyes. There was a big flying object hovering about 20 feet above the three-storey apartment. It was a flying saucer measuring about 942 square feet. The object lights were not blinding blue, yellow and purple of color. Every time I've seen or experienced paranormal activities, time seemed to stop around me, as if everyone else was on pause or their minds were sleeping and the earth had stopped turning. These moments always brought me tranquility and peace of mind. This object definitely had some living beings inside it. In my imagination, an image of what the beings looked like was telepathically transmitted to me. I have to admit that I was skeptical about the actual existence of these creatures because my eyes saw only the machine. Anyway, these creatures had ideas similar to ours. They appeared to have developed the ability to provoke and

The event

change natural activities. They looked like human beings, though darker in color and with a crown on their head which was part of their body, just like the image of Ramsey's or like a lizard. At that moment, with time standing still, a conversation between a couple was telepathically transmitted to me. They revealed this to me:

- We live in our temple, (meaning their body), for one thousand years before dying. We have one partner only to live and work with during that time. If we disobey the laws, it will affect the star system and could cause a tragedy. I asked them why they never walked on earth and they replied:

- If we are in contact with air, we'll die very quickly.

They also told me they could see me and the entire path of my life since the beginning of the existence of my soul. They were surprised to see me. They recognized me from long ago and this gave them hope and faith in the existence of an eternal life. These creatures were happy about being able to communicate, hear and see me. I think it was the electricity from the cloud, which illuminated my soul, which made it possible for them to see me. They also didn't want the earth to be destroyed because they said the planet wouldn't remake itself and they had the power to try and stop whatever might destroy it. Those creatures seemed to like earth and some of us, but they saw us as animals who were still stupid. They told me they were going to help me get the funds or the things I needed. Just before the saucer went back up in a straight line, the female asked her husband if they could adopt me because she liked me. But, as I said before, I was sceptical about the messages I received because I couldn't see them and this machine could have been something else, like an atomic bomb, a small visiting planet, an object created by humans, or even a tangible apparition sent by angels or the devil. Anyway,

I saw what I saw and while the saucer was still there, I wanted to go get the neighbours in order for them to see it too. Hypnotized as I was, my only reaction was to start singing the song that was playing on the radio. I know someone has the proof of the existence of this

The event

object, because that night someone recorded me singing "Heaven" and another song I had composed. I heard this version on the radio with the amazing music of the flying saucer in the background. Therefore, I know someone has the original recording from that night. If scientists know how to analyze extra-terrestrial sounds, they'll have to listen to this recording and analyze the sound to confirm that it came from a strange enormous flying object that had the power to send telepathic ideas and images. After the couple left, the communications stopped. I wonder if it was these creatures in the flying saucer who had recorded me and broadcast it on the radio. However, I find it more logical to think that it could have been Hydro Québec with their meter outside or Rogers AT&T, since I believe the police had planted a bug to monitor me. Regardless of who did it, I was broadcast on air and someone said my name only once. Then, from all they recorded of me, a false name was used. I presume that they had done that in order to steal my acquired rights.

I do believe that the paranormal activities I had been made to endure unblocked my telepathic communication. However, I have reason to believe that either the spiritual substance or the extra-terrestrial creatures was responsible for many of earth's natural disasters, but I cannot say which ones.

***

Chapter Three

The dream of a royal member's departure
***

I can't remember what year it was when this happened, but it was a little after the events, so it could have been around March of 2002 or 2003. Outside it still looked like winter. At that moment in time, I really thought that the end of the world that we had been expecting was very close, and that we had barely escaped it. I couldn't find my friends; they had all moved and changed their phone numbers. My

The dream of a royal member's departure

father was somewhat angry at me and I didn't understand why, but I guess he had taken my ex's word over mine. He didn't want to help me, even though he owed me my share, which he wanted to steal from me to give to his new children. At that time, I had no work and at the government agency, they refused to give me the help I was entitled to get. I had just got back not long ago from my mother's and everyone was closing the door on me. Even my family told me:
- Ask your father, We don't have enough to help you.

I was discouraged. I had no food and all doors were shutting in my face. After 2 days without eating, I was no longer able to try to find a job. It made no sense to me that my father wasn't helping, since I had done no harm and since he

was in a position to help me because he was a millionaire; the worst thing was that he was rich because of me. My uncles had helped my cousins and some of my friends received help from their family, but right then no one was helping me. I'd even seen parents go broke to help their kids. I just needed to eat and they were all letting me die. The situation didn't make any sense at all. My father used to love me; I couldn't understand why, he had become the way he was. It was painful and made me angry. I tried to see what I was doing wrong but I wasn't taking drugs, I had no problems with gambling and I hadn't hurt anyone to a point where they would want to see me dead. I had no choice but to go to the hospital, where I might get help since I was too dizzy to do anything else. I had just 50 cents left in my purse, so I used it to make a phone call because there was no time left on my cell phone. I went down the stairs but I didn't think I'd be able to make it to the hospital, because I felt as if was going to faint. I reached for my phone in my purse because, even without minutes left, I could still call 911. I called the ambulance and waited for them to arrive. When they came, the ambulance drivers put me on a stretcher and brought me to the hospital. At the hospital, the nurse gave me a bed in the corridor. I wondered if they had any information on the cloud striking, so I decided to ask her, even though

The dream of a royal member's departure

it had been a while since it had happened. I spoke in a low voice, afraid that she would take me for a liar, which is not something I enjoy being seen as.

- I was hit by lightening but it happened a long time ago. But since then, I've been dehydrated. I also haven't eaten for two days.
- Don't worry. Relax and try to rest; you'll feel better afterwards.

She hooked me up to an IV and left. In the morning when I woke, the doctor came to see me and didn't ask me any questions. He just told me:

- All the blood tests are normal. I'm going to release you; you can go home now.

I stared at him, wanting to ask him about the cloud, but I decided to do it some other time. I went home without eating. I arrived back home with my situation totally unchanged.

My neighbour Diane, who is the girlfriend of one of my father's friends, came to invite me for supper. I felt bad because I was usually the one helping others with grocery money, even taking them on trips. This image of me being like those drunks and drug addicts depressed me, especially knowing I was none of these things. I couldn't live, like this; it just wasn't human. I had no idea what to do, so I decided to call a friend of mine, whose phone number I had found. Diane let me use her phone so I could make the call.

- Hello, Jacques!
- Yes, Jacques speaking. Who is this?
- It's Christine. Do you remember me? We went out together a couple of times and you said I could call you if ever I needed anything.
- That's funny. My name is Jacques but I'm not the one you want to talk to. He was my roommate but he no longer lives here.
- That's weird. Sorry, then. Bye.
- No, wait! Don't hang-up. Let me guess: you're calling Jacques because you want to go out or something. Well, I'm a lot better than him! Would you like to come to dinner with me tomorrow? You seem like an interesting girl!

The dream of a royal member's departure

- No, I don't think so. For crying out loud, I don't even know who you are! On the other hand, the Jacques that I know is your friend and if you only want to take me to a restaurant without any other expectations, I might just accept your invitation. Let me think about it. I'll call you back later.

It was a crazy idea, but I needed to eat tomorrow, and I needed to find a solution to my problem, so I thought I should just accept his invitation.

- Diane, come here and give me your advice on this invitation.
- Me? You're asking me?
- Yes, would you go out to a restaurant with someone you have never seen before?
- Well sure. You can tell us where you're going and if you don't call us by a certain time, we'll call the police.
- That's a good idea. I think I'll accept the invitation. Let me just call him back.

- Hi, Jacques. It's Christine again. I finally decided to accept your invitation.
- Good, I'm happy about it. Tell me, where do you live?
- I prefer to meet you at the metro station, near the restaurant in the shopping mall downtown.
- That's fine with me. Is around six good for you?
- That's perfect. I'll see you then. Oh, before I forget, I want to tell you in advance not to expect anything more from me than a night out at a restaurant, is that understood?
- Don't worry; we're going out to eat, that's all.
- Ok then. I'll see you tomorrow.

The next day, I got ready to leave for my rendezvous. I took the metro and arrived in no time. I sat and waited in a little café that had many windows. I wanted to be able to see my date arrive, without him knowing that I was there. I suddenly had a bad feeling and felt like backing out.

I wasn't sure what I was getting into. Meanwhile the chef of the

The dream of a royal member's departure
restaurant looked at me and came to sit beside me.
- Are you all right, pretty thing? You seem afraid of something.
- No, that's not the problem. I'm waiting for a date and I feel like going back home. I've never been on a date with someone I didn't already know.
- Well don't worry; I'm here. Let me buy you a coffee and whatever you want to eat.
- That's very generous of you, but it's not necessary. Thank you.
- I insist. By the way, my name is Ahmed and I've been the cook here for two years.
- Do you think I could get some work here?
- Maybe. Let me see if I can help you.
- I have so many problems right now; I really need help a job or something.
I proceeded to tell him a little about my situation.
- My ex is causing me problems and my father owes me money but he refuses to give it to me. I've been waiting for too long and am at the end of my rope.
I stopped for a moment and wondered why I was telling my life problems to a stranger. Meanwhile, through the window,
I saw a man waiting at the designated meeting place. I thought that it had to be him, Jacques, the other Jacques. I was glad that he didn't know what I looked like, because this guy, with his ripped jeans and long hair, didn't look safe. Just looking at him, I guessed that he was a dirty drug addict.
I decided to let him wait there; after all, he'd never know that I was inside the restaurant. Meanwhile, I sat at the table with Ahmed. He had his head down and started talking.
- I also have some problems. My girlfriend kicked
me out and I have been staying at the house of one of the bosses, but he's fed up with me and wants me to find a place soon. How about you; do you live alone?
- As a matter of fact, yes, I do live alone.

The dream of a royal member's departure

- You wouldn't happen to have a room for rent, would you? I could stay there only until I find a new place. It could also help you until you find something.

I thought about the fact that people rent out rooms all the time and that this could be my temporary solution.

- Are you serious about this?
- Yeah and if you want some references, just ask the boss. One of them will be coming here soon.

I drank my coffee, thinking about my father's unrealistic behaviour, which always got me into dangerous situations and usually ended up making me feel disgusting. I definitely didn't like this system of modern harems, which let you be fucked by just anyone, for no real good reason other than that the person is there. If Ahmed were to come to my home and decide that he wanted to get laid, I'd have no choice but to let him do it, unless I wanted to get beaten up. After some thought, I decided I didn't have many options in my situation. Therefore, I decided to accept his offer.

- Okay, Ahmed. When would you like to come over to my place?

He looked at me with a kind smile.

- Well, I'll be ready as soon as I'm finished in the kitchen, if you want to wait for me, that is.

I'll never forgive my father and his new wife for making me live this way. I love them but when I realize that they do not love me enough and that they are only trying to steal my money, it gets me mad. I am not going to talk about whether I had sexual activities with this weirdo or not. I don't really know why I'm writing about him when it makes me feel ashamed of myself, but I had some memories about this man and he might be an important piece of the puzzle for someone else's life. This Lebanese man appeared in an image at the end of the 18th century. In this picture, he worked in a restaurant like the one where I met him and his boss was an older Spanish man. It was in England or a city in Ireland, close to England somewhere. In my memories, I saw him leaving the restaurant through the back alley

The dream of a royal member's departure

door. He was hitting on fake Fred, or was it my Spanish step-cousin. Anyway, before Fred got near Ahmed, he was carrying Sidney, who lay unconscious in his arms. That's when Ahmed came out, screaming, as if he knew him:

- Hey, man!

Then he took the girl from his arms to put her on the floor. He got closer to fake Fred, grabbed him by the collar, and continued.

- You owe me money for some drugs! Tell me what you did to that poor girl! Didn't I tell you

not to hurt girls!

That's when I saw him take his knife and stab it into fake Fred's stomach.

In this image, Ahmed left Fred's body, spurting blood, in the alley and summoned his boss.

- Look at this shit! Could you help me to clean it up? I have to bring the girl to the doctor's office.

- What? I have to clean up your mess! Did you see how disgusting that asshole is!

The Spanish cook continued sounding very angry.

- No problem! I'll start picking it up while you're gone to bring the girl to the doctor's, but you'll have a lot of meat to cut when you get back! You better be ready!

- Yeah. Yeah, thanks. I'll see you shortly.

Ahmed finally reached the doctor's doorway, rang the doorbell, left Sidney in the care of the clerk, then paid the doctor's bill and disappeared. Time passed, then I saw Sidney waking up in the doctor's house. Beside her was the female child murderer all tied up in a strait jacket. As soon as Sidney recognized her, she got up and ran out of the office, afraid for her life. She knew she had identified the criminal woman to the authorities at an earlier time and she presumed the guilty woman knew about it. This story ended with Sidney watching a sleigh being pulled by horses and in it was her distant female cousin married to a Prince Frederick of England.

The dream of a royal member's departure

It was supposedly that cousin, along with her mother, who was making the checks for literary art and for the insurance claimers. These images from my memory ended, but another one also appeared, featuring Ahmed and my ancestor. It seemed to be during the first century because Ahmed was dressed as a barbarian and was one of a gang of people bringing me back from Egypt to Ireland. Sometimes these images were very weird.

We finally arrived at my apartment. Ahmed was tired, so we went to bed right after eating. That night, I fell asleep quickly and had what I believed to be a significant dream.

I awoke in my dream, seeing a woman waving and screaming at me.

- Come close! Come here!

She was standing beside her white Mercedes or Jaguar limousine, just in front of the mortuary.

She looked nice and seemed to have something important to tell me, so I slowly approached her, and as soon as I was standing there in front of her, she gently took me in her arms and said:

- I love you.
- I'm sorry, but I don't know who you are, madam.
- There's no need to worry. You'll find out soon enough! I must tell you that I've known you for a very long time!

She kept holding me real tight, not letting go. I saw another woman sitting in the car. She had black hair, her smile was like a dead person's, and her eyes were not moving. I wondered if she was alright, so I put my head in the car.

- Hello. Nice to meet you, madam.

I didn't get a response. She had no reaction whatsoever. The woman outside invited me to sit in her car and started explaining something to me.

- You must remember this: there's a flower shop just beside the cemetery. It's my store. If ever you get lost, just go there and you'll be able to get everything you need.

She looked at me with her warm, comforting smile in the same way a

The dream of a royal member's departure

mother would. I felt as if I was her own daughter.
- Do you know your way to the cemetery?
- No, madam, I don't know my way to the cemetery!
Then she said:
- Ask me one question, and afterwards, I'll disappear.
That was the last thing she said before I woke up.
When I opened my eyes, I was sweating a great deal and wondering who these women were. I didn't recognize them. Ahmed was awake and he told me that I had been screaming or talking. I told him about my dream, but he neither reacted nor responded. The next day, I decided to go downstairs to see my neighbour Diane. I knocked and she invited me into the living room. I didn't have time to sit down, as a special news bulletin on her T.V. caught my attention.
- It's impossible, Diane. These are the two women I dreamed of last night. Diane, shh! Don't make a noise. I want to listen to the news. The news said that the mother and sister of the Queen of England had been found dead yesterday in their car.
Was this true? Was this real news? I couldn't be sure, but I knew that those two women on the TV were exactly the same as those who had come to see me in my dream the night before.
- What can this mean? I asked Diane.
- There has to be an explanation for this! Why did I dream of them last night? Why is it that today they are talking about them on the news? Diane, do you know what it means?
- No, not really. But look now. They're showing Jesus flying in the middle of the screen.
- How strange is that! Where did the news go?
- It's always like that around Easter.
- The news seems to be finished. Anyway, what did you come here for? Did you want something?
- No! I forgot why I came, but I'll see you later. Bye, Diane
Bye Diane.
I went back home for the day.

The dream of a royal member's departure

I wasn't too excited about Ahmed arriving, even though he was going to bring me supper.

I didn't go out at all that day, and around eight, Ahmed arrived with my supper and his bags of clothes.

I hesitated before opening the door, but since I had given my neighbour all the information about him, I felt safer, not that it would change anything if he decided to hurt me. The night ended early and the next morning came fast.

That morning Ahmed wanted to have a serious conversation with me, but I didn't know what it was about.

- Christine, it's nothing important. I just have a question for you!
- Sure, what is it?
- I want to know if you've ever killed someone.
- What kind of a question is that, Ahmed! Why are you asking me that? Have you ever done something like that?
- This is what I want to talk to you about. I killed a friend of mine!

My heart started pumping, and ideas were running wild in my head. I had to control my stress and think fast.

- Ahmed, did you do this on purpose or was it an accident?

I had to find out if it had been an accident or if he had killed him in legitimate defense. If neither of these were true, I was in a great deal of danger around him.

- Okay. Well, tell me the story about what happened, I'm curious.
- I lost my temper when he called me an asshole.
- Come on, this can't be the only reason!
- Yes, this is how it happened. I was holding a gun, but became so frustrated by his offensive term of abuse toward me that I lifted and pointed the gun at him and while I was saying:
- 'Don't you ever talk to me like that again!', the shot went off and killed him. This is the main reason that I left Lebanon. I'm telling you this because they might still be looking for me.
- Oh, boy! Your story sounds complicated but let's change the subject. Tell me when you're working till today!

The dream of a royal member's departure

- I'm leaving very soon and should be back at around 7 o'clock.
- Okay. I'm going downstairs to see Diane while you finish getting ready.

I hoped he was going to let me go and wouldn't start any kind of craziness.

- No problem, Christine, I'll knock to tell you when I leave.
- Great! That's perfect. I'll see you later, then.

Wow! That was close. I hurried to get downstairs.

I went into Diane's living room and sat there until Ahmed had left. I went back home and packed all of his things back in the bags. When night came and I heard a knock on the door, I called the police in case Ahmed lost his mind. I waited a little bit before opening the door to Ahmed. I saw the police car arrive and knew I was safe.

- Ahmed, I'm sorry about this, but you have to understand that I have an issue about mistrusting you and you're going to have to leave. You can no longer live here.

The officers were standing in the street, looking at Ahmed.

- Fine. Never mind. I'm going to come back later to pick up my stuff, but I first have to see where I can go!

Ahmed left. I didn't want to have any contact with him, so I put all of his bags in the empty apartment next door and gave the key to Diane. I didn't want to take any chances because I knew how people get if they're angry or unhappy.

It was 5 o'clock in the morning and I was still sleeping when I heard someone knock at least 20 times on the door.

- Oh, no! It's him and he's not happy. But what if he kills me!

I went to the door and told him that his things were all in the apartment next door and that Diane would give him the key. I looked through the back door window and saw him go down the stairs, but at that same moment, I heard a loud, thundering noise that sounded like an airplane that was very close. It felt as if the airport was right beside my home. I started thinking it could be a bomb, that maybe Ahmed had set off a bomb and that I was going to die. So I looked

The dream of a royal member's departure
everywhere outside to see what it was and I saw the most beautiful sunrise I had ever seen; there were two suns rising at the same time, but not at the same place. One was the normal everyday sun, but the other one was something else, and it made a loud noise.

The big ball of fire was rolling like a ball, passing just beside while being so close and by the optical effect of its enormity, I would say it was only 40 feet away from earth. The ball kept rolling and went back up in the sky. It was so beautiful, but its energy was absorbing all of mine and took all I had left. But I started shaking and was very dizzy, so I just went back to bed.

Later, at the end of the day, I went outside and on a balcony on the other side of the alley, I could see mercury residue, still glowing, which probably had come from the big ball of fire. I reached my neighbour's door.

- Diane, come see this. I need you to call the army or something.

But she was a little drunk, as always, and told me that she was going to take care of making that call. The ball of fire must have been a falling star or a kind of meteorite. I started wondering if it could have been the explosion which was expected to cause the end of the world. Fortunately for us, we had barely missed this explosion.

The next day, I looked around to find my passport, but it seemed to have disappeared and I suspected that Ahmed had taken it. I needed to go downstairs to make a call to report my missing passport and at the same time I wanted to try calling my father again. I reached my father, whose voice had changed from his usual bad-mood tone. He sounded sweet and concerned. He finally decided he was going to help me and told me:

- It's not funny what you're going through. I'll come to see you tomorrow and bring you some money.

Why did I have to be in bad situation for him to answer my call for help? Many days passed and a friend I had been seeing on and off for about 2 years arrived at my door. I would have called him but he didn't have a phone number for me to reach him. As soon as I had let

The dream of a royal member's departure

him in, I said:

- Mustafa, I'm so happy to see you but you're a little too late. I needed you last week.
- Hello! What are you saying? I came over to have a beer with you. I sure didn't know that you were back. When did you get back from Mexico?
- It's been a little more than 3 weeks.
- Listen, Christine. I have many things to do tonight but I want to come back to see you tomorrow. Are you going to be here?
- Yes, of course. I'll tell you all about my adventures since I last saw you.
- Okay. Bye, Christine.

He kissed me.

- See you tomorrow.

After he left, I felt better and more secure knowing that he had come by, but I wasn't sure if I should take him back into my life. I went back to sit in the kitchen. It was very quiet in the room, and the light was on. I remembered the dream I had had 2 days before, and began thinking about what the woman told me. In particular, I thought about the question she said I had to ask her and wondered if I had to ask her one simple question, what it would be. I didn't actually decide what I'd ask, but I had this thought about what my name could have been in my past life. Then suddenly, without having a chance to change my mind, a blowing whisper in my kitchen said:

- Sidney. Your name was Sidney.

Just like in a fairy tale, another noise went 'poof' and a plume of white smoke invaded my kitchen. I believed it was that woman from my dream who was disappearing, since she said that she would only leave after I had asked her a question. I knew that somewhere this could have been true, because ever since she called me this, many memories from a past life came to life within me. This event reminded me of this kind of gift that angels have, which has existed since the beginning of time. This gift of hearing and telling others

The dream of a royal member's departure
their name was attributed to royalty many centuries ago. That must be why people used to bring their newborns to the king and queen, in order to get their opinion before naming the new baby, often asking them to do so.

***

wondered if I had seen these women before somewhere other than in the news. Well there was another memory coming back to me and it was from another dream I had had when I was a young child. Nevertheless, a dream is very different from a memory and from an astral voyage, since it doesn't always come from an image of a real-life scene, from a scene that actually occurred. Dreams are often only our imaginations being active and a result of everything the mind had seen. Or maybe dreams are the passing of life without the human body from hell, before arriving somewhere. Whatever they are, I've always been impressed by the capacity of my soul, when I can remember a dream from as far back as when I was 3 or 4 years old. Then again, why it is that I remember specific dreams? I knew that I would solve these puzzling messages somehow, but at that moment, I couldn't seem to understand them. When I had had this dream, I was in my room in a small apartment in the city, which badly needed renovating. But I had the most beautiful Book of the Jungle wallpaper.

In this dream, I was a baby, sitting in a banana baby seat in the middle of a yard in the country, in Europe somewhere.

My mother in the dream was that woman who was the sister of the Queen. She was talking to a 12-year-old boy:

- Sweetheart, could you keep an eye on your little cousin for a short period of time? You won't have much to do. She should be sleeping until we get back.

- Sure, I can do that. No problem, aunty.

- I want her to get the fresh air while she takes her nap, If she awakens or if you have any kind of problems, the servants are inside; just ask them to come and help you.

The dream of a royal member's departure

I was experiencing this dream as if I was the baby.
I watched the woman leave, thinking she didn't love me for leaving me like that and she disappeared with her sister. The boy also left, but to get something in the shed. He wanted to shoot birds and the door to where the gun was, was unlocked. The young boy filled the gun with ammunition and returned to the baby. I again thought that the boy hated me (these baby emotions must be kind Page of a phase). He approached me.   - Why are you crying, little girl?
He tried to take me in his arms, but while putting down the pistol, he accidentally pressed on the trigger and the bullet went straight into the baby's stomach. I felt him holding me while the blood dripped from my stomach. The boy was traumatized and whispered.
- Stop crying! No! No! Please, this can't be happening! I love you so much. No!
The chauffeur/gardener arrived.
- Oh my God, boy, what have you done?
Hurry, get inside and change your clothes, I'll take care of her.
The boy came back after he had cleaned away all traces of blood on him and gave the dirty clothes to Raoul, the gardener. Then Raoul rolled the baby's body in a blanket and put it in the trunk of the car.
- Kid, you have to keep quiet about this and never tell anyone. We're going to say that we saw the Nigger run away with her.
At the end of the dream, I woke hearing the screaming, crying sound of a baby being born.
I remember being in shock, telling my mother about my dream.
- Mommy, I was shot and I died. I'm scared.
- You're not dead. You're right here with us and very much alive. It was just a bad dream, darling.
I remember that the following day was when I first saw the person whom I call Charles.
As soon as I saw him, I felt as if I needed to talk to him because he felt so familiar to me. I named him Charles because I think it had been his name in a past life as the king of Southern Ireland. I always saw him

The dream of a royal member's departure

as a very handsome man whose presence warmed me. Anyway, I watched him standing at the entrance door, and I paid close attention to what he said:

- It's funny; I heard a story that's identical to the one from Christine's dream. This kind of coincidence makes you wonder if it comes from a memory transfer or from the soul. It's hard to identify its origins. Charles was nice to me. I always sensed that he trusted me.
- Christine, we'll see if you'll accomplish your task in life.

He smiled self-confidently.

I wondered if the Sidney the woman called me was that baby from that dream. But it doesn't make any sense, since in my memories of being Sidney, I didn't die at the age of five months, unless she was also named Sidney as a dying baby. I know that my blood mixtures are not the same as the baby's, but there is a bloodline connection between those people and me.

I thought about how to forgive such an accident. The only way was to imagine that it had been planned by angels, telling myself it was not my place to be reborn. I had to be able to detach myself from the love of these connections. However, I had a chance to remember what it was like to be their blood and what their ideas from their souls were like. They also knew the person that I supposedly was before. I still wonder if this story was real or if it was just a dream.

*****

Chapter 4

Departure and new encounters

If I were to make a movie, I would probably start it with this chapter. It was the life just before I was born. I suppose I am lucky to possess the memory of the day I made my way down into this body. Some souls have the choice to decide to come down or not. From up there, I could hear my parents calling me, asking me if I wanted to come

Departure and new encounters

along: - Many people miss you. It's been a while since you were here. Apparently, not everyone can choose if they want to come or not. Some souls have no choice. As for me, I knew I could change my mind and stay up there but I wonder if I would really have been able to stop the process if I had decided not to come. I only had to remember and again saw these images, after the cloud had hit me. I remember having these memories when I was a young girl, as early as before I could speak, but I lost all memories of earlier times after an accident I had. I can remember being in a dimension invisible to the human eye. I was a transparent image illuminated by light and I could fly and create any place I wanted to imagine, as it was my responsibility to imagine being able to live in the kingdom of heaven. Nevertheless, like everything and everywhere, there was a law which always interfered with my direction if I was unable to stop myself from having bad ideas. Anyhow, I could see my mother from up there. She was a young, 17-year-old woman with long, shiny hair. I could feel the love she projected around her. Even if the peace and love party was attracting my desire and exciting me to be here, it was not my reason for coming. It's a special kind of place up there and I was able to see and hear every thought of the person I chose to visit with my soul. In heaven there are no secrets for humans to hide since all thoughts are revealed by whispers. Anyhow, while I was up there, I went into the secret registry to set an objective for myself to achieve on my journey to earth. I had the urge to be on earth so that I could taste and feel the heat of having blood running in my veins. From up there, everything seems much easier than it really is. I also remember that there seem to be a lot fewer people since only those with souls are visible. Before leaving the beautiful place where I am linked with my lover, I need to choose what I'll be doing down there. On the designated planet we had to leave a handprint and accomplish our plot to perfection or start over again until we succeed.
At this moment in heaven, my lover arrived, wanting to surprise me with the decision he had made of going on a journey to earth. I spoke

Departure and new encounters

to him: - It's about time you arrived! I couldn't hold on any longer. I was about to fall into the dark passage forever!
- You know it's not forever.

His soul is now getting very close to me and the life of his light is palpitating and totally invading me. The whisper reveals his inner thoughts and warns me of his desire to go down to live a bodily life.
- If we go down, my love, I'll find you. I'd like to go to help someone save their life and then will come and meet you wherever you are. You need to go choose your path of life.

As soon as I realized we were leaving, I lost control over my emotions but I had to accept his decision while keeping the secret that he loves me. It was too easy to be disappointed, so I just couldn't keep myself from projecting the thought to him.
- You can't say that you love me if you are about to leave me.

I didn't really mean it but it was too late to take it back. Because I had committed a crime by not believing that his love for me was sincere, the law was pulling me down before I could even know for sure that he did love me. It was too late; the suffering caused by his absence was making me feel a pain akin to dying. In the celestial paradise where I was it's the faithful loyal being which is the eternally reigning one since he is the strongest one.

I'm still hoping and waiting for my lover to come back, but I'm not sure I want to go down. All of a sudden, the soul of someone else, a Japanese-looking person, appears. What does he want? Maybe he's here to make me be unfaithful or to test my level of strength but I know not to let myself succumb to love which is not nourished by me and not for me. I can hear in me the loving words and ideas he is thinking but I know they are not dedicated to me, even if I am the only soul present at this moment, unless he his only a messenger from my lover. I finally understand what he wants: he has come to ask me for help with his own lover. He tells me that before being transferred to the body, often the idea doesn't reach the person to whom it is intended and if I'm not disappointed when taking a

Departure and new encounters

message, if it's not for me, I should be able to help and receive the help that I need.
- This is my secret from me to you to, solved.
He then disappeared. I am still expecting to see my lover come back and I am waiting for him. I am burning with pain. Two angel children arrive with a bucket of water, which they pour on me, to ease the wound caused by my lover's absence.
This very magnificent creature who changes back to an adult-age figure when it moves away from me tells me:
- You will always be my mom.
Time passes and, being all alone, I know that I
will soon be leaving our bed cloud, which needs both of us to hold us there in paradise, and which is going to fade away. In the process of going down, there is a stopping point, where the soul's clouds of animal forms live. They are the bosses of the function of thought for the functioning of the human body and they have the natural-medicine cure for some human diseases. Mine was a kind of tiger and he tells me that if I break laws, it will be an impasse for me to be immune and treated against some diseases. They are also what make us different, so that we can accomplish different tasks.
   I finally feel myself fall into a deep hole and I hear my lover yell:
                  - Why did you leave?
          That's when I fell into a deep sleep.
                            ***
At a very young age, I had to face facts and become conscious about the existence of the soul's eternal life. As much as we want to believe in its existence, most of us just wonder about it. For those that are forced to become conscious of it being a reality, life becomes different and they are often seen as being different from others.
I experienced my first paranormal activity when I was involved in an accident at the age of about three years old.
It is the year 1975. In the kitchen, a Janice Joplin song is playing and my mother sings along

Departure and new encounters

while-making lunch. While my mother is occupied, I worm my way onto the front porch. My father isn't here so I think I'll venture to the second floor; my mother won't find out. In search of sensations, I decide to just slide down the banister from up there all the way down; that should be fun.

I climb up the stairs, put my hands on the banister and slide all the way down.

- Yippee!

I hear my mother shout:

- Christine, come inside! Your food is ready.

- I'm coming, Mom!

In spite of this, I climb again and again until I feel so confident that I forget to hold myself properly. I then fall from the second floor on my back and head, breaking my arm on the cement. I finally fall unconscious.

I am no longer moving. At that point, I enter into limbo. The man who lives on the corner passes by, sees me unconscious, leans down and takes me in his arms. The man climbs the stairs, knocks on the open door of my home and says: - Is there someone home?

My mother, standing in the long corridor, sees me motionless, resting in his arms. She runs towards me, yelling.

- Oh, no! The little devil went past the fence! Oh, no! Is she dead?

Then my mother says hysterically:

- What happened? Was she hit by a car?

I want to talk to her while I am watching the scene but I'm paralyzed, so I can't.

- Calm down, Ma'am, she's alive and still breathing!

Please come inside and lay her down here.

The man puts me down on the brown suede sofa in my dad's private living room.

As for me, I'm somewhere between life and death. I'll always remember it.

I'm still unconscious, but wide awake and seeing my father sponging

Departure and new encounters

my head.
- Please, Christine! Wake up! Did you do something to her, Jina?
- How dare you say that?

When my mother pushes his shoulder, he moves his arm away and the ring on his finger scratches her hand. She lets out a frustrated sound.

I watch and try to get back to my body but the wind is pulling me the opposite way, I hold the door handle to stop myself from flying away, but the wind is just too strong and I'm forced out the door. I end up 20 feet from the ground, right in the middle of the street. This is when two women dressed like witches grab me by the arm to catch me. One of the women is my grandmother; the other woman is my mother's grandmother.

I scream and fight back, afraid of never waking up in my body again.

- Stop moving, you silly girl.

The woman takes me to the doorway to watch my parents.

- You see how sad they are! It's entirely your fault; you never listen!

The woman goes back to the street and the wind is still pulling me away from myself; my legs and feet are floating in the air.

- Can you help me, Ma'am? Please do something! Change me back into myself, please!

The older woman has a terrifying look that is so mean that she scares me.

- Girl, don't be scared. I'll protect you, just like the others, as long as you don't hurt anyone.

The loving feeling she sends me makes my frightened impression of her disappear.

The younger woman, my grandmother, shakes me a little and asks me:

- Are you sure that you want to go back?...

Departure and new encounters

...- It won't be the same now that you have awoken the memory of existing on the other side!
- Yes, I do want to go back home!

The older woman comes near.
- Leave the poor girl alone.

Then she smiles.
- I think you've been in between long enough. You will now follow me to heaven. It's time for you to leave the ones you love and go explore up there.

Bring the girl back and block the way by following me. You deserve it. I feel a kiss on my forehead; the wind is whirling around and finally, I wake up on the sofa. I believe that day was the spiritual departure of my grandmother. From that day on, my life journey to integrate with others was going to be more difficult, since my conscious being was no longer asleep and wondering, but awake wondering when. I guess it was not for me to choose who would be living their journey knowing.

***

There are people who were present in my life and I wonder if it was important or not for them to have crossed my path. Reality showed that there were no important links between them and me.
However, they could be one among those who came to save my life. I'm not sure of this and won't ever be.
Therefore, I could only turn the tables, saying I was glad that they came into my life, if indeed they were those people who later came to help me.

I was three or 4 years old and my mother, her friend Cathie and I were going on a vacation to the Bahamas. We arrived on the island and anyone who has visited those islands knows how hypnotic it is there. Entering the ambience of the Bahamas is like going into a trance. The fragrance of the flowers enchanted me, making me feel like I was in a dream, lost in paradise. The people were very friendly but in a wheedling way. In the lobby, the same song, Hotel California,

Departure and new encounters

played every day at around 7 o'clock. It sounded like a welcome ritual. Thinking about it, the singers could have been the hotel owners, wanting people to listen to their music.
We were lying on the beach and Cathie got up.
- I decided that I am going on a two-day expedition.
Just like that, Cathie got up, went packing and left by herself. My mother and I spent all day on the beach. I was toasted.
- Get your things; we're going back to the room. Look at yourself! That's a real bad sunburn you have there.
The week went by fast. At the reception desk, the hostess was very kind and friendly, a dark-skinned woman with her hair done up in a bun on top of her head. She spoke to me:
- Do you know how to swim?
- No, not yet; but I'll learn how.
- If you're interested, there's a swimming class in the morning. My son attends it every day.
- Wow cool! Mommy, please, can I go tomorrow?
- Sure why not? We'll go check it out tomorrow.
- Yay! Hooray!
I jumped up and down.
The second week went by very fast. I learned to swim and everything was all so sweet.
We only had couple of days left and Cathie had still not come back to spend her vacation with us. The phone in the room rang and it was Cathie. She spoke to my mother:
- I'm not coming back with you guys.
Jina didn't agree with Cathie's decision.
- I won't leave you here alone, Cathie. Come on. It's the atmosphere here that's making you not think straight. Your son and husband are waiting for you at home. I'll give you one more week, but if after that you still don't want to leave, I'll have to drag you home by force.
Well, we had to extend our vacation.
At the end of the week, the friendly hostess wanted to bring me into

Departure and new encounters

the life of her private home. She came to talk to my mom and me:
- Can I bring Christine to a carnival? It's a little far from here, so it would be easier to take her to my house for her to sleep over.
My mother looked at me with her confused angry eyes and I started jumping.
- Please, mommy! Can I go?
- Well, it would give me time to go look for Cathie. Let me ask the authorities around here and I'll give you my answer afterwards.
I finally ended up going to the hostess's home.
When I got there, it was a little dark outside, but I
was amazed at how nice and cozy it was. As I walked behind her, I remember seeing the empty swimming pool in front of the house, surrounded with flowers.
- Why is there no water in your pool?
- No time for that! Besides, I swim at the hotel.
I suddenly felt afraid, wondering if I was there just to go to the carnival. What if she decided to keep me there and what if I disappeared forever?
- My son will be here soon. I'll have you sleep with me in my bed.
I started crying and complaining that I wanted to go home.
- Don't worry. Let's call your mommy and daddy. It'll make you feel better.
She gave me the phone and I called.
- Daddy, come and get me.
- Don't worry! I spoke with the nice lady and she's going to take you to a carnival. Didn't you tell her you wanted to go?
- Yes, but I miss you.
- Are you going to be all right? Because she can bring you back to the hotel if you want.
- No, it's okay. I'll try to stay here.
That was the extent of the conversation. I was finally calmed down and fell asleep next to her. Sometime later, I woke up. She wasn't in bed, but I could hear her talking on the phone.

Departure and new encounters

- What are people going to think, seeing a black woman with a white child? They sure are bad people, especially when they start saying that she is sick for being white. There's something particular about her name and the old recording we found has the same name as that girl's name. It could be her.

There was a silence, then she continued.

I have to go work outside the country to sing in a big club and I will need someone to baby-sit the boy. Can you help me?

The conversation calmed me into a deep sleep.

When I woke in the morning, her son was there and we went, as planned, to a carnival.

While we were there, eating pink cotton candy and walking hand-in-hand with the boy, a white woman stopped and looked at me. She approached and asked me:

- Hello. What's a pretty girl like you doing here? Do you know where your mother is?
- Well, yes, ma'am. She's at the hotel.
- How polite you are! Well, let me ask - are you sure everything is all right?
- Yes, ma'am. I'm fine.

That woman looked like the one I had dreamed of who was the queen's sister. Anyway, she left and the young boy pulled my hand, saying:

- Come on! Let's go on the Ferris wheel.

I don't remember why, but I started crying, feeling really bad, and the hostess had to end the day sooner than planned. The hostess brought me back

to the hotel, just after stopping at her place. The young boy said to me, before I left:

- You will no longer be alone.

She then brought me back to my mother as planned. Our vacation was over and we all went back home.

Often after that I wondered about the identity of these people.

Departure and new encounters

The woman reminded me of the father of the boy at my insurance company. It was as if they were having an affair somewhere in time. As for the boy, I have been confused about him since I met Bill because he always kept asking me, every time I saw him, if I remembered the carnival. I never understood why he kept asking me this question. Even if he was adopted, he had told me he never had been to the Bahamas, unless he was lying to me. I don't know why, but since the song I sang has been on the air, I've had some thoughts about seeing the hostess and her son again. Nevertheless, it is of no importance, because if anyone were to come and tell me they are those people I'd met, I wouldn't believe them, since anyone could come up to me and pretend to be them. Therefore, this could turn out to be too dangerous for me. When Arnold came my way, I did get some clearer images from those memories. I believe it could be because his father lives there. However, it did let me see the system of meetings of big company bosses which showed me that if someone commits a crime, they will be revealed to a worldwide group of the richest people on earth. It made me understand that the truth would always be revealed to those that one day could help. So I wondered if, when Arnold came to help me, he was sent by these people I knew or if he was that person. Anyhow, I wonder if there is a reason for the people we meet. If there are reasons, maybe those who appear together when I think about them could be those they needed to connect with each other. If that were so, I would say that this boy was one to meet with one of Kurt's sisters as I saw them together. Although, its odd that, in the past she was murder in her twenties and maybe this bad situation of the past shall not have to repeat itself.

However, I guess it's not any of my business anyway.

*****

Chapter 5
Visitors

These next 10 pages offer just a brief glimpse of my childhood. I had a normal childhood and was not an abused child. There is no secret formula to caring for a child at home. My mother knows how, although it's hard to keep me from playing outside, so she can't afford to keep me inside every day. She has no car, but works all night at the old port of Montreal. She pays for courses for me and I have lots of cousins but they live too far from us to be able to walk there, so I can't see them all the time. My friend who comes most often is Paul, one of my mother's best friends. When I got back from the Bahamas, he had something to say about it. I remember in my back yard how frustrated he was. Our conversation went like this:
- Christine, you went on a trip!
- Well, yes. I even made a new friend.
He starts being aggressive with his manly authority.
- Tell me, what did he do to you? Tell me now!
Paul has been my friend since I was very little and he is very possessive of me. He then holds my hands and holds me down so that I can no longer move.
- Let me go or I'll beat you up.
- Ha! Ha! You're not strong enough and it's your new black friend's fault if you don't love me
anymore. Paul always plays a bit roughly with me since he takes judo classes but he always end-up hurting me. Most of the time, this is why he leaves early.
My young age makes me wonder what kind of laws for living I would want to have in my next life. Also, I have to consider the age when my sexual activities will begin: how I can have what I am curious about without running outside to who knows who is a difficult question and task to add to the home problem that has to be fixed. Therefore I am not sure yet of what kind of rules or ways for living I need to have imposed on myself in order for my life to be better in the next one. My parents did the best they could. I think I heard them talk of the

Visitors

subject once or twice. I heard my father say:
- How do you want me to know which one is the real one? She is so young anyway.

Deep inside I know most of the people outside are not important. I also unconsciously know when someone should not be important because I sense they are intruders or I just have an attitude of unawareness towards them.

I wonder if the one I can still hear will come and find me as he told me he would before leaving heaven!

We are in the seventies, the decade of peace and love. It is the end of a revolutionary war and the Japanese just signed an agreement to provide technology. Europe introduced the lottery, which will also bring social assistance to the poor. Life in America is now much better and hunger should be disappearing.

I am now 5 years old and Charles's sister in law's wife comes for a visit. She is accompanied by Flint's reincarnation. Although he is young like me, he must only be 5 years old. Anyway, my mother invites her to sit down, but she refuses, preferring to stand up as she speaks to my mother:
- Jina, I think these two have known each other for a very long time, even in past lives. I believe they will recognize each other.

Flint is tall and stands behind the table near the exit door. He looks twice his age.
- Why are you here?
- Well, Flint's grandmother lives just on the corner and he's here for a visit.

The woman looks at Flint, who is making a face at him.
- Come on! Ask her what you wanted to ask her.
- Christine, who gave you that black eye?

My mother comes close to me, rubs my head and says:
- Christine has an admirer. Every time he plays with her, he hurts her. Go ahead, Christine. Tell him what happened.
- Yes. It's Louis from across the street. He was demonstrating how to

Visitors

make someone fall with
his leg, and I slipped and hit my face on the ice.
- Well, if he ever hurts you again, tell me! I'll show him how to make someone fall by using my leg!
My mother, shaking her head no, looks at Flint.
- No, young man. This won't be necessary, because Christine is no longer allowed to play with him.
From the way our visitors are talking, we surmise that they no longer believe that my parent did this to me.
Charles's brother's wife puts her hand on Flint's shoulder and says:
- That's my Flint showing his protective side. Well, if ever Christine goes somewhere far on her own, you can call me and I'll send Flint so he can keep an eye on her. He's a very good-hearted protector, it seems.
- We'll see later if that might be necessary.
Even after this conversation, I'm not sure what the family connection is between Flint and the woman he is with. The woman and Flint leave and my father arrives some time later. My mother tells him about our visit, but as soon as he sees my eye, he raises his hand at my mother, saying:
- Did you do this to her?
- How dare you even think that!
You'd better not raise your hand to me again, you.
And she explains what happened. My father puts
his hand down, moving his lips very slowly to say:
- Sorry. Forgive me.
He then says to me:
- Ha! Ha! You've had an encounter with Flint. Do you know that I know another boy who looks exactly like him!
My father knew what he was talking about and I also know since I myself have difficulty knowing if this Flint was the Flint of the past. There's also the boy from the insurance company who looks exactly like Flint, but to my knowledge was an Alexander in a past life. All

Visitors

these look-alikes make it difficult for me to recognize which one is important for me!

***

3 years have passed. It's a warm night and my dad takes me on his Harley Davidson for a ride, as he often does to go see the summer fireworks. Tonight, we are unexpectedly caught in rain and we're not very near our home.

My father stops on the side of the road, removes his helmet and lifts mine on the side so he can talk into my ear.

- We're going to stop at Charles's place until the rain stops. He lives very close to here.
- O.K.
- Now, don't worry. I'm going to drive slowly. Hold onto my belt tightly.
- Yes, daddy.

The road is slippery and the rain is falling hard,
but we make it to Charles's place intact.

Charles has two boys and one of them is Flint, but I wasn't sure because it had been two years since I last saw him and I only saw him for 10 minutes then. Charles's father is there. He looks familiar and is very nice. I feel good in this house, as everything is nicely renovated and I get a warm feeling here. Charles's wife takes my jeans and shirt, then gives me a T-shirt that goes down to my knees to put on while my clothes dry. Flint, or the one who looks like Flint, asks me to come see his room and collections on his shelves.

There are two beds in the room. One of the brothers is lying on one and when I approach the other one, Flint pulls me down the way Paul does to me. Suddenly I feel as if I've known Flint longer than Paul, which is not the case. This is a very weird emotion. He says in my ear:
- Do you prefer my brother to me?
- Why do you ask me such a question? I don't know. What I do know is that he seems to dislike me because the time I saw him when he came to visit me in my room he criticized me for no reason.

Visitors

Finally the woman enters the room and gives me
back my dry clothes. I then hear my father call me:
- Hurry! It's time to go.
Anyhow, the rain has stopped and we go back home.

***

If I recall correctly, I believe I had seen Charles's brother before on a frightening night.

Again, I am maybe three years old. I wake in the middle of the night after having a bad dream. No one responds to my screaming. It seems like there is no one at home. I get up to take a peek through the living room window. My mother is at work at the old port. On the balcony, I can see my father standing, talking to some men. In front of the house, there's a car with a trailer. The men standing on the balcony have a sort of disguise and one of them is sitting on a chair, his head down, dripping blood. He has a bag of potatoes on his head and seems to be dead because his face has bruises, his complexion is very white, and he seems stiff. Seeing that image scares me so much that I start screaming.
- Help! The man is looking at me! Help! He's coming for me.
Frank, my Dad, is still on the balcony,
Finally the woman enters the room and gives me
I think they heard me screaming because they covered the man's face with the potato bag. I then hear the handle of the door turn to open and my father comes inside. I try to hide but he's blocking my way.
- Christine, what are you doing up at this time of the night? Go back to sleep immediately. It's two in the morning.
He then approaches to grab me.
- You have to go to bed now. I'm with some men and you're too young to be here with us.
- Where's mom? I want to see her.
- She'll be here soon. Now that's enough.
Then either Charles or his brother, I'm not sure which one, since they look alike, pinches my cheek.

Visitors

- Don't be scared, little girl. What you saw isn't real. It's just like a dream and you won't remember a thing in the morning.

My dad puts me back on the floor gently, slaps my bum and orders me to go to my room.

I leave to go to my room but turn into my parents' room while no one is looking so I can hear the men's conversation. I hide under the pillows and blankets. My parents' room is right beside the living room and up on the wall there's an opening between the two rooms, so I can hear some of what they're saying. One man says

- Children shouldn't see any outside action after midnight. It's unfortunate that such a young face was in the window. Anyhow, it took us a long time before finding and capturing him. That fucking bastard must have killed and raped at least 20 children.
- How horrifying this pig's ideas are! I don't even want to imagine what he sees. Imagine if he had escaped from the psychiatric ward for longer, how many more children he would've grabbed. And how disgusting he is, making the whole neighbourhood panic with fear.
- Anyhow, it's still awful that he had to be killed, said my father.
- Well he gave us no choice and it's better that way. When we finally found him, he was holding a knife, trying to stab us with it as he attempted to get away. The bastard also had the nerve to say They like it and I'd do it to your boys, too! As he fought back with his knife, the shot went off. We then tied him to the chair and brought him to some of the victims' parents so that they could know he was really gone. I'd say he was possessed by a pig, that one. An incurable disease! While we were looking for him, his own family told us to end his life - he was too much of an insult to them!

I hear my father coming close to the room so I hide, putting all the pillows on top of me, but leaving a hole to peer through. Luckily, he doesn't turn on the light nor does he look my way. He opens the bottom drawer of his bureau and puts away a set of handcuffs. He leaves the room very quickly without seeing me. The men are now getting up and leaving. While my dad is on his way outside to watch

Visitors

them leave, I hurry into my room and fall fast asleep. I never knew what really happened but I also heard my uncles talk with my dad about an F.B.I search to capture that disgusting man who was also tortured by gangs of mad parents.

***

Growing up, I was taught and I understood the importance of following the right path and was reminded all the time to be good and strong and honest. Everything I heard and was told gave me no choice but to make the right decision about my actions; therefore, my mind was always clear about the difference between good and bad. What I describe next is not so important to remember, but the victim does seem to think that it's funny enough to still talk and laugh about 30 years later, so it's worth describing.

It's just a couple of days after that scary night.

It's my parents' night out, so I have a babysitter and I always feel insecure when I am babysat, because I have this notion that I will end up being kept by the babysitters forever.

This night, it's my father's girl cousin Lisa who's babysitting me. I have a big Doberman and Lisa is scared of the dog in a very paranoid way. The dog senses it because he growls at her all the time and if she raises her voice, he barks. I am always on my guard and do not feel safe with her reaction towards my dog. She makes him so mad that he is now slobbering from barking so much. I have to hold the dog by his collar to prevent him from running towards her and she's screaming, so I have to put him outside. Unfortunately, she forbids me to play outside.

- Lisa, please stop being scared of my dog.

I become bored and think about a game I can play. I take a paper bag and place all kinds of objects in it. I open my father's bottom drawer, remove the handcuffs and hide them in the back of my pants. I go over to Lisa.

- Lisa, do you want to play a game with me?
- It depends what kind of game.

Visitors

- Well, it's an easy game. I'm going to cover your eyes, then you just have to put your hands in the bag and guess what the object is that you choose.
- Okay. I can try it once!

I go ahead with the game and cover her eyes.
I help her put her hand in the bag. While she is doing this, I take the handcuffs and use them to attach her arm to the chair.
There! I did what I wanted to do.
Let me tell you, if you want to see someone panic, try this. The poor girl starts screaming a lot. It's kind of funny because I don't have the keys to unlock the handcuffs. Lisa starts calling everywhere and ask her mother to come over. Meanwhile, my dog comes back in and Lisa starts crying and screaming even harder until my barking dog runs to her and starts licking her everywhere. She's very scared of dogs. The poor girl could have had a heart attack. I even felt pity for her.

- Lisa, stop crying. You'll be alright. My dad will be here soon and he has the keys. Please don't be too angry.

Lisa's being nice now, but is still tied to the
chair. Her mother arrives and laughs when she sees her. Lisa has to wait, tied to the chair until one o'clock in the morning, when my parents finally come home. She even pees in her pants.
My father's the first one to come in the door. As soon as he sees Lisa complaining and showing her uncomfortable position, he also starts laughing and decides to joke around, saying:

- I don't have the key. You're going to stay like that until morning.

Knowing this is untrue, my mother pinches him and says:

- Stop fooling around. It's not that funny, Frank.

He finally unlocks the handcuffs and Lisa hurries to the door, still crying.

- I'm never coming back. Your daughter is as much of a monster as you are, Frank. I swear to you: I'll never baby-sit again.

It's true that she never came back. I played this trick another time on one of my father's friends and he also never babysat me again.

Visitors

Sometimes I wonder if I just needed to learn how to handcuff someone, to know how to do with all the criminals who came my way.

***

I'm eight years old and we're living in our first house, located across the street from a mortuary.

It's a Friday night and my mother has a night out with her sisters, so my dad will be babysitting. He has invited someone to come over to play cards and chess. Our guest is Charles's father, a nice man. As soon as he arrives, the house is suffused with a warm feeling. He and my father sit at the big table in the dining room to play. On the table, the guest's glass is filled with a strong alcoholic drink. The two men seem to be getting along and are laughing. My father acts very politely with the man, as if he's an important person, ensuring that he is comfortable and has everything he needs. This scene makes me think that this man could somehow be a member of the family.

As I listen to them, I interrupt to ask my father:

- Daddy, is he your father or uncle?

- No. Don't you remember seeing him before? He's Charles's father.

- Oh, Charles's father. Something makes me think that he's a member of our family.

My father replies:

- You never know. He just might be.

Then our guest says:

- You remind me of someone: one of my grandmothers; in fact, she even had the same family name as yours.

He then starts to name some names which gives me a feeling of déjà vu. I'm experiencing a hypnotic moment.

- I'll come back. I'm going to watch T.V.

My dad points his finger at me, saying:

- Not too late! Don't think you're getting special treatment because mom's not here.

I open the French doors which separate the living room and I take my

Visitors

dog with me to the second living room. I am watching a love story and a train robbery, but my ideas about what the man had said to me are triggering my curiosity. I am suddenly anxious to know more. What if I didn't ask him enough questions and what if he leaves before I have a chance to ask him and I never see him again.

Frank decides to put on some music in the dining room, when all of a sudden the lights flash a couple of times and the radio starts crackling. Finally, the music comes on and the song "Spanish Train", by Jet Rethel, starts playing on CHOM F.M. I don't know why, but I feel somewhat different because all of a sudden I realize that I remember having lived before. A feeling of safety heats my stomach up but makes me feel that I am old in my soul.

The next song on the radio is "Money" by Pink Floyd. My dog just loves that song, so he runs to the speaker and starts howling.

His reaction is so funny. Every time, with no exception, the dog goes nuts over the song and he does it only for this particular song. My father starts laughing as he looks at his guest, who is freaking out and saying:

- The dog's going to bite me. Is he going to stop?

The dog was also jumping in circles, scaring our guest.

- Don't worry! He's not going to hurt you. He obeys me. All I have to do is stop the song and he'll stop. He's a crazy dog.

To prove it, my father gets the record for him to see that it really is the song that makes him react this way.

Anyway, he plays the song a couple of more times and the dog howls away.

Finally, after a while, the dog show is over and my father and his friend resume playing. As for me, I go to my room but come back as quickly as I had left. I have an urge to talk more with this nice man. I see a whole lot of hundred-dollar bills, even couple of thousand-dollar bills. It's the first time I've ever seen big bills like this. The man speaks to me:

- Come closer, young girl.

Visitors

He then takes my hand, patting it gently.
- I think I know you. ...
... -As I said, my mother's mother had the same name as you and memories of her come alive when I see you.
I have to admit that he does seem very familiar.
- She used to tell me that I was her favourite. It's difficult to say for sure if you are or not, since there is a name missing in the puzzle. Also, you're too young for me to see the resemblance.
He starts again, this time sounding serious:
- And poor Beatrice! How she must have suffered! I wonder if you remember a girl being without her mother? How many times did Nicky tell me how guilty she felt when her mother spoke of her!
- Do you remember Nicky?
My boys will know. I already told them that if you ever have kids, they'll be welcome as family.
I'm not sure what the man is talking about, although all of the names he reveals to me make my stomach flutter when I hear them.
The man smiles sincerely at me, a smile from the depth of his heart.
I know now what the missing name he was seeking is: it is James, which is hidden in my mother's father's name. The reason my grandfather's kids did not have the name in their papers was because 100 years ago, the law added a new name to the present James name, to protect the mother. Anyway, at that moment,
I did not know about the hidden name; therefore, I couldn't have told him.
The man asks me again:
- Do you remember Joe, Fred and Henry?
He adds other names and I became hypnotized by dreams, seeing reruns like a movie of a life. The people I was seeing were real and maybe back just like me.
- Somewhere there's a boy who loves you a lot and when he gets here, he might be angry, but for sure he will defend you from everyone.

Visitors

I will tell you something and hope you will remember. If ever you meet an adopted boy and he starts to act not so nicely toward you, forgive him. It might not be his entire fault. It could be mine for not raising him.

Everything the man tells me kind of confuses me, but I listen, as I am very curious and interested.

He looks at my dad and says:

- The grand loves her, but don't bother with him too much; he'll only be there to do his job.

He looks back at me and says:

- Poor you.

I have to admit that each of the names he spoke to me about brought back a memory, and therefore a story. Looking back at scene the man was creating felt like watching an old cowboy movie inside the house of some rich people. It also awoke a dream of a good-looking Italian-Spanish boy with a bent nose. All of this makes me wonder when in history there were so many kings named Frederic at the same time! There was one in England, one in France and one in Spain who was looking for his beloved Isabella.

All these kings with the same name must have made it easier to trust one another when communicating. I am not sure why I think or was thinking about this, but the Italian sure had something to do with this.

The man is also mumbling about a story which doesn't concern me.

- There's a boy staying at my sister's.

On the other hand, did he say half-sister? I cannot remember.

- His father was married when he conceived him and his mother left him because she got married and didn't want to miss the opportunity because she had a child.

I'm not sure, but I think he's referring to this story as if he's the father of that child, but I'm not sure that's what he said.

He continues:

- I'm going to keep him just for you.

Visitors

Even today, I still see some images from a faraway life before.
The images of the young man are those of the nephew of a Janice Kennedy married to a Joe Maxwell. In my memory, the boy was her son from before she got married and she had left him with someone else, in order not to lose her chance to marry the rich man.
The man speaks again:
- Since I was my grandmother's favourite, I would like do something for you one day. If your dad or anyone else doesn't give you your share, someone will take care of the problem.
The grand will help you because he will need you to get his own share. If ever my grandson tries to steal you, or to hurt you the grand will protect you. Here, everyone has to respect one other within the family. Now don't forget to forgive the boy if he hurts you because he will only be jealous, so tell your husband not to kill him. It won't be his fault. If he doesn't understand and if he does hurt you, he will be punished by us.
My father turns around and shrugs his shoulders, to show his confusion.
- That's enough, now. Time to go to bed. Say goodnight and go to your room.
- Well, goodnight. I'm happy to have met you.
I then kiss my dad on the cheek and go to bed.
It's morning when my mother arrives home.
When I get up she's in the kitchen, talking to the two drunk men who are still playing cards. My dad is winning the game and the man pleads:
- Let's play another game, double or nothing.
- No, sir! Forget about the debt and keep your watch. I am now going to call Charles and send you home in a taxi and you don't owe me anything. A game is just a game.
- No way! I owe you 40 thousand. I always pay my debts.
- No I don't want it. It's just for fun, not a real debt.
My mother interrupts the conversation.

Visitors

- Frank, you'd better not take advantage of the man there or you'll have to deal with me. It's
terrible, you men still drinking in the morning. Plus, I never see you drink, Frank. What's happening with you!
- It's a special occasion.

The men start laughing again.

My mother Jina takes the keys to the truck and stands there in front of the front door, waiting for me.

- C'mon! Hurry up! You'll be late for your ballet class. Get your things; I'm waiting for you.
- But I'm too tired to go.
- Now, don't give me any excuses. You wanted to take dancing classes. Well it's time, so hurry up.

Before I leave, the man tells me:

- Don't forget what I told you about kitty girl!

Obviously, I did forget all about what he had said only a couple of days later. It was only much later that I did remember, around 23 years later, before the memories of Nicky and other images from the past life came back to me to warm my soul. This happened when I got a visit from those people. I am having trouble telling which is which. It was also during those same moments that the memories of what the man had told me came back as pieces of a puzzle that I had to put together. Once again, this proves to me that I have to be in the presence of souls that I had met before in order to have a déjà vu experience.

Steven often comes to visit here in my little apartment. He has become my lover but I'm unable to endure his presence for very long. He is one of a kind but sometimes he invites four people in an hour and he acts stupid and makes everything he walks next to fall. He fights with his friend in the small apartment and he is so hyperactive that he drives me so crazy that I want him to leave after just a half an hour. The young guy has good intentions for sure. He's protective and is a good lover but he has to correct his behaviour or he won't ever

Visitors

find a girl who will endure him.
Therefore, I really think I'm going to leave him, because we really are not compatible. When he comes later I am going to tell him that we should date other people.
As expected, Steven arrives and comes in the back door.
- Hi Christina, I'm so happy to see you. My phone is ringing. Wait just a minute.
I obviously hear his conversation.
- Hi, Cavrone. When are you going to pay me back? I'm going to put my pinga in your culo pende. Ha, ha, ha!
I watch him in the kitchen, pacing quickly from one side to the other, looking out all the windows, then running into the corridor, looking through the other window.
He is definitely going to drive me nuts, that one.
- Steven, please stop running. Please calm down, for Christ's sake.
He laughs.
- Chupamé la pinga. Ha! Ha!
He then changes from a happy mood to a serious one.
- Come sit down. I want to talk to you, Christine.
He then takes out five or six rings.
- Which one do you want? Try them on. Do you want to marry me?
- Oh my God, are you serious! Honestly, this is too kind of you, but we don't even get along. It's never going to work. The answer is no and I think we should stop having an intimate relationship.
- But why? I love you.
- You know why. Now, come on! Don't pretend that you don't see the facts.
It did not seem to have hurt him too much because he didn't scream nor did he cry. When he left, he just added:
- If ever you change your mind, call me to let me know, and keep the rings.
The short visit ended.
Many months have passed since that break-up but I still want to find

Visitors

the right guy.
Someone unexpectedly arrives at my door.
- Hi, I just moved in across the street. My grandmother used to live there. Maybe you knew her. May I come in and talk to you for a while?
- Yes, sure! Why not. I do know your cousin and your grandmother. Come in, but don't look at my place. It needs to be fixed up.
The young man sits in the kitchen and starts to tell
me about his sadness.
- I had a friend whose name was Christine but she died not long ago. I felt guilty knowing I could have saved her but I got there too late and never knew if it was a suicide or a murder.
He looked sad. He then asked me to come closer and give him a hug.
- You remind me of her.
- Well, let me go. I don't even know you.
- You don't remember me?
- I think I did see you somewhere, but can't seem to remember where.
He continues talking to me, as if I had known him forever.
- I wonder if I should only keep you as a friend!
- I can't say, but it would be better if for tonight you go back home. We can talk about this tomorrow or another day.
This young man is tall and handsome. Why does he want to have anything to do with me? I suddenly realize that he looks exactly like the guy from church. I also remember seeing him with my cousin. She came to me, with him standing beside her, and told me that he was in love with me. I had no idea who he was and he ran away. Still sitting in the kitchen, he looks at me and says:
- Are you sure you don't want to have sex with me right now?
- Are you joking with me? Let me tell you that I
haven't had sex for many months, but I should get to know you first, so give me time to think about it.
He finally decides to leave because he says that his daughter is

Visitors

sleeping and he needs to get back home.
- Good night, Christine. I'll come see you soon.
Sweet dreams.
- Yes, good night to you, too.
- Don't forget to lock your door tightly.
- No, I won't forget.

Could he be my guardian, I wonder? I close and look the door, then take a shower and finally go to bed. Between my flower-scented sheets I start wondering.

Who is he? I can't seem to remember. I do see him present at many places during this life, as well as in sequences of past lives. The week goes by and finally I know who he is. It's Flint, the one considered to be the grand, but I wonder why he never came to talk to me whenever he was in the same place that I was. It's been such a long time since the last time he spoke to me; actually it's been about 25 years. I gradually have some memories of seeing him in a bar in Cancun. I'll ask him if that was him the next time he comes by. I don't have to wait long for his second visit.

- Come in. Do you want something to drink, Flint?
- Do you have a beer?
- No, I don't drink beer, but the store is right downstairs, so I'll go down to get you a couple. What kind?
- No, I can do that myself. Wait for me; I'll be back in 2 minutes.

He's back in no time and takes a seat in the kitchen.

- I want to ask you if you ever were in the Daddy Rock Bar in Cancun last year!
- Yes, I did go there. In fact, I fell for a girl named Lorna, a tall girl with long black hair, but we didn't get along. She wasn't my type.
- I see. Well, are you married or are you with someone? You know, these days, guys come along and if I don't ask them, I'll never know if they have someone until they're finished fucking me.
- No, I'm not. Are you?
- No. Do you remember once when you were young and came to visit

Visitors

your grandmother and you stopped by my house?
- Maybe. It's possible!
- You'll have to ask if it's your mother or your aunt who comes to visit my dad every Christmas.
- Ok, I will.

Unexpectedly, he grabs my hand and pulls me towards him. I fall in his lap and he starts to kiss me. I push him away.
- I don't think we've known each other long enough.
- C'mon! We've known each other for a long time, plus we'll get to know each other more!
- I have to admit I'm excited because I haven't had sex for about eight months.

He becomes even more excited, wraps his arms around me, lifts me and says:
- Which way to the bedroom?
- First door on the left.

He carries me to the bedroom, placing me on the bed, caressing me all over with his big hands.
- Turn around.

I obey him, getting on my hands and knees. He holds my buttocks with one hand, pulling me towards him while he enters me. He makes love to me for about an hour and after ejaculating, he just lies there, motionless, smoking his cigarette. He looks quite satisfied but gets up to get dressed.
- You're leaving already?
- Yes, I have to go to sleep. My daughter's coming early in the morning.

He gives me his phone number and goes home, across the street. The next day, I wonder what to do now, whether he needs my help. I am very confused. My nearly 10-year-old relationship with another guy ended and it's difficult to know where to start or whether to build a new relationship or not. Anyway, I decide to call him and invite him for supper. He answers the phone sounding really mad.

Visitors

- I'm sorry. My ex-girlfriend came to see me, saying she wants to get back together. I think that's what I'm going to do, so don't call me anymore.

I also get mad, not that words would hurt him anyway, but it just might make him think about how he should behave in the future.

- Stupid asshole! You do what you want, whenever you want you, without taking responsibility for your actions. You're just like these other stupid fuckers!
- Christine, my girl friend's moving in tomorrow, so please, I don't want you to come over.
- Don't worry about that. I won't! But what makes me mad is that I will be stuck with your inner presence. And how are you going to deal with the situation? I won't fuck just anyone so that you can get rid of me. Do you know you make me sick? I'm so mad at myself for having succumbed to you. Do you know that cheating can cause heart attacks, stupid asshole? Go to hell!

I hang up.

I think I took the opportunity to spill out everything I wanted to tell all of the stupid jerks who have made me endure the same thing. Anyway, Flint was the one who had to hear it.

I have to be patient and endure the pain until I find the one person who will ease my heart from beating too fast because of the cheating. But this was the kind of situation I have been experiencing in recent years. A little less than six months have passed by and I still haven't found the one who will fulfill the role of lover/friend in my life.

Steven still comes to visit me at times but not as a lover. He brings friends over for me to meet, and this evening is an example:

- Christine, my cousin is downstairs and he says he knows you. Can I let him in? He'd like to see you.
- Sure, but I'm working on filling out papers. Just let him in the living room. I have time to talk.

I'm surprised when I see that it's one of the look-alike Fred's. Don't ask me how many false Fred's there are because all those I have seen

Visitors

look like twins. Anyhow, I had known this particular one since I was a teenager.
- Hello, Christine. I'm so happy to see you.
He hugs me and kisses me on the cheek.
Oh, my God! Is he ever good looking! I look at him and his blood seems to be heating up and a warm feeling seems to come over him. Standing beside the window, he's smoking a cigar and laughing.
- Do you remember when we were young and your dad grabbed me by the neck.
I still think about it at times and it makes me laugh to remember how I panicked. I think it was one of the most frightening events of my life.
- That's funny you remember that, I hadn't thought about it since it happened. Well, you had to remind me about it for I to remember it seems.
- Steven, we have to tell you the story of what happened the night that Fred and I met.
I was 14 years old that particular night. I didn't feel like going back home. I had just come back from a 2-month visit to my mother's house on the island. It was the first time I had met up with my friend Josée since my arrival.
At the end of the evening Josée left to go home and I was supposed to also leave 5 minutes later, but I lost track of time and I missed my bus. I had to stay there to catch the next bus about a half an hour later.
Meanwhile, my dad decided to come and find me, but didn't know where I was. He called my friend Josée, since I had told him that I was going to be with her. Imagine how he panicked he was when he found out I wasn't with her. Speaking on the phone with Josée, he said:
- Where is she, Josée? You'd better tell me right now.
- Okay. I'll show you where she is.
- Perfect, I'll be at your door in 5 minutes.
Josée, all frightened and shaking, tried to call us to warn us that my dad was coming. The music was so loud that no one heard the phone

Visitors

ring. I left the room where I was kissing the boy who had just become my new boyfriend. I needed to talk to my other friend's boyfriend about something important, so I went to knock on the door of the room where he was hiding.
- Who is it?
- It's me, Christine. I need to ask you something.
- Sure, come in.
Fred wasn't dressed because his girlfriend had just left and he was hiding behind the blankets.
- Come sit closer and tell me.
- I want to know if you are Charles's son! It's so crazy how much you look like him.
- How could I know? I'm an adopted child.
At that moment, I started telling myself that he might be the boy the old man had spoken to me about. But there are so many adopted children that there's no way I could be sure it was him. In addition, it had been such a long time since the man had spoken to me that I barely remembered. I started daydreaming, trying to remember what the old man had asked me about the boy, but Fred took advantage of my distracted state to jump on me and remove my clothes.
It was crazy; my boyfriend was in the next room and his girlfriend had just left. He was good-looking and I remembered I was the reincarnation of one of the old man's grandmothers or half-sisters. I was still feeling sort of bad about what was happening, although I felt as if I knew this guy more than any of the people who were present that night. Suddenly there was banging on the door and a man screamed:
- Get out of there! I know you're there!
All of a sudden, the door burst open and my father came into the living room, screaming:
- Where's Christine. Are you youngsters on drugs? Because if I find any drugs, it's not going to be one of your better days.
Fred said to me:

Visitors

- Hurry! Get dressed.

We didn't have enough time to do so because in a flash, the door opened wide. My father stood there, smaller in stature than Fred, who was just about 16 years old, but he was able to grab Fred by the neck and placed him up against the wall. Fred's feet were dangling and he had tears in his eyes, nearly crying.

- Sir, no! Please, no! I haven't done anything.
- Christine, grab your things and hurry. Let's go; we're leaving.
- Let him go, for crying out loud! He hasn't done anything bad.

My father looked very mad but did let him down.

On his way out, he stopped at the living room door and yelled again.

- You boys had better watch it and get rid of your drugs if you have any, because I'm going to send my people after you tonight.
- Daddy, stop it!

When we got in the car, my father seemed to be calmer. I was afraid of what he was going to do to
me, but he just started laughing quietly.

- What have I done! Poor kids! Christine, you have to call them when we get home to tell them I'm sorry. They must be scared as hell! Just tell them I was mad, thinking I was going to find a bunch of stone-drug kids. Don't forget to ask how much it will cost for the door I broke down, I'll pay for the cost in full.

It took me about an hour before I was able to call them and when I did reach them, it was as if they were waiting for end of the world to come.

- We're going nuts here. Thank God you called. Do you know, every time we hear a noise, we hide in the closet, thinking it's the gangsters coming after us.
- Ha! Ha! That's too funny.

I couldn't stop laughing on the other end of the line.

- You have to calm down. I swear there is no one coming for you guys, I promise. My dad is very sorry and even wants to tell you so himself.

Finally, we finished with the apology but during the night, one of the

Visitors

boys left and decided to play a trick on those who remained. He called many times, threatening the other guys, and that was one of the most frightening nights your cousin ever had.
He still looked scared, just thinking about it.
- Well yeah. That was something I never forgot.
Steven smiled, impressed.
- I had heard about this story many times before.
- It was a long time ago.
- Yes, it was. And you, Fred. I heard you're married now.
- Yes, but.
Steven interrupted the conversation, saying:
- Fred and his wife separated not long ago.
- Oh, I see. Well, a separation isn't easy. I should know about it.
- Christine, I have to go home and take a shower. I just finished work, but do you want to come over to my place later? I'm inviting you. Here, take my phone number.
- I'm not sure. Let me see how I feel later on. I'll call you to let you know if I'll stop by or not.
Fred had a drug problem, cocaine. I tried the drug myself a couple of times. I even can count on one hand the number of times I tried it. I just wanted to try it, but was lucky never to get hooked on it. I think it was my father's stories that scared me away from it. I remember him telling me:
- I never take that shit and if I did, in my position, the people looking out for me could end my life. It's a very bad thing. You should know that I only smoke and sometimes I help those who are hooked on cocaine.
That particular conversation stayed in my mind
and it probably is the reason I never wanted to imitate my friends when I saw them use it, even though, as I said, I had tried it. It must be 15 years since the day I used that drug or any drug and I am surely not in the mood for that kind of tripping. I was tempted by Fred's invitation, so I decided that I would stop by there later. We would

Visitors

probably talk about everything that had happened in the past years and since we both knew many of the same people, we would have a lot to talk about.

I walked to his place and arrived at the door. My heart was pounding fast as the door opened and he stood at the top of the stairs.

- Hurry! Come up. I was waiting for you.

He was as attractive as he had been when we were kids. He had just come out of the shower and was dressed in his navy-blue bathrobe.

- You know, I haven't come here to have sex.
- Stop that! Just come in and sit down.
- Okay, then. Well, tell me what's new in your life.
- You know that we're not like you. Most of us still take drugs and we've never stopped since we started.
- I pity you. It's so sad.
- It ain't so bad. I have a good job. Actually, I have the best job among all of the guys. I work in a big hotel.

I looked at him and saw even more clearly the resemblance with Charles's family members and how similar his taste was to theirs. I saw them when looking at him.

- Let me tell you that life has not been such a thrill for me. Let's say that life has been difficult since my ex-family with Fly's family plus the judge and police gang associated with them and the dead guy's family decided to use me as their prey. I lost my kids, was put in jail, and they tried to have me locked up and killed. There were times I couldn't take it anymore. I ran away to Mexico and that's the only reason my life was saved, because all of the other preys were killed. The worst is that I didn't get any help from my family since they were probably scared. Listen to this. The last guy who beat me up said that my step-mom, his boss, had offered to pay him to kill me. His story was a little scatterbrained but made me lose trust in all people. In conclusion, things aren't going very well for me. That's why I'm filling out the lottery papers.

- Yeah, it's bad around your home.

Visitors

- Yes. I'm scared to get mixed up with others. I did have a friend who decided to help me, but because of the situation being so bad, it only made it worse.

I can only say that he saved my life. His ways were not anything I would support, but it did save my life. For sure, I don't want to join the angels so soon. There are more things I want to accomplish in this life before leaving!

- Your stories are kind of scary but you look like you're in good health! I'm separated and have to travel from Ottawa to here in order to visit my kids. This apartment isn't mine. The woman who babysat me when I was a child lends me her place when I come. Do you want a line?

- I'm not sure it's such a good idea. Maybe I will, but just a little one. I haven't taken any for such a long time. I don't remember what it does. In addition, I'm usually way too smart for that.

He became very attentive, sweet-talking me, smiling at me and looking in my eyes as if trying to illuminate me. His charm was almost potent enough to make me give in to his advances.

Everything seemed good but this time I wanted some kind of assurance before getting into the sexual act. I was tired of being abused by men who didn't want to take their responsibilities. Fred suddenly looked excited and suggested:

- Let's make love!

- Fred, no. Please, not so fast!

His sense of warmth gave me the chills but I didn't want to make love before I was sure I could get into a more durable relationship than the ones I had experienced before. I wanted more than a one-night stand.

- I have to be honest with you. I have the hots for you, but I'm not interested in a sex night with no attachments, so I want to take my time.

- Come on. Come to my room. I know you want me!

- That's not the point. No, I don't want to right now.

- Can I at least kiss you?

Visitors

- Well, not today. Maybe I shouldn't have come!

I could see in his eyes and by the way he was shaking his head no that he didn't want me to go.

He stood in front of the door to block my way. He then took me in his arms by force. I fought back but I felt the pain getting stronger where he was holding me, so I stopped resisting, knowing he was stronger than me. In addition, I was going to harm myself if I continued fighting. I had seen many die, so I was aware that it could happen to me, and obviously I didn't want an accident to happen.

He placed me on the bed so I grabbed hold of my pants with my two hands in order to stop him. He then put his hand on my throat, saying:

- Don't fight back. Just let it be.

He finally succeeded in pulling off my pants, then ripped my panties. He still sounded angry because I was still pushing him away. His manly pride for love seemed offended, so he tried to hide it by gaining control.

- Did you ever get it in the ass? Now calm down and don't fight back.

He gave a good swing and I felt him enter my ass so forcefully that he actually damaged me. I then shivered as though an electric shock had passed through my body all the way to my brain, giving me a bad migraine. He had hit a nerve, the bastard.

I stopped fighting, which I should have done way earlier, and with my hand changed the location of his penis nicely so as not to get killed or something.

I put my mind back to where it had been when I had the huts for him, just before I had told him no.

When the rape which had transformed into lovemaking ended, I stayed in bed next to him. That's when it happened. It came from nowhere in my head: the sound of the voice of the old man playing cards with my dad, saying to me:

- Damn pervert.

I fell asleep listening to the voice of the man talking.

Visitors

At sunrise I got up, got dressed and noticed a photograph on the little table in the corridor. It was a picture of Fred on a football field. By an odd coincidence, behind him stood Flint.
Fred woke up.
- Christine, where are you going?
- I'm going home. I'm going to call you later.
I rushed home. Outside, the breeze calmed my nerves but made me dizzy. I wondered if he had intended to hurt me or if it had been an accident during a moment of pressure? All of a sudden, my emotions from a time in the past awoke in me. This déjà vu was no longer a flash of a memory but a place which had become part of the present. I felt that I was in the beginning of the 19th century. I felt my soul filling itself from a taste I could recognize.
When I got home, I decided to call Flint because I needed to know about his relationship with Fred and also because I needed advice since I had this thought of wanting to kill Fred for hurting me. Even if it was not my nature to kill people, I still needed to calm these ideas down because they were making me sick.
- Hi, Flint. Do you have a minute for me?
- Yes, sure. What's up?
- First, I wanted to know something. I saw a picture of you with Fred at Fred's house and my question was is Fred your friend or family?
- Fred? No, I don't know any Fred. The person you saw isn't me or maybe I was in the picture by coincidence or it could be someone who looks like me.
- That's bizarre. Anyway, to change the subject, what am I going to do about him? I get so mad when I think that he's hurt me on purpose. I can't stop telling myself that if I kill him, I'll heal better and when I think about these bad thoughts, it eats me up inside and I don't like it at all.
- Do you really think he did it on purpose? If you want my advice, don't do anything foolish and you'll get better, don't worry.
- I won't do this for sure, but I keep thinking about it and it's …

Visitors

... - making me sick.
- Take your time and call me if you think about it again. I'll help you change your state of mind.
- Of course. I'll take my time and think good thoughts. Thank you, Fred. You're so kind to take the time to talk to me.

I concluded that if I had let him do it in the first place I wouldn't have gotten hurt.

- Well, okay, Fred. I'll let you go now. And thanks again. I'll call you some other time. By the way, you must know that you're no longer in my presence within.
- Do you want to come over?
- No, thank you. I've been alone for 10 months. Being with you isn't such a good thing.
- Ok, then. Call me back anytime, but are you sure you're all right? You don't need me to do anything for you?
- No, thank you. Maybe next time. Bye.

***

Things were not going badly enough for me already, and then I was unable to get any kind of money and with my life constantly in danger I didn't know where to look. I was legally entitled to government assistance, but even the government was giving me a hard time. They didn't want to give me the money. As for my father, he was at it again, not helping me, but buying himself a new 100-thousand dollar car.

I had no food in my fridge and had no time to find a job, plus I was scared to be an easy target for these hunters who continued to threaten me.

I was just going to try my father again before I fainted alone by myself.

- Father, you still owe me my share, and I have problems: I'm hungry.
- It's not my problem. I don't owe you anything.

Click! He hung up. My father owed me a third of his fortune but he kept denying it, saying that he had other children who he loved more

Visitors

than me and I would never get anything.
As far as I was concerned, it was finished. I got angry and unsympathetic so I called him back one more time.
- Hey, you! I don't care about your other kids since they don't care about me. They are not my problem. The reason you owe me money has nothing to do with me being your daughter and you know it. If it weren't for me, neither you nor they would be living such a secure and good life. I need you to help me now, or I could die!
- I don't give a fuck. For all I know, die.
- Can you tell me what I ever did to you beside love you and make you rich!
- Eat shit! Stop calling me and harassing me. I don't care.
- Really, you mustn't be the one you claim to be if you don't care about me. It's not normal the way you are toward me and if you want me to die, well you die, too. This is your tricks, to take my share and give it to your other family. Think about it! They are going to let me die. Well, I'll put a bomb in your house; this way, no one will get my share and it might even put you robbers in jail, where you belong, for doing this to an innocent person.
He hung up again. I was so furious for not being able to understand the reason for his behaviour that I grabbed my table and toppled it, sending it all the way to the end of the room. Then I started crying and screaming with rage.
Somewhere else, about five minutes later, my dad was driving his Harley Davidson bike and was punished by angels because he was involved in an accident in which someone ran right into him. I believe it was inflicted by the laws from the unknown.
My father ended up in the hospital for three months with a broken hip and broken leg. This made me feel very bad, knowing I had told him to die just before it happened, even if logic would say he deserved it, because in my heart I loved my father and didn't really want him to die. The idea of wanting vengeance toward my dad was never real because my love for him always made me end up forgiving

Visitors

him for his illogical and mean behaviour. The worst is when I tell myself that he just might not be cloned. I think that this fight made us come to our senses a little bit because his behaviour improved. He now speaks and listens more to me when I call. But he still doesn't want to give me my share and if in reality he has been cloned, I would understand why he became the way he did with me.

***

Fred still came to visit me every 2 weeks. He stopped by every time he came to visit his children. This love affair lasted until I realized that someone had taken me for a fool. That particular night, Fred arrived at my apartment and, as usual, we ended up in bed but, while naked in bed, I noticed that his body was not the same as it usually was. He seemed to be missing a freckle. Overcome by the feeling that I was being exploited I grabbed the sheet and covered myself.

- Fred, you're not the same as usual. Why is that?
- I wanted to tell you before but...

He lowers his head guiltily and says:

- Sorry, I'm not Fred. My name's Bernie.
- Who sent you here and how were you able to get to my door? Why do you look so much like Fred and why didn't you tell me this before?

He had no answer for me and that made me mad so I screamed.

- Fuck! Did someone sell me to you? If so, you have to tell me right away who it is. I'll have him or her arrested. Tell me who it is.
- I'm so sorry I was going to tell you but you were so happy kissing me. I don't know what more to tell you. I wonder who my parents are. There are so many of us who are adopted and who look alike. Can you tell the difference between us? Can you tell which family each one of us reminds you of?
- Why didn't any of you say it to me before abusing me and taking advantage of me? Imagine! I could have gotten killed. This is so bad! How can I be so stupid? Don't you have a heart or any kind of respect?

I felt so dirty and disgusted that I started to cry.

Visitors

He asked me:
- Which one did you prefer?
- What kind of a question is that! I can't even remember or know which one was which. Don't you feel bad about knowing you're cheated?
- I don't know. Maybe.

The man whom I did not know left and I just stayed home and meditated to try to solve this situation. I had to think of some way to make it less uncomfortable so that I wouldn't be too affected by this humiliating situation.

So I tried to see if anything good had come out of being in their presence and I did find some good things, such as the dreams of the memory of Nicky. While in the spiritual presence of these men, I created two new songs, in addition to the songs already existing which they added my voice to in the background.

"My Immortal" was one I composed. The inspiration came to me while I was filling out the lottery papers. I was remembering the time when I was in the bar "Slice" in Cancun, a time when many of the black members of C.K.U.T. were also there visiting. I told one black guy who kept looking at me while I was talking to someone:
- Pepe is being a pain in the butt. He's run away every time I've tried to ask him a question.

The black guy who was looking at me was the same one as the one on the video of "Call my Name". He got up and punched Pepe right in the stomach. I hadn't asked him to do that, but I guess we didn't have the same understanding of things. During the inspiration, I saw Pepe sleeping in a bed and watched the image of his soul fly into the sky in the direction of the apartments next door, as if he had died or had gone on an astral voyage. I felt a lump in my throat, thinking he could be dead for real. Somehow, that's what inspired me to create the song.

I also composed "Call My Name" from a multiple vision of memories. This one came on the morning that George Harrison had a heart

Visitors

attack; anyway, that is what they were announcing on the radio. One of my thoughts was of a person whose help I had asked in order to find someone in Playa, and his European girlfriend, who I thought was a pretty girl with blue eyes and who seemed to have had the same type of life as mine. Her mother had remarried over there when she was young, so she had traveled a lot to visit, just like me. Anyway, another memory came up, from the opening night of a bar in Playa de Carmen. Pepe was working as a bartender and after I had been there many months, I was lost and he called my name. That is when an extraordinary emotion filled me, with all the memories of myself that I had forgotten about. This person had a magic power within him and this is what inspired me to create that song. I knew Pepe, but couldn't remember who he was. Anyway, that emotion of the memory of myself when I was young inspired me. Not forgetting the image when on the street, I asked Bill to bring me back the person I was looking for.

There were other songs from me that they recorded and used, which I do not remember much, although I remember they used the lyrics. "Am I good enough for you?

Try me, choose me, me, me, meeeee." Another one I sang was "My mother told me to wear the mask. Why do we have to do so? I don't know which one to wear! Can't I just be who I am?"

When I heard this last one on the radio, I felt so bad. I don't know why, but I remember being with the Japanese-Spanish guy who worked at the bar "Christine" in Cancun. He had come to visit and I said to him:

- Oh, no! They didn't put that on the air! It's making me feel so bad! As if by magic, I never heard the song played again.

However, I did forget the melody which came from my emotions when I created the song. "Broken". It was also me singing, but the other person's voice was coming from an old western song that was playing. In addition, I don't know why they recorded me singing at least two of Celine Dion's songs and played them on the air with my

Visitors

voice in the background. I saw many suspects among those around me, which made me suspect many people of being guilty of doing the hacking. I know my phone was hacked for a while, but I also saw one of the tenants in the store downstairs, a Chinese man who had told everyone he was millionaire, give some c.d.s to a black dude who bought himself a new Harley after my songs were sold.

Like all the others, they never gave me my share of my creation, nor did they pay me for hacking. All my compositions together brought millions of dollars to the recording studios. In conclusion, it was my being with Flint and those I thought were the same person which brought to life a real person's image from the past. It happened simply, magically, out of the blue, just like that. Sitting in my office chair, I could feel a taste of blood from a soul that had not yet arrived, which was familiar. The girl in the image is 16 years old. It's around the late 18th century or beginning of the 19th century. She's calling me from a phone booth at a store in Ireland. The girl is beautiful, with her blue eyes and dark hair. The light blood of her soul is the same as mine, but mixed with an emotion, the taste of which I recognize. She tells me that she has run away from her caretaker, which her husband-to-be's family had provided for her. I see that she met up with her future husband at the dance and she left to make love for the first time. It was kind of a lucky circumstance for her that he was the boy she left with. She tells me on the phone:

- Mom, it's me, Nicky. Please come to get me.

I see this image as if it's happening now for real. Telepathically, the echo of her voice is like a live person, like a person talking on a phone, and her fresh image is like that of a person who just left a few minutes before. It's so real that it brings me more memories from that time in a past life. Somehow, after all that, she's the one who brings me the strength to heal from the shame the men's abuse had just made me endure. I wonder if one of them is the reincarnation of her father of the past. But how would I know which one it is! On the other hand, maybe one of them is the father of her husband's, which

Visitors

she tasted through me, giving her the desire to come back. Anyway, I am unable to solve this mess, so I decide to relieve myself of this burden, at least until I can discover the last name of that man, the father of that daughter which is the mother of my great aunt's. I also know that I am not the only one to whom the look-alike Fred did that abusive trick to. With all of this, I came to understand why, in the past life, Eduardo or Geraldo chased Fred and, when they did that, which appears to be the case, while one of the girls who was their sister died, it is difficult to identify which one is the guilty one. I also had a vision, which showed me one victim identified as the false Fred, when in reality the victim was a missing Italian man named Tony. That particular arrangement was created so that his wife and daughter would get the insurance money.

He was not coming back for the rest of his life, but he also wanted to protect himself from the hunters. In conclusion, there are many different stories in doctrines and in memories, but to know which one goes with which is still a mystery to be solved.

***

After being a witness to cloning and victim of abuse, I started questioning myself about the identity of my father also about who could have organized this mischievousness. I am starting to be aware that there are many dangerous living people around and they are still after me. I will have to dig further to make sure the man there playing the role of my father Frank is really Frank, my father. All I can say is that if the facts prove that he is not Frank, it would explain his unusual bad behaviour toward me.

While my father was still in the hospital, Hector offered to help me. Hector came back to Canada from Argentina with his wife and daughter a couple of years ago, but he just got divorced from his wife. This man has been a friend of my father's since preschool and he just moved into the apartment next door. To help me, he had invited me for supper more than two weeks ago. But the mayor's accountant called the office and made threats saying he would find any

Visitors

fraudulent workers. Anyway, he made me go to a church, where they gave me a check for the time being.

Tonight, I'm going to Hector's house. I walk in and I sit at the table and see Hector's daughter.

- Josephine, aren't you pretty! Do you know that you look like my daughter?

She smiles, happy to receive the compliment.

I look at the table, already full.

- Hector, what's that weird thing you're eating?
- Dried tomatoes.
- What, Christine. You never tasted dried tomatoes? asks Jo.
- No, never!
- Let me give you one. You have to try this. It has a special taste.

Hector changes the subject.

- Did you know that Big John, who you were talking about the other day, is my cousin?
- No, I didn't know that. All I know about him is that he went with my dad to India and that he was working on the construction of the extension of the Montreal Convention Center.
- Well, Hector, did you know that one time big John tried to teach my friend Steven a lesson after he or his friend came to my house and stole my T.V.?

John wanted to teach him a lesson, so he went to his house, took his guitar and brought it to my dad. I'll always remember how he came crying to me like a little boy.

- The guitar my grandfather gave me when I was a kid was stolen. Who could have taken it?
- No, Christine. I didn't know that Big John came to see you.

All I know is that a gang of black guys beat big John to death and I came to live near you. Since I have a daughter now, I thought it would be nice to get to know you. I want Josephine to meet people who will be there for her if ever I die. I'm not getting any younger, you know.

- No problem. That's a very good idea. We could find a way for her

Visitors

meet my children. They are the same age.

- John had brought me some papers and was leaving my place when he was attacked. The couple who he was living with told me that he owed the attackers drug money. You must know that the gang of murderers has done lots of damage around here. But there are many of them and they are not all murderers; I even know some honest ones who even are spies for their own kind. You have to know them to know which ones are dangerous. There are bad people everywhere in this world. Hector, I have another problem. I seriously think that my Dad Frank is not the real Frank. I think he has been cloned!

- You look like a clone yourself, Christine! And what is that supposed to mean, cloned!

- Well, it means someone who takes someone else's place, pretending to be him. In simple terms, he's been duplicated.

- Come on! I've known your father since preschool! I know who he is!

- Really? How many years had it been since you had last seen him before you came back here? And why doesn't he ever come to talk to you when he sees you? In addition, explain this to me. When I was in the car with him and you passed by, I asked him who you were. He just shrugged his shoulders and said "I don't know Hector, I think."

- He didn't look sure, so I asked him, "Well, do you know Hector? Who is he to you?" He then started to smile his sarcastic smile and said "I don't know, maybe!"

Hector appears to be in a bad mood.

- Stop this nonsense! I have no idea what you're talking about!

It was now my turn to be in a mad mood, but I resisted screaming at Hector. After all, he had invited me to his home.

- Never mind, Hector. I'll find a way to know who he is. I'll find fingerprints hidden somewhere and until then, I'll try to avoid doing anything about it. Hector, something funny has happened since last week. I had some vision of you from the past. Tell me if what I am going to tell you reminds you of anything. We are in Ireland sometime before the Second World War, but there's a small war going on

Visitors

because of the hurricane which left only potatoes on the land. The house where I live with my mother went up in flames so I'm staying at the house of a nice man named Flint. We are all in Ireland just before a train departs.

Hector has some German Italian and French blood and looks like Picasso.

- Hector, in this memory, you were living with this man Flint, too, working as the chef. Your wife was the housekeeper and Josephine was there, waiting for her first love to come. You had run away from the orders of the German authorities because you didn't want to gather your family together for them to kill. I'm not sure why they were at war, but my guess is that it was due to the fact that there wasn't enough food for everyone. Your wife being Spanish, the Italians made you turn against them since they were asking to get the Spanish first. That was why you came to hide them among the rich farmers of Ireland. You were reporting all the information of their upcoming attacks. I can see this as if it were yesterday. The weirdest method of capturing people that I saw was good-looking Italians asking women in order to capture their family at their gathering. I can see a family gathered together, being shot at. It was thanks to you, Hector, that a group of people from the P.D.G. of the United Nations was able to capture many of the enemy. I can also see the departure of a rich German-Englishman who was in Ireland, also hiding. So, Hector, does it remind you of something?

- I don't know. Maybe, but I'm not sure. My memory doesn't see that far back.

- I can remember that you had exchanged the information and in order to legalize the payment. You had given them some of your paintings, for lots of money. You had then helped with the construction of the structure and statues for my house, in addition to the house of your daughter who was close in age to mine. Josephine was often in Spain but came back every summer and on vacations. You even hid some of the most dangerous dead assassins in cement

statues.
- No, I don't remember.
- It doesn't matter. It's only a vision and has been erased by rebirth. The intelligent Japanese, who are not at war, also helped a lot with the capture of the corrupt Italian murderers, the ones willing to take someone else's place and the ones raping and hurting women. The Japanese who helped did so because they said they were the Iris rots from far away and they were the ones who had named my family emperors. When they decided we were a distinct race, they brought technology in exchange for the criminals. They cut their fingers paying their family to let go and letting them out for the hunt to begin. Whether you remember or not, they are only memories, which are not so very clear anyway. The only thing that has remained the same is that you're still building structures of buildings and that you're still willing to build one for me, too, but will I receive my funds before it's too late in order for us to achieve this? I thank you for your hospitality, Hector. I'll repay you one day. Good night and see you later.

***

Chapter 6
Love destroyed by a war

I'm filling out my lottery papers. I have all the combinations, starting with one and twenty, up to the end. I should be finished in about 4 years. Looking out the window, I notice a man I've seen before. The man is entering an apartment next door. Under his arm, he is carrying a case that has the shape and size of a rifle. I finally recognize him. It's that judge who works at lotto Quebec, the same one who keeps telling me to stop taking papers. I had to check if what I was doing was illegal. I found out that it wasn't illegal, so I decided not to listen to the man, who I suppose just wanted to give an order and be obeyed even though there was no real legal restriction. I once saw him bother my father in his miniature collectible car store. I

Love destroyed by a war

wondered what he was doing there, and I realized that it was that same asshole who had signed papers to get me arrested way before I was filling out the lottery papers. I remembered him asking my dad stupid questions.

That night I came into my dad's store and saw the man standing there. As soon as he saw me walk towards the back, he came behind me and followed me all the way to the back, without even asking permission. My father was sitting on a chair and quickly got up, laughing and being shy because he had just inhaled a cloud of smoke from his hash cigar.

Right away, with no hesitation, I asked my dad:
- Who's this man? Do you know him?
- No.

Then he started laughing, probably because he was stoned from his cigar.
- Why is he going into the back store then?
- I have no idea. Why don't you ask him?

The judge didn't give me a chance to talk. He started asking questions:
- Sir, what are you doing here and what's that weird-smelling cigar?
- Sir, do you want some?

My father started laughing.
- I can give you a little bit if you want, but it's mine and I won't have any left if you take it.

He laughed again then smiled warmly at me.
- No, I don't know him.
- Father, I think I recognize him. He's a judge.
- Whoops! He is bizarre! He looks like he's never seen a hash cigar.

My father looked at me, winking and smiling at me, then said:
- Watch the man carefully. I'm going to make him freak out.

He was preparing a silly joke.
- Sir, I sell drugs. What do you think of that?

The cars are there for nothing. Ha! Ha! Ha! Do you want some?

Love destroyed by a war

The man made a funny face, frowning and seeming confused that he was the object of our laughter. Then the other man who works with my dad got up, looking very serious, and looked at my dad, shaking his head.

- Frank, would you stop making fun of the man? I'll take care of him.

He then approached the judge, started showing him the collections of cars, and explained their value, trying to turn him into a good customer.

I didn't stay much longer, nor did the judge, who was getting ready to leave. I felt a great deal of danger around this man as if he was a dangerous man hunter.

- Daddy, be careful. I don't trust this man. Don't stay around him. I sense danger. I'm leaving now. I love you and will come by another day soon.

I kissed him on the cheek and went home.

Today, while filling out papers, I thought about this and realized that this judge came to spy in order to create a war. I suspect this man of being part of an arrangement that was behind my father's motorcycle accident.

It's not normal that this man, who bragged about having 100 thousand dollars in his bank account, moved into a messy apartment next door to me. He's up to something for sure and it makes me scared.

I know that two days ago, police officers refused to obey his orders to arrest me again.

I overheard the conversation between him and the officers who said:

- Sir, no. What she's doing is not illegal. I cannot arrest her on these grounds. Don't ask me to act against the law, sir. Take care of your business elsewhere and without us.
- You'll see what I'm going to do! You'd better arrest her, I said.
- Yeah, yeah. Right, sir.

That was how the officers refused to obey his orders. Since then, he has been sitting in the third-floor apartment next door, with his rifle

Love destroyed by a war

between his legs, waiting. What I see is making me quite nervous. When I go out, I'm very scared because one of my friends was shot on the corner of the street when a rifle shot came from a rooftop. They weren't able to catch the person who did it. So I look everywhere, on the rooftops and behind me, when I walk outside. It's driving me crazy; I'm going to have a heart attack soon. The worst is I know he's after me because he told me so. I told other people about it and they called me nuts, saying I was overreacting, but he's there with his rifle, looking at my window every day.

I decide to go ask the new Chinese woman at the store if she saw him and if he told her why he was here. The woman is a doctor from a research laboratory in California. She came to study my phenomenon in order to diagnose it and tell me if it's dangerous for me to have contact with others because of the events. Anyhow, as for the judge, no one knows why he is here, but I heard many different hypotheses. One is that it's because the girl next door was killed and the killer is still at large and they want to capture him. There is another story which says that the judge and another man, who also recently showed up and is carrying a rifle, are here to capture my ex-boyfriend Mustafa, who could have been involved in some shootings. Anyhow, these are all only suppositions. Whatever, the reason is, I seem to be either the bait or the target because there's no other logical explanation.

Meanwhile, on the T.V. news, I see a little boy on his bicycle getting hit by a car and the judge talking to the announcer, saying.

- I want to offer my apologies to the parents, in hopes that they will forgive me because I didn't see him. I feel so bad not to be able to turn back time, to change the circumstances.

Sadness overwhelms me and I began to panic. This has to be a coincidence.

That boy has to be another boy, not mine. In my mind and good heart, I can't believe and it is not possible that someone could be so angry, seeing me fill out papers, that he would go out and murder

Love destroyed by a war

a child, then hypocritically say he's sorry. There has to be an explanation but I have no idea what it could be. I just close the idea to acknowledge it could be my son who was just hypocritically murdered.

The next morning, about two days after Lesley came to my place with the American visitor's daughter, Lesley knocks at my door and says:
- Hello! Christ, please open the door! I need to talk to you. Please, I just bought some furniture. Look, I have the bill; it cost me 5 thousand dollars and they are coming to deliver here.
- Lesley, I have to tell you that you can't stay here nor leave your things here anymore. You need to take your things and not come here anymore, so don't bring any more things.
- No problem. But just for today, because they are already coming here with the furniture. It's too late to change the order. Stop it! Don't do this to me. Another truck will come pick it up 2 hours later. Listen to me! You'll have nothing to do! Please, I have no place to put the furniture before much later.
- Fine, I'll have them leave it on the balcony.
- Oh, come on! I'm not sure that I'll have a place for two days. My mom hasn't finished with the renovations yet.
- That's not my problem, Lesley.
- Ok, I understand. But I have to go now and they're coming tomorrow, so please let them in when they get here. I'll try to be here, okay? In the meantime, chill, girl!

He leaves, almost running. I close the door, angry but not showing it. Elsewhere the two men with rifles are watching and waiting for something. I know there is something fishy about the delivery of Lesley's furniture. At this moment, a scene comes back to me of an event which had occurred about six months before the murder of Lyndsey, the daughter of my father's friend. I'll go talk about this with Diane downstairs, because I seriously think that my life is in danger. I go downstairs and as usual, Diane is there, already drunk.
- Diane, I've got problems.

Love destroyed by a war

- Sure, tell me about it. Do you want to have a cup of tea or coffee?
I sit down on the old kitchen chair.
- Yes, thanks. I'll have a cup of tea with sugar and milk. Diane, I need to know if you found out if they found the girl and her kid from across the street.
- No! Nobody knew anything about it.
- You know, I was the last one to have seen her in her apartment. I remember watching her and her son in her apartment. There were five black guys running from one room to the other. That night, all her curtains were open and all the lights were on, then all of a sudden, I couldn't see anything because she closed the curtains. I didn't do anything to call the police because I thought she was buying drugs and because I hadn't heard anyone scream for help. Unfortunately, the next day I saw a moving truck and the black guys loaded two big boxes but nothing else. You must remember me panicking, asking you to go see next door. The week after, the owner put all the furniture and personal belongings on the side of the street, with a funereal look on his face. No one knew where the tenants had gone. I had seen these guys before and Lesley wasn't here on the night I last saw them. But he was driving the moving truck that day, picking up the two boxes. I saw him very clearly.
- But why are you talking about this? What does it have to do with you?
- Well, I think they're planning to do something to me tomorrow because tomorrow some furniture is being delivered to my place, then another truck will come pick up the furniture. They might be planning to steal my papers or even murder me, as they did with the others. I've been working on these papers for 3 years and don't want some druggie murderer to get a hold of these papers. In addition, he could want me dead, since I'm sure it was he who stole some of my songs and some that weren't mine that I sang. He's a deejay for C.K.U.T., the Jamaican crack heads. I know he recorded me because he went downstairs and then broadcast me singing Bryan Adams's

Love destroyed by a war

song "Heaven" with the noise of the machinery which was outside at the time. His name is the one said to be the accompanist with Jeanie, which is not my name, but me singing. Not that I have any rights over a song which I didn't compose. However, he did also record some of my compositions.
- Well yes, I totally understand. Call me as soon as they get here. Anyway I should see them arrive.
- Okay, thanks. And be on your guard. They're dangerous. They're not new at committing crimes.
The next day, the deliverymen arrived.
- Please, leave the furniture on the balcony.
- Ma'am, I can't do that. I need to put them inside somewhere. I can't leave them outside.
The deliverymen aren't from the black gang. They come from the store and are white men. I decide to let them put the furniture inside, but I go downstairs to make phone calls. I call my father, but there's no answer, as usual, so I leave him a message telling him:
- There's something abnormal going on; I am a bit scared.
I explain the whole story to him, hang up and go back home.
Lesley finally arrives and the deliverymen have left. The front door is open and there's a police car parked in front of my home. He looks at me, wondering if I know what he was planning and becomes nervous.
- Oh, no! I have to go see someone right now.
He leaves very fast, but purposely doesn't run too fast in front of the officer, so as not to appear suspicious.
After about a half an hour, the officers leave and I go upstairs to work on correcting the papers, because someone had taken a pile, so I was missing some. An hour goes by before Lesley returns, this time with a Spanish girl and another guy. I let them him since I know they're not his usual murderer friends. After they came in, I go back in my room. I hear them talking in the kitchen, but I don't dare join them. I only go into the kitchen once, to tell them to hurry because I want to take my shower. I even lock my bedroom door. 20 minutes later, I hear a knock

Love destroyed by a war

at my door. It's Lesley, saying:
- Christine, let me in. The box of papers is mine, okay?
- What did you just say? Have you gone crazy or something? Come on! There's no way that I'm going to give you my papers! In addition, there are some pages missing, so I need to correct them. I won't let someone play them, knowing they could lose. Imagine if they spend all of their money, then lose when I knew there were some missing. No way! They'll come back and kill me or something. Anyway, who do you want them for?
- I want them for me.
- Don't take me for a dummy. I don't believe you. By the way, did you intend to pay me back with the furniture? Because that's not what I want. I want and need land.

Diane arrives, right on time. She starts yelling very loudly.
- Christine, are you alright?
- Yes, for now. But Lesley wants to take my papers and I don't know want he's going to do!

Lesley starts jumping in the hallway and says:
- I haven't done anything.

Diane gets mad at him and again yells:
- Hey you! You'd better hurry and get your things. I'll be watching you from downstairs, with a piece, so don't you dare try anything.

I open the door to accompany Diane to the door. As I watch her go downstairs I notice Arnold sitting on a rocking chair across the street. Supposedly, he heard that I was in trouble and came to my rescue. I don't bother with him and go back upstairs. Then, minutes later, the Spanish girl comes and knocks on my door, saying:
- Your friend outside is at the door and he wants to see you!

I climb down the stairs and see Arnold standing there.
- Christine, is everything alright? We're worried about you!
- I'm not sure, really!

Arnold starts shouting in the hallway.
- Don't let me catch any of you laying a hand on her or they'll have to

Love destroyed by a war

deal with me. I'm watching you and am ready for you.
Lesley looks at me, frustrated and confused, his eyes almost popping out of his head from fear. Arnold is two and a half times his size.
All of a sudden, someone else arrives.
It's Mustafa's friend and he's running down the street, yelling:
- Christine, are you alright? Someone called to tell me you needed help. I'm here for you.
Arnold sees him and decides to try to capture him, knowing he was suspected to be part of a shootout. Today's a crazy day. So many people have come by at the same time, it makes me wonder who has sent whom.
Arnold is panicking on the balcony:
- Come here, you. Don't wait for me to catch you. Yeah, you'd better run fast.
Arnold goes off in pursuit of the Arab man. Meanwhile, Lesley is calling someone on the phone:
- Yo, never mind. Don't come here. It won't work. I need to leave this place now or I'll die. Call the other one to come and help me bring my stuff.
Finally, after about an hour, some people come, load the truck and then leave. In my mind, I start wondering if he really did want to hurt me. I want to give him the benefit of the doubt, since he had helped me the times I got out of jail after being falsely accused, but on the other hand, I don't trust him and no longer wish to see him.
Unfortunately, Lesley comes back.
- Hey, Lesley! You forgot some things upstairs. Take them now.
- Oh, yes. But I'll come back for them tomorrow.
- Okay, but you can't stay here because I'm leaving. But do you want to drop me at the metro station?
- Sure, no problem.
While locking the door, I notice an armed man, but it's not the judge. The man has a round face, but the judge has a long, thinner face. The man resembles my father or Arnold's uncle, the ambassador,

Love destroyed by a war

although I'm not sure, since he's wearing sunglasses and a cap. He's on the roof, pointing the gun at Lesley. He's signalling towards me with his arm to move away. Then he yells:
- Move away, girl.
Lesley turns and sees him.
- Oh, no! Not me! Fuck! Fuck! Hurry, let's go.
I look again at the man and make a sign to tell him to calm down. In my heart I feel relieved and happy to see that some people have come to my rescue, especially since I saw the disappearing attack which took place.
That night I came back home, safe and sound. The next day it's Pierre's turn to come visit. He comes to fix my washing machine. Lesley arrives while Pierre is here to take the rest of his things. Something's wrong. Lesley has the eyes of a demon and walks toward my drawer of knives.
As soon as I see him open it, I know I have to react fast. I've been on my guard around him since I saw him next door at the murder scene. Not wanting to see his next move, I unlock my back door, but just before going outside, I see Lesley take out a knife and hear him mumbling "I have to save my mother."
I look at Pierre, remaining calm, and tell him:
- I don't know, but if I were you, I'd follow me, right now. And hurry up.
I run out of the apartment to reach Diane's place, Pierre following behind me.
- Christine, what was that? Is it me or was that guy very weird? What the hell was he saying and trying to do? Let me tell you, I never saw anyone so fucked up.
- I don't really know. I think he was scared, but I believe this guy is dangerous.
- Was he going to use the knife on us for real?
- I don't know, Pierre and I sure don't want to go back upstairs to find out.

Love destroyed by a war

- Me neither. I don't want to know.

I look out the window and see Lesley leaving with none of his things. I hear him saying:

- Not me! Not me!

Pierre and I go back up and bring all of the rest of Lesley's belonging out on the balcony.

It makes me feel relieved, but I know that danger is still wandering around me. In the evening, Lesley comes to pick up the rest of his stuff. The girl downstairs let him in even though I had called her to warn her not to do so. It seems she never listens to what I have to say anyway. Well, thank God, he doesn't do anything to harm her and he stays around all night, slowly taking his stuff out.

Seriously, I don't understand Lesley. One day he shows me how to fix my back door since it wasn't safe and could have been opened easily. He acts nice, making my place more secure one day, but the next day he wants to harm me. He makes no sense. I can only believe that he is a kind of traitor.

In conclusion, it troubles me to see that there are some people who are so insensitive to other people's rights to live. The effect on me, to unconsciously know that murders are occurring every day, is definitely not the same as the effect of seeing and knowing that I am a target chosen to be the next prey of war, with premeditated intention to kill me. These attacks, which have been active for months, or rather, years, have completely terrorized me and made me paranoid about some people's intentions toward me.

Many months have passed. It is now winter, Christmas is over and I believe it's the end of January of the year 2004. I think I just saw a ghost. Even if it's not the first time I've seen this person, it was the first time I saw her as a ghost. I had a vision which showed me she was one of those once named Joan of Arc. She has the same physical characteristics as a killer in the distant past, the type of person I would have preferred not to have crossed paths with in life. When I think and read about it, I still wonder why those who praise her

Love destroyed by a war

haven't deduced that she is sick and needs to be treated. If her fans didn't praise her bad achievements, I wouldn't consider them to be lovers of horrors. It seems that they consider it to be something to be proud of. Those ideas from the admirers, in my opinion, will become an encouragement to give birth to others, who will cultivate similar ideas of action.

In conclusion, this proves how and why others get sick believing it is the way to behave. Therefore, there are still problems on the subject of humans with animalistic behaviours.

Anyway, I have not left the country for many years and it has been two years since I last saw my children. My ex has moved and refuses to tell me where he now lives and no lawyer wants to help me.

I get up from my chair to look through the window of the front door that opens onto the porch. I am still afraid of being attacked, so I am on my guard. The sun has gone down and outside it is starting to get dark. I see a faint light in an apartment on the other side of the street in the apartment building beside the Laundromat. The glow from the light attracts my attention because the curtains of the place are wide open. It must be the tenth time I've looked through the window today. I'm feeling kind of nervous because earlier I saw a little girl, who looks exactly like my daughter, enter the downstairs apartment, where people moved out last week. Anyway, since then, I've wanted to go down there, to see who the little girl is. But every time I was ready to go there, something stopped me. The first time, I was stopped when a truck parked in front of the door where the girl with green eyes and long blond hair entered. Driving the truck was the Chinese family who previously rented downstairs. The Chinese man used to tell everyone he was a millionaire. I don't trust these people anymore because my father came to speak to me about them, saying:

- The Chinese man made an offer to buy, but when I was at the restaurant with him to finalize the signing of the contract, he told me he didn't have the money to pay for it.

He then said some words in Chinese but I didn't understand so I left.

Love destroyed by a war

My father implied that the man had bad intentions. The most confusing thing which made me suspect there was something fishy going on was that when these Chinese people came, there were two couples at the same time, one on one side and the other on the other side of the street and both were identical, like two sets of twins pretending to be the same people. Let me say that what was happening around me was very confusing. What stopped me was seeing the little girl get in the truck and the truck taking off right away. Obviously, I could no longer go see her, since they had taken her with them. One hour later, I see them come back and the little girl has her hair cut short and dyed black. The young 9-year old girl gets out of the truck by herself. She's the same one I had seen earlier; I recognize her without any doubt. She then enters the same door as before. I know the Chinese people aren't the child's parents and she looks exactly like my daughter. I stay in front of the window, watching.

I see the truck move to park on the other street corner. A red car follows them and parks right behind them. I know there's no one living in that apartment yet and I think that possibly the child is one of the 7 children of the family who lived there before.

So I try to remember what she looked like. I think she might be lost and forgot where her family had moved to. With that idea in mind, I postpone going down to see if she was my daughter. I still keep an eye out to see if she needs help because I suspect that something abnormal could happen. I look again at the truck and I see a man getting out of the red car behind them. He's walking toward the door that the girl had entered. I sit for a second to analyze what I'm seeing. I know the man and wonder what he's doing here. His name's Claude. He's the one who looks like Fly, the murderer of another Claude, who was the son of a well-known bar owner in the upper Laurentians. Changing the subject, I'll tell you a story about this Claude fellow who looks like Fly. Steven brought him to my place as a security guard after my neighbour was murdered and I almost kicked him out right

Love destroyed by a war

away after he did something.

It's the third day that he's with me. Sitting on the sofa, Claude reaches into his pocket to get his bag of cocaine.

- No, Claude. Sorry, I don't want any. I had enough when I was with Fred and I don't want to take that stuff anymore; besides it's not me: I was always against this drug before.

He looks at me, surprised.

- Are you sure you don't want any?
- Yes, I'm sure. I'm finished with that drug for good.

He takes his hand out of his pocket and a big knife falls to the floor. Without asking myself any questions, as fast as lightning, I grab the dagger, run to the back door and hide the knife in a box outside on the balcony. I then use my key to lock the door and come back into the living room. I then say to him:

- What the hell are you doing with this dagger in my home! Didn't I tell you not to bring any weapons in here?
- No, I didn't know!
- Really, don't play games with me or pretend as if you didn't know. Today was the first time that I didn't pat you down for weapons before letting you in. Are you telling me I was doing it for nothing before?
- I don't care! Just give me back my knife please.
- No, you will not get it back before you leave.

While he looks everywhere in my apartment, trying to find his dagger, I wonder if this man could be Fly! He could have changed his identity to save his life! He looks so much like him and that confuses me. Then again, the last time I saw Fly was 13 years ago and he supposedly had been killed since then.

That's why it doesn't make any sense to believe he could be Fly, although the newspaper might have been tricked in order to protect him. No matter who the man is, he's still dangerous, running around with a dagger. The next day, I kick him out of the house, but that makes him mad and he goes to the downstairs store, pulls out

Love destroyed by a war

another dagger and holds it under the Chinese doctor's neck. The police intercept him right away in the front yard and now he just got out of prison. So now that I see him entering the apartment, I fear for the safety of the young girl. What if he is here for vengeance!

I am about to go out again, when I see another person enter the apartment, a 16-year-old boy with a Mohawk haircut. Very soon after, I hear a scream for help. Immediately, my heart starts beating fast and my veins are heating up as if I have a bad sunburn. My imagination tells me a rape is occurring, but I'm not sure that's true. What if she is my daughter? That would explain my physical reaction. I have to go help her now! Before I leave, I need to call someone to let them know where I am in case I don't come back. I call my father, as he is always the one I report to, but as usual, he doesn't answer, so I leave him a message.

- Dad, you have to do something to help. I'm not sure what to do. The Chinese people dropped off a girl and...

I tell him about everything very quickly, in a mixed-up way, then hang up. I don't wait for him to call me back. I'm ready to go rescue the girl. So I go down the stairs but as I reach the last step, I back down, seeing Claude and the boy with the Mohawk leave and run away. I stop again and look at Claude getting into his car. He starts the motor. The truck in front of him with the Chinese people in it does the same and they both leave very quickly. As for the boy with the Mohawk, he just runs into a street somewhere and disappears.

I'm standing on the sidewalk when the boy who used to live there comes out. I know him, so I shout to him.

- Hey, kid! Tell me something. Is there a young girl inside the apartment? I saw and heard something weird a couple of minutes before you got here.

- No, there's no one else in there besides the people who just left. They came here to visit the apartment for rent.

- Are you sure there's no one else in there? I saw a young girl go in there!

Love destroyed by a war

- Yes, I swear. No one else is in there. She must have all ready left. I'm sorry, Christine. I have to get back to our new place now. I have no time to chat. I'm already late.

- Ok, I believe you. Thank you and be careful on your way home.

He left and I went back upstairs again, confused and wondering where the little girl was. A couple of hours pass and again I am looking outside. A light glowing in the apartment attracts my attention. It's just upstairs from where everyone was earlier. Since the light is shining and outside it's dark, I can see inside very clearly. The curtain is wide open and I see the little girl appear, standing at the window, facing me. I can see her from her head to her knees. She looks terrified and her tear-filled, illuminated green eyes can be seen as far as where I am, on the other side of the street. I can't seem to be able to acknowledge what I'm seeing, because it doesn't make any sense. This isn't possible, but it is what it is and I am seeing it. Next to the girl stands a tall woman with short black hair, blue eyes and freckles on her face. The woman is dressed in her police uniform and holds her firearm firmly in her left hand, pointed at the temple of the young girl. The woman is looking everywhere, as if she wants someone to see what she's doing. Holding the girl's shoulder with her right hand, she makes sure the girl doesn't move.

I then see the soul of the girl, which is so scared that it came all the way over to me, asking me to help her.

I can see her body, not moving, but her soul is talking and doing what she wishes she could make her body do. The woman turns around to look in my direction. I quickly crouch down so she can't see me. I run to one of my neighbour's house. I knock many times so he knows to hurry to the door, and finally he lets me in.

- Hurry! Look at the window. Can you explain to me what this women is doing? I don't understand.

He looks at the window and seems not to want to see. He closes his eyes, then shakes his head no and says:

- No. No, Christine. Don't look at that.

Love destroyed by a war

He then puts his hand on my head, pushing it down so I can no longer see. He then closes his curtains and says:

- Hurry, follow me into the kitchen.
- Hey, neighbour! Where's your gun? You told me you had one hidden somewhere! Give it to me! It's an emergency. Hurry! I can't let this happen. Come on! We have to help her. What's wrong with you? Hurry! Do something.
- Just calm down! Are you sick in the head or something? You'll be killed if you go there. I lied. I don't have a gun here.

I just told you that to see what you'd say.

- But what are we going to do? She's a police officer! Who are we going to call for help?

At this confusing moment, I'm very disturbed, thinking that if I call her friend the other police officer, she'll lie and they'll believe her more than me. What if they handcuff me, then I'd end up alone with her and she could shoot me, throw my dead body somewhere, anywhere. So calling the police is not an option. It's out of the question.

Well, since my father knows some people in the R.C.M.P., he should know what to do and who to call about this before it's too late. While waiting for my father to call back, I tell my neighbour what I know about this female officer.

- That woman was always present when they came to arrest me, those times that my ex and the organized criminals were falsely accusing me, in order to extract money from my family. I remember one time, when I was all alone with my youngest child and people knocked and banged on the door so many times as if it was the end of the world or a fire.

I hurried to the door in case it was an emergency, but it was that stressed-out policewoman going crazy.

I opened the door a crack and through the small opening I answered:

- I'm just getting out of the shower and I'm not yet dressed, as you can see, so could you wait five minutes, please?

Love destroyed by a war

This woman pushed hard against the door and entered with no respect.
- Look, my baby and I just got out of the shower. Please wait here while we get dressed.
- No, we'll stay right beside you. We're here to take your baby.

I thought the situation was absurd, and I was on the verge of losing my mind. She gave me the court order, which I took and looked at.
- Okay. If this is true, I can understand, but I don't want to give him to you. So I request that my ex come here himself. I don't want to just give him to you. I don't know who you are. I still have rights, don't I!

At that very moment she puts her hand on her gun and releases the lock. We're in the small corridor. I'm wearing only a towel and she's standing right next to me, saying:
- Come on, give him to me now or I will take him by force.
- Would you wait a minute.

I am so stressed out from her weird behaviour.
She still has her hand on her firearm, this time almost taking it out. It's not as if she would need a gun;
after all, she's twice my size and I'm almost naked and am putting shoes on my son's feet while I hold him on the bureau in the corridor. At that moment, in the position I'm in, it would be impossible for me to take the offensive. I have no way out, my life is finished, and I'm going to die today.

I have no choice but to give in and follow her orders, in hopes that my son's life and mine will be spared. Her mean way of talking makes me think that she wants to do more than her job, and it scares me.
- Just let me finish putting his shoes on. Be human! It's cold outside.
- No, that's enough! Give him to me now.

She takes him from me abruptly. Her partner looks at what's happening and doesn't seem to agree with her.
- Calm down! Let her finish dressing him, for crying out loud.
- No! There's no time for this. Let's go now.

They leave in the police car, with my baby, but there's no baby seat in

Love destroyed by a war

the car. At this moment, I become aware that these women are used to behaving illegally.

The legal paper was probably fabricated by friends within the system. They arrive at my place like this, without my knowledge, and with my ex not being present, and they take my child on an hour-long drive with no car seat; all this doesn't make any sense to me from a legal point of view.

I should not have opened the door to those officers. At that moment I never suspected them of bad behaviour and I was wrong. I am seriously scared and I wonder what she can do to me or to any innocent person, even a child. I am more scared and I know for sure she is sick, now that I see her holding her gun to the temple of an inoffensive 9-year-old child. I think hard to find a way to help and I remember that my other neighbour has a gun for real. He told me I could come in an emergency and he will try to help.

I look at my neighbour who seems to be absent-minded.

- Give me your phone. I have to call my father back.

I take the phone and make a call, but there's no answer.

- What's going on? It's the damn answering machine again. He never answers when it's important.

I leave him another message:

- Dad, please! You have to help. It's the police; a kidnapping.

It makes no sense; the female officer seems to have lost her mind. Please, Dad! You have to help. She's going to murder someone. Bring a gun! Do something, please. I'm scared.

I hang up and shake my neighbour on the shoulder in an attempt to rouse him from his stupor.

- I'm leaving now. Can you try to do something about this, like call other authorities while I go see my neighbour who has a pistol?

- You're not really going out to get a gun, are you?

- Well, I won't go next door empty-handed, because she'll kill me too. The woman there has gone wild and if I am dead, it won't change what's in store for the child, will it?

Love destroyed by a war

My neighbour puts his hand on my shoulder and says to me:
- Don't worry too much. There's nothing you can do about this. Go home. I'll take care of this.
I sincerely think that he won't call anywhere and I can't wait for him to do something. The child might be my daughter.
So I run to my neighbour's home, the one with the gun, I knock very hard on his door. What mischief is this? He's not answering. I knock and knock, over and over again, but still no answer. He's probably not home. A feeling of panic invades my insides.
I'll never be able to save the child and she might even be my daughter. Oh, my God, she's going to die and I will, too, if I go there with nothing to defend myself with. I start trembling all over, thinking hard to find a solution, but nothing comes to mind. I go back inside my apartment, using the back door so that the woman doesn't see me. I barricade my doors with heavy furniture and wait for my father's call or for his guard's friend to arrive. There's one thing I'm sure of: I won't let the police officers in in case they are with her. I don't understand what's happening and that it's happening for real. It's impossible for me to believe that a person could harm such a young, pretty, defenceless creature such as that little girl. I want to understand the reasons but it's out of my range of knowledge. I've tried to see all the possible aspects and I've been able to deduce many reasons that could have motivated her, but I still can't believe it. One of my suppositions is that maybe this woman wants me to be part of what she's doing, thinking I will support her bad behaviour, because she was in court when my ex tried to tell lies about me. He did so in order to get custody and take away my rights to our children. As an aside, during the trial with my ex, I always believed that those who knew me would think of me in light of the times I had been good to them and that they knew these bad accusations against me were false, since I was always nice and would never think of hurting anyone. But no one came to help me; as a result, those who didn't know me continued to doubt me and they maintained this

Love destroyed by a war

negative perception of me, even if I had never committed a crime. Getting back to my main concern, the female officer at the crime scene, while looking at this woman, I begin to think that it's a bluff and I give up the idea of getting myself killed to save her. I can't anyway so I wait, thinking that she won't kill the girl. I can't imagine such an evil act happening because these ideas do not exist within me. In general, humans are not capable of believing that others will act in ways they wouldn't think of acting themselves. However, what I am seeing is happening for real, even if I refuse to believe it. Maybe this woman wants something, like my papers or money, but I don't know. I tell myself if that is the case, she will call or ask me somehow. Meanwhile, my neighbour had given up the idea of calling the authorities and my dad had not called back. For Christ's sake! Why doesn't he call me back?

Claustrophobia starts to invade my soul. I am trembling all over and even though I'm not the one in the skin of that little girl, I'm feeling her emotions. I wait, but nothing happens. No one comes, no one calls, and there are no messages on my phone. I become very upset, feeling so stupid for not being able to rescue her, but I still don't think it's possible that she will kill her.

I become aware of how vulnerable, weak and defeated I am, so I start crying. Time passes and nothing happens. She doesn't call to ask for something. Why is she doing this if she doesn't want something? Did someone she loves rape the girl? I don't understand her.

Suddenly I hear the loud sound of a gunshot and I no longer see anything in the window. I sit down and have a vision of a little girl lying in a bed dying. I see her soul vibrating incessantly. I then fall into a state of shock or trance, hearing her voice repeating:

"Why doesn't anyone love me? No, I don't want to go. It hurts too much. I am hurt. Please, someone, help me! God, I did everything to be nice to everyone else. Please, God, tell me why no one loves me."

The vibrating soul suddenly stops moving and silence sets in.

The image of her tear-filled green eyes looking through the window is

Love destroyed by a war

now the image stuck in my head. It stays for days and days, just like a film on pause. It's so sad that it makes me cry and I still cry when it comes back to me. That night, a couple of hours later, I hear many other gunshots outside, but cannot see what's going on.

I get up again, go look through the front window and see her again. But this time she's driving a police car and the passenger beside her is a man who looks like Flint. But I think it's his look-alike, the young man from my insurance company, or even Charles's son. I'm not sure, as they are so similar in appearance, just like twins, especially when seen from a distance. The poor guy's head is tilted towards his shoulder and dangling backwards, his eyes are wide open, and his face is blue and white. He looks dead: his lips are purple and there is no sign of life in his eyes. I feel a cool breeze of loneliness, as I tell myself that I waited so many years for him to come meet me and now that he is here, it's too late. Regardless of my intention towards him, he was here to talk about family matters and he still was important to me. Therefore, what I see appears to be a big loss, which breaks my heart very deeply. I tell myself that he might have known who the person was that his grandfather had spoken to me about.

It's also a big tragedy for me if the man is the one from my insurance company, since he is the person who can help me with all the bad things I have endured. Let me add that since misfortune came to haunt me, I have became the target for the provocation of wars. Those who put me in such a bad situation allowed easy access for criminals to come and attack me. They made me the target and prey without paying me. But how could anyone let that happen without saying a word, especially knowing that my life was in danger and that these criminal murderers had run away with my personal assets? The female police officer slows her car down for me to see what's in the car, then she stops in front of my window to make sure I have a good look at her prize, the dead body of my friend and business partner, also a phantom member of the R.C.M.P.

I can't comprehend that he is also dead and that he got killed while

Love destroyed by a war

trying to rescue someone.

What is happening is terrible, because I am seeing it happening for real and not in a movie, and I am powerless to stop it. I only hope that someone will come and arrest her before I lose my mind.

This woman is shattering my life. She's completely crazy, a very sick psychopath.

I let out a scream in my apartment. I become aware that there is a war happening here. I become more scared than I've ever been in my life because I don't have a weapon for protection. I sit on my bed in a state of shock and an hour passes by. It's the end for me; she is now coming for me.

She's on the balcony and is knocking on my door. I see her from the little window of the upstairs door. I won't open the door because she's alone and doing her bad thing to everyone who sees her. Unfortunately, my phone's batteries are too low to make a call. My body is sweating all over like a pig. I am shaking so much that I have trouble walking. After much banging on my front door, she goes to my back door and finally decides to knock on the door of my downstairs neighbour. Her mother is alone and the female police officer takes the woman away in her car somewhere. About a half an hour later, she is still alone and has the keys to the downstairs apartment. She enters and starts hitting the ceiling with a stick, trying to break a hole in it. Unfortunately, there's a hole where water had leaked previously and it wouldn't take much for her to be able to poke through into my apartment. I start to agonize, saying my farewell prayers to life. I think of how I can escape, but she has both doors open and if I try to leave, she'll catch me for sure.

Also, I can't escape through the roof because I don't have a ladder. I hear her talking to me through the walls and she seems angry.

- I know you're in there. You'd better let me in or I swear you'll regret it.

I can hear her walking with her boots from one end to the other non-stop, as if she's running after something. She then starts hitting the

Love destroyed by a war

ceiling again. I can't handle the stress so I sit on my bed trying to think of an idea because I know that as soon as she comes in, it will be over for me because she's going to end my life just as she did the others.

Panic takes hold of me and suddenly a vision comes to haunt me about the Queen of England, which gives me the idea that this female officer could be a European. During this moment of anguish, I see that dream I had when I was a child. In the dream there's a gardener holding the body of the five-month-old child cousin of the young boy who shot her by accident. I have no idea why, but I think that if she thinks I know who she is, she just might get scared enough to give up. So I decide to scream loud enough for her to hear what I am saying.

- No, Raoul. Prince Charles is not here! Try calling me later.

Raoul is the gardener from my dream and also a hypnotic time change. I think she personally knows this person because she lets out a scream of panic.

- What? Who?

I don't know why, but she runs away.

I presume she knows the names. Anyway, it's a miracle and I am saved by the memory of a vision from a dream. Probably an angel sent me this image from her soul and I have reason to believe it's the queen's sister who saved my life.

30 minutes later someone's at the door again. This time its Flint. On the other hand, it just might not be him, as it can be his look-alike. Well, I don't care since I need help.

After knocking 20 times, someone speaks,
so I decide to open the door and let him in.

- Are you all right? I heard so many gunshots! Did you see anything? I did. Someone has to do something; it's all so terrible.
- Just don't worry. Nothing will happen to you. I'm here. Be quiet and calm down.

He decides to bring me to the bed, holding me tightly in his arms. He puts me down on the bed, then puts his hands on me and starts to

Love destroyed by a war

move them all over my body. He gets to my pants and pulls them off. While all this going on, I can't stop talking about the little girl, still seeking a solution in my effort to rescue her. But he tells me:

- Don't move and don't say another word. Just be quiet and turn around.

He takes his clothes off then comes near me, pulls on my buttocks, wile entering me then makes tender love to me. I am still trembling with fear. However, I feel a sensation of great comfort and tenderness which brings my soul back to me. He continues to hold me as if meaning to be sincere and say's:

- If I were to die, I would want it to happen while-making love. It has to be the best way to die.

He continues to mumble and says:

- You won't die today because I'm here to protect you. Don't worry anymore and stay calm.

He continues to caress my back and buttocks with his big hands.
He finishes coming and stays on the bed smoking his cigarette, then gets up in a rush and leaves quickly.

- I'm sorry but I have to go do something important at home.
- Okay. Promise me that you'll go see if the little girl can still be saved, but be careful; if the officer is there, don't go.

I have reason to believe that she has lost her sanity.
I give him a hug and say to him for the last time:

- You also could die. I am very scared for you too.
- Don't worry. But lock your door and let no one in, under any circumstance.

The morning arrives after a night of no sleep. I still won't go outside, as I am stricken with fright and I'm tired. I feel like such a coward for not being able to save the girl and if I had known to call the R.C.M.P. that night it could have changed the situation. Thinking about it, it probably wouldn't have changed anything since my father probably did because the dead person in the police car was such an agent. All of a sudden, I hear a loud knock on the back door of my kitchen

where I am sitting.
- Open your door!
It's the female officer again, but this time she's not alone; her partner is with her.
I stop moving and don't answer. I tremble and sweat drips from my forehead. I think she's going to break my door down.
I hear Diane coming up the stairs, screaming.
- Would you go away? Can't you see she's not home? Just leave her alone. We'll take care of her.
While Diane is talking to the women,
she has no idea what the officer did last night and she thinks they came to help me since that's what they said they were doing here. The women finally go back down, believing Diane and leaves. I didn't see her with my eyes but I was able to recognize her voice.
I wait a while, sitting in the chair. I get up and look through the window to see if the coast is clear. I see the weirdest thing happening. There's a truck just like the one on the news which was used by people who kidnapped and raped girls under 10 years of age. The truck is parked right next to the store downstairs. Someone opens the middle door and throws a big metal stake dripping with blood out next to the sidewalk, then drives away, tires screaming. I see the new Chinese doctor from the store come out of the store, so I shout "Ma'am" and point towards the weapon left by the side of the street. She looks at me, then looks at the stake, leaves it there and goes back inside the store.
I can't understand what is going on and I now want to go downstairs to get the stake as proof but I am panicking and am too scared of losing my life, so I go back to sit in my chair in front of my papers. Minutes go by and I look out again because I want to go down, but it's too late. Someone had picked it up, because it was no longer there. The stake probably was used for one of the many murders, which took place yesterday, but it was now impossible to know which one. I again sit down, trying to calm myself down and feel not safe

Love destroyed by a war

enough to go out because I still cannot stop agonizing. Meanwhile, I put my head down on my desk. I can still hear the echo from the voice of the little girl saying:
- It hurts! Why me? It hurts! I'm so scared!
I get up and go into the bathroom. There's a hole from an open space in the floor. I put my hand in it, checking to see if it reaches the downstairs ceiling, because if it does, I will have to barricade it. Right when I am not moving, I feel a little child's hand stroke me softly. It's a different kind of touch, making me feel good, just like a breeze, which has come to ease the heat. All of a sudden, the name Malenfant comes to my mind. I remember the old story of Aurore Malenfant, and think of the disgusting images of the poor girl and all she suffered. But the situation here is very different, so why am I thinking of that story?
I now fall into a trance. I am probably hallucinating, but what I am seeing now goes on in my head with my eyes closed. Even if I feel my soul leave my body, I am not completely gone, as it is just slightly seeing the other side.
It seems to be a passage to the spiritual world. I see a long, dark tunnel, and the young girl is in it. At the end of the tunnel a light shines. I follow through it with my soul and at the end of the light the little girl is awakening in a body beside a tree, on another planet similar to Mars, like in the movie Dune. Her body isn't the same; she's dark brown and she has the head of Ramses, but the light around her new body is the same image as she was before she died, like a child. She doesn't understand and her soul feels the desire for revenge. I hear that this place is the hospital planet for lost souls. Most of the souls there are trying to get revenge while trying to bring their murderers to their death. From the time they arrive there, the victims are anxious to send the criminals' souls to hell.Only then will they be able to make them experience frightening moments; for example, they can make them fall into a hole with no bottom or make them feel all possible types of unpleasant emotions. Soon, when the

Love destroyed by a war

female officer has no body, the child will be able to make her suffer every imaginable type of suffering, until her soul reaches an understanding and she is able to forgive her. Children are more likely to be unable to understand what happened to them; for this reason, they are very unhappy while waiting for them to arrive. In such cases, the victim often tries to find their killers which can cause earthly disasters when they pass through the door that separates the other side of the world and this one, which is somewhat forbidden but offered by the muse. After this notion was explained in a room inside a mountain, similar to the Tibetans, I awaken and no longer feel the living presence of a soul around me.

The afternoon comes and finally my dad appears.

He's standing on the corner of the street, right in front of my kitchen window holding a hockey bag in his arms.

He looks at me while talking to a black man, then points towards me. I can hear him talking:

- Protect her. Make sure nothing happens to her and don't let anyone come close, not even the police.

- Yes, sir. You can count on me.

As he opens the bag, I can see the guns inside. I feel rather insulted, because I want to have a gun. Now I am troubled, knowing that I have to trust someone else for my safety and that doesn't please me. But it makes me feel better to see that my father understood my messages and came to my rescue. Thinking about this situation, I might need to know in my next life, when my insurance friend shows up in my bed, that I will have to be ready for the female killer who will be nearby and will start committing her crimes just like in the past, since her actions are probably related to the jealousy she has for Alexander. Therefore, if I could know it before it happens in my next life, I might be able to plan her capture, before she loses her mind and starts killing innocent children. However, this could be something very difficult to accomplish, since it is so difficult to become aware of reality, which often proves that future lives are subject to repeating

Love destroyed by a war

past lives. Two more days go by before the street war outside ends. It is early morning and I am in the kitchen, listening to the news on the radio, when I hear the announcer talk about this war tragedy.

- The R.C.M.P. has recovered about 128 dead bodies. They appear to have been transported and put in a train after their death by someone who planted a bomb in an effort to hide any evidence. The officers got there before the fire had decomposed the bodies in the train. They were hidden in the Via Rail station.

They found two young girls, both with gunshot wounds in their head. One was in the train and the other one was on the side of the street in the city of Laval.

They are still trying to identify the victims.

The broadcaster continues:

- We have many witnesses today here at the courthouse and they all want to talk at the same time. The judge declares the case to be disorganized, and she doesn't understand what happened, so she asks the lawyers to straighten out the facts.

Everything is too messy and tangled up and no one says the same thing; as a result, we will not make this a public matter in order to avoid causing a scandal. I request that anyone with information contact the Quebec Provincial police, where each case will be handled separately. Thank you. This has been a special morning news report.

The radio started playing music.

After this tragedy, I never knew if the woman wanted something from me. I heard that all of the witnesses had pointed at me, saying they thought I was the center of the whole event. But I never left my apartment while it was taking place and if I was the target, well it could only be for my fortune. After all this, I have not been able to find out if it was my daughter who died that night. In addition, my ex moved and he doesn't want to tell me where he's living. And, for the moment, I don't have the money to get a good lawyer. Even if I did try using all possible sources of help,

Love destroyed by a war

they would all refuse to give me their help or support. I have to conclude that those behind my case were scaring them too much. I am taking care of it myself until I can at least get part of my fortune. I am unable to provide my children a safe life and for that reason I had to abandon them to where they would probably be better. In conclusion, I have reason to believe that if the first ones to be against me for my fortune are members of my family, I will never be able to accomplish anything without running into many problems, because the illicit ideas to hurt me will be what people around will hear from them to do to me.

***

I have no idea how much time has passed since the incident of war. It could be days or weeks or even months. I don't remember; however, I know that I was still in denial and traumatized by it. That day lotto Quebec decided to change the lottery papers. All my work is no longer any good and I will have to start over. However, my family and the law still owe me a lot, so I shouldn't have to be filling out these damn papers in order to get my funds back.

Can someone please tell me where all the honest people have gone? I see this world filled with criminals and robbers. I notice that we have the second biggest church in the world and war is not permitted in our country, and yet they still attack me and some people around me. They took it out on me for a week; I who need all my energy to be able to live, someone who doesn't even have a penny to play their unpleasant games. Well, I suppose they don't have the courage to face someone strong that would be willing to play their kind of destructive games.

Facing the facts that I really was the one, they took it out on, even after I projected some inspiration which brought millions of dollars to them. I saw that no matter what they said to get away with it, I was still the one they sucked the energy out of while they were at it. Nevertheless, I have tasks to accomplish and I will find the right way to achieve them. It is astounding for me to see that they preferred to

Love destroyed by a war

steal from me instead of paying me the fair price. Some even preferred to die. I presume this to be so because it is what happened to some of those who took advantage of my fortune in spite of seeing that my intention was always to reach a goal, which could only bring good. As for those who blame me for their suffering and misfortune, I will tell them that I didn't encourage death, since I don't take drugs and even if I did, if I couldn't get any drugs, I would abstain and wait for the end decided by God before getting any.

I know myself and I want my soul to stay legal in order to be respected by others. I do have exceptions to my ideas about people who behave like animals, but these types of people don't concern me because the members of my family with such behaviour are all now in the beyond.

I lost 3 years, working 10 hours a day. Thank god I at least got the opportunity to meet many important influential people of this world. A couple of days before the papers changed, I'm
 home with Kirt, Diane's niece's boyfriend.
We are talking in the kitchen after, I finished cooking him a meal .
Suddenly, Kirt jumps on me to cover me.

- Christine, there is an infrared light on your back. Look, it's still glowing. Oh my God; you could of been killed.
- Hey, what are you talking about! A what? An infrared light? Oh, no, not for real. I wondered what that was. I can consider myself lucky and I must be protected by angels because every other time, I had moved away before they could have a clear shot. The funny thing about it is that I didn't even know what is was.

My heart starts to beat faster but I am trying to keep my cool because I want to see who's targeting me. I open my curtain, staying on the side of the wall and take a small peek outside.

- Kirt! Come look! He's running away.

I'm able to see his silhouette but it's impossible to identify him. He's on the rooftop, directly opposite my kitchen window.

I must be stupid because it took me many months and Kirt to tell me

Love destroyed by a war

before I could realize that the red light came from a pistol aiming at a target.

I only met Kirt a couple of years ago but he is one of those I knew in my past life.

- Kirt, do you know that I remember you? The memories are kind of crazy, but in the past life after my husband passed away, you lived with me, helping with the garden and I told you that it was time for me to go. I could no longer continue without the love of my husband and daughter, who is still angry with me about her younger kid, who I think is the father of Charles. As for my other kids, I never was able to find them. I want to leave and start over again. Please call your cousin and finally make my journey end.

I still can see you there, saying, "No, Sid. I've loved you forever. Don't leave yet. I'm going to treat you. Please, what will I do without you." But, I couldn't suffer any longer and I went and called your cousin myself. The next morning he arrived and suffocated me in my sleep, saying "I'm not a cannibal". I then watched you crying from the in-between world.

You came in the room screaming, "No, not so soon! You fucking asshole! Didn't I, tell you not to! Why did you do it anyway?" You then took a shot at him, punching him in the face and you were mad at him for a long time afterwards.

- Wow! Christine, it's possible, but I'm not sure I remember.

Kirt is a Haitian and he has been trying to help me find Nicky's father.

- Kirt, I can also see in these images that I used to babysit your child. Even if you still have that same child with that same girl and you want me to babysit him again, I can't help you understand that, because since the robbers came along, it's dangerous.

Kirt will be staying over to sleep tonight, he will sleep on the sofa as he always does when he sleeps over. Night passes and no one comes to kill me.

A couple of days go by. I am now home alone and I am looking at my no-good papers, telling myself that at least I have saved all this paper

Love destroyed by a war

for recycling, because usually in the stores they end up in the garbage and I have 10 big boxes full. My desk is in front of the window in the kitchen. The judge is still in the third-floor corner apartment on the other side of the street. All of a sudden, the lights are out and he disappears. 5 minutes later I see the red light appear again, but this time it's shining on my chest. I move away fast but it follows me around. I get up to hide and at the same moment, I hear a gunshot. In slow motion, I am able to see a gold light coming faster than lightning in my direction and then suddenly the electricity goes out. The bullet has hit the electrical box on the wires outside. I open my window and see a man running on the roof.

- Help me! Someone! Help! Someone just tried to shoot me. Hurry! He's on the roof.

In just a couple of seconds the firefighters arrive. They probably were passing by at the same time or something. The men in the truck climb their ladder so he can look on the rooftops and the fireman shouts at the man come down from there. They move the truck from one roof to the other, trying to capture the guy but they can't catch him; he has disappeared. At the same time, one of the black guys who was in the apartment where the girl and her son disappeared arrived at his place, which is near mine. I am so confused and scared that all I could do is scream.

- Catch that black guy over there.

I'm so scared that even though I know they have nothing to do with the shooting,

I still want all the criminal suspects around me to be arrested. The judge finally appears. He's standing on the sidewalk in front of the place where he's been waiting for many months. I recognize his jacket, the same one that the guy shooting at me was wearing. He looks at me smiling guiltily with a, straight in the eye. I become hypnotized and can no longer speak. As a result, I can't tell the fireman that its him who had just shot at me. Nevertheless, I know he had been hunting me for some time. I only have my doubts about

Love destroyed by a war

who sent him after me. One of these days, I will find out who is the source of these attacks and someone is going to have to pay me back for the money stolen from me and pay for the injustices that have been inflicted on me while they were planning their robbery. I have never been able to live like other people because I had to live with the idea that someone was coming to kill me since it had happened so many times. These ideas that suffocate my energy prevent me from trusting people around me even if I want to believe that there are good and honest people like me.

My emotions are justified and it is normal for me to be a little paranoid because of what I have been through. In conclusion, we cannot understand what we have not experienced. This is a type of reasoning which turns out to be the truth.

***

Chapter Seven
Murder

After all these attacks, I worry and wonder who could have asked this judge to come after me and hunt me like an animal. I do suspect four families of being associated with him. But a criminal can also do things on his own, and to seriously believe someone did it on his own for no reason does not bring the intrigue to a satisfying conclusion. These criminal mediators are often unknown and always arrive when they find out that a conflict is taking place somewhere. They probably think they will be able to put the blame on those opposing the conflict but we are not so stupid that we don't see them coming. I told myself that with my book, I'll let the whole world know that my family and I are not guilty and have nothing to do with the gossip and these false accusations. This could resolve some conflicts and leave the mediators with no one else to blame but themselves for their bad behaviour. I am going to tell you the story that caused a stir, created many problems for me and spread a lot of gossip on the streets about the fact that my family and I were at war with a well-known family in

Murder

Quebec. These stories got to the point that a mediator was destroyed and even tried to end my life. For sure, it was the mediator who planned and did bad things, because the victim's family had called us and said that they already knew the situation and the truth. I know that if I had access to prisons, I would arrest all the criminals connected to the robberies and crimes against me and I probably could fill up an entire prison. I sometimes think that these criminals believe that we are not aware of their propaganda and that we are liars like them.

Everything began after my first break-up with Marc.

I'm 18 years old, and Marc and I have been living together for two years. I am still very young and we fight a lot like stupid dangerous kids and sometimes hurt each other. Perhaps I need to live a little bit more before settling down, since I still want to explore other relationships. I am still unaware of many things; therefore, my curiosity has not been satisfied yet. When Marc ends up hurting me while we are fighting, my pride makes me hate him very much. Even if I love him, I end up breaking up with him for all of these reasons. I have been living alone for a few days and I'm excited because my girlfriend Carina is coming over to spend the week. This will help me, as I am disoriented with Marc being gone. I'm always happy when she and I are together. I have known her since I moved into the small mansion and we went to high school together. When she finally arrives at my door, she greets me:

- Christine, my sunshine! I'm so happy to see you.

She jumps into my arms then goes to sit on my big sofa, sinking into the big white cushions.

- Carina, I miss Marc so much. How will I ever be

able to forget him? We used to make love everywhere, in the park, on boats, at people's houses, and we were together all the time.

- Don't worry! You really don't deserve to be treated the way he treated you and next time, you might not get just bruises; you might end up in a hearse.

Murder

- Don't exaggerate! He's not that bad.
- Probably not, but accidents happen fast. Just remember that when you lose one guy, there are 10 others around to replace him.
- It's easy to say, but not thinking about him isn't very easy since all my recent memories are all about him.
- You have to meet someone else.
- Yeah, maybe. But what kind of guy will I get? I just left college because I smoke drugs and can't concentrate, I have no future other than waiting for my dad to give me the share he owes me, so that I can run a business, which will provide me with a living so I can make my way in life.
- I work and even if I smoke, it won't change anything since my job doesn't require my total concentration.
- Talking about smoking makes me want to roll a joint.

I take a cushion, place it on the floor and get down on my knees to cover the hashish and roll a joint on my glass coffee table.

- Thank God I don't have a coke problem, anyhow.

Carina, do you have to get ready or do something before going out to the disco?

- No, I'm fine and ready to go.

We're so happy to see each other again and we look so stupid jumping around in the living room like crazy girls. When we get to the bar, Bill is there, happy as can be to see us and to show his friends that he knows me. I introduce him to Carina. He starts acting silly and joking around.

- Ha! Ha! It's Carina, Christine's new girlfriend.
- Bill, don't start making up stories. We're just high school friends, not lesbians.

An hour later, I look around and everyone knows my name. It's Bill's fault since he's gone and told everyone about me. We drink zombie shooters all night, and way too many.

I get so drunk that I can't remember how I got home. All I know is that I wake up and see Carina sleeping beside me, still dressed.

Murder

A couple of weeks later Carina moves in.
She even brings the same plant she had in her room when we were kids. It's now early on a weekday evening, and Bill arrives at the door. He's come to ask for a joint because he is way too high and hasn't slept for 2 days:
- I need a downer. Please help me.
 Bill's having a bad trip and it makes him feel better to be around us. In fact, it's a compliment, since I have this effect on many people.
- Christine, I have someone for you to meet. I keep thinking of you and I believe you'd make a nice couple. Besides, this guy has trouble meeting girls because he's extremely shy.
- I don't know, Bill. I'm seeing someone, but I found another girl in his room, so he probably isn't serious about me. I'll tell you what: let me think about it and I'll get back to you in a couple of days.
Bill starts laughing for nothing. The hashish joint has started to have its effect. There he goes again, with his clever jokes.
- So, girls; do you lick each other's pussy at night?
- Hey, Bill. Would you stop it with your stupidity? We're not lesbians. You know that we both like men.
- I'm just asking to make sure. But come on! Tell me the truth! That's what you're doing together.
- Come on, admit it!
Bill has his eye on Carina. He keeps telling her that she is very pretty and as soon as he becomes shy, he starts again with his insinuations about me and Carina having sex together. Carina's never had an interracial relationship and it's so funny to see her intrigued about Bill.
Now she looks at me and laughs.
- Christine, Bill's too much! He makes me laugh so hard that I am about to pee in my pants. Make him stop saying that I'm pretty.
The evening is calm and funny and Bill finally is no longer high, so he gets up to leave.
- Bye, girls. And Christine, do you mind if I give your phone number to

Murder

that friend of mine that I spoke to you about, Fly?
- Of course! Give it to him, but tell him not to expect that I will go out with him.
- No problem. I'll tell him you just want to talk and see if he interests you.
- Ok, Bill. That's good. Bye, now. And be careful on your way back.
- Bye, girls I love you. You're the best and I'll be back to see you soon.
- Bye, Bill. Don't take that dangerous drug anymore. Take good care of yourself.

A couple of days later, the telephone rings. It's Fly calling.
- Hi, Christine. My name is Fly. Bill gave me your phone number. I hope my calling doesn't disturb you!
- No its fine. Tell me, Fly, what do you do in life?
- I'm a businessman. How about you? What do you do and how old are you?
- I'm 18 years old. I just left college and I'm looking for a future. I just broke up not too long ago.
- My sister has a new boyfriend named Marc and he says he knows you.
I heard that he's your ex. Well, if I see or find out about him hurting my sister, I'll get back at him. Bill told me that you still had some bruises caused by him.
- Yeah, but they weren't bad wounds.
- Would you like to come to the restaurant with me? I'll take you to a high-class place in old Montreal.
- Hmm. It sounds good. I don't know if I can refuse such a tempting invitation!
- So it's a yes?
- Yes, I accept.
- Super! I'm happy. I'll come pick you up tomorrow at 7 o'clock.
- Okay, see you tomorrow then.

Carina's not working tomorrow and she'll wait with me for Fly to arrive.

Murder

The next day we're sitting on the sofa waiting. There's a knock on the door and it's Fly. I'm nervous to see him for the first time. Also, the fact that his sister is going out with Marc, whom I still love, is a chance for me to find out what he's up too. Before I turn the door knob, I look at Carina and say:

- Carina, you have to give me your opinion of the guy. You know me. I'm not a good judge of character.
- No problem. If I give you a nudge, it means not to go out with him.
- Okay. Shh! Be quiet. I'll open the door now.
- Hi, Fly. Come in. Wow! I'm impressed. I wasn't expecting to see you dressed so classy.

He's wearing a purple satin shirt, with a tie and designer jeans worth 300 dollars. He's not tall, about five foot seven and he's wearing John-Lennon-style glasses, which give him a Mafia accountant look. He comes in, sits down and starts a conversation.

- Bill told me that you girls smoke hashish!
- Yes, do you want some?
- No, it's just that I have some Jamaican gum and wanted to roll one and smoke it with you before leaving.
- Yes, sure. Take your time and roll a joint if you want.

Carina makes a sign to follow her into the kitchen, which I do.

- What is it, Carina?
- Don't you find this guy to be a bit of a weirdo? He stammers when he talks.
- I'd say he's just shy. Remember what Bill said the other day about him being so shy with girls?
- Yeah, maybe, but I still find he looks like a psychopath.
- Well don't exaggerate. His sister is going out with Marc and Bill knows where his family lives and we're only going to a restaurant. I find him somewhat attractive.
- Okay. I must be worrying for nothing. You know,

I don't want anything to happen to you. I tell you what. I'll ask him for his cell phone number before you leave and the name of the

Murder

restaurant where you're going. Also, call me every hour or so.
- Sure, I'll call you.
- Ok, it's your call. I gave you my advice. Let's go back to the living room.
- So, girls. What did you talk about? Not bad things about me, I hope!
He giggles and offers Carina a big joint.
- This one is for you later, when you're all alone and bored .
He then looks at me with a smile and puts his head down, saying:
- Christine, now that you've seen me, do you still want to go out with me tonight or have you changed your mind?
- No, I haven't changed my mind. When do we leave?
- Right now!
- Okay, let's go now.
- Cool! Bye, Carina; I'll call you later.
- Bye, you two. Fly, take good care of my friend.
- Yes, I will. Don't worry; I'll bring her back safe and sound.
We arrive at the restaurant, a splendid place with a baby grand piano in the center and a big fireplace with a glowing fire. It's a classy restaurant with, an expensive menu. Fly orders a 100-dollar bottle of champagne.
- You're crazy. It's way too expensive! Are you sure you can afford it? I sure don't want to do the dishes.
- Don't worry, I had a very good day today.
The evening goes very smoothly, with pleasant conversation.
- I want to tell you what I do in life. Bill told me I could tell you anything, that you're a trustworthy person.
- Well, of course. If you feel like telling me, I'm curious.
- I cook cocaine to make rocks then bring it to some black guys in a music station.
- Ah, okay. But can I ask you if you're a user?
- No, I only smoke hashish. Do you use cocaine?
- No, I've never even tried it. My father is against it. He says that too often rat poison is mixed with it.

Murder

- The only reason I do this job is because I am one of the few who is able to change it into rock. In addition, if these people don't get their drugs, they'll kill women and children in order to get it.
- Oh! Why would they do that?
- They're narco-terrorists who can't live without their drugs.

The big guy that has the supplies is scared as hell of them. Therefore, I'm the one stuck doing business as an intermediary. I work with my childhood friend and I will be finished with this shit as soon as I finished building my business. I'm going to leave this crazy job.

Fly's phone rings and he leaves the table. Waiting for him to come back, I sip from my glass of champagne while listening to the soft music of the pianist playing. He walks back and sits down, looking mad.

- We have to leave fast after we finish. I have a job to go to and have no choice to hurry. That fat bastard always spoils my night off when I go out.

Fly mumbles under his breath.

- One of these days, I swear, I'll show him who I am and he'll regret not having treated me with respect.
- Fly, don't worry! It's nothing. We can do this some other time.
- Really? You're willing to go out on another date with me? He looks surprised.
- Sure, it all depends on what we're going to do!
- Would you like to go horseback riding?
- Yes, sure! I love horses. I used to have a female horse, a Spanish purebred for competition. We bought her but she is boarded with friends. I can't ride her anymore because she's into making babies now.
- Wow! You're lucky! What would you say if we were to go to a ranch this weekend?
- Yes! That's an excellent idea! Can we bring Carina too?
- Sure, and if she wants to come, I'll ask Bill and maybe some other friends to come too.

Murder

- Super! Let's organize it and call each other back tomorrow.

He's not the kind of guy I should be seeing but since he wants to get out of it and build his own business and since he doesn't actually use cocaine himself, I'll give him a chance. I finish eating my nice steak and my vegetable with melted cheese as fast as I could. He then takes me back home and leaves in a hurry.

The rest of the week goes by quickly. He calls me every day and talks to me about my ex and his sister. The weekend comes and we have a group of five going to the ranch. The ride is relaxing; nothing special happens except that I lose my shoe.

It's sunset and we're going back home but we stop at his place, just he and I.

I meet his roommate, a Spanish guy, and his girlfriend, a beautiful model.

Their apartment is a dump, with piles of dishes all over the table and counter. His room has piles of dirty clothes everywhere and the drawers are half-open and all messy. It's terrible and I wonder how someone can live in such a mess.

Fly looks at me, not even embarrassed about the disorder and says:

- I need to hire a maid. It looks like a dump here.
- I can see that. I have an idea: pay me to do it! I haven't had a job since leaving college and I no longer have my job as a store manager. It would help me. How much you would pay me to do it?
- Come on, I couldn't let you do my cleaning!
- Well, yes! Why not? Just give me $250 and I'll do your whole apartment, including inside the drawers, the windows inside the kitchen cabinets, the dishes, and your laundry. Let's say that I am in need of pocket money.
- Okay, if you insist! I'll give you the job but wait here. First I'll go ask my roommate to make sure it's okay with him. Just wait here in my room.

I sit on his bed, looking around the room. There are many papers on the bed, full of numbers, and some firearms on the floor. I pick one

Murder

up to see if they are real, or just toys. Fly enters the room and sees me looking at his gun. I might have been too curious, but I am young and still very innocent. I had seen lots of guns in my life my father has some at home through his army permit and he also has a collection of old firearms. I was intrigued.

- Be careful with that! It's a loaded 9 millimeter.
- Oh, really? What are you doing with it?
- I need them to protect myself from my boss friend. He threatened me with death. He told me he'll send his guys to kill me if I don't pay him back soon. I was arrested twice with a kilo of cocaine. I have to reimburse and pay him back two times 10 thousand dollars for bailing me out plus the cost of the drugs.
- Oh, he's not allowed to do that. Have him arrested. He should take his loss, too. Isn't it a risk of the business? Isn't it he that asked you to work for him?
- There's no way I could have him arrested. They would kill me for that. I've known this person since I was a kid. I even used to go to his uncle's mansion up north when I was a kid. He always treated me bad when I was a kid. His uncle even told me once: "Don't let him talk to you like that. Personally, if someone threatened me like that, I'm not sure I would let him live".
- Just stop hanging out with him.
- I can't. He wouldn't leave me alone. He's always on my back. I always have to do what he tells me. If I don't, he threatens to hurt me or members of my family.
- Your story sure sounds complicated.
- Yes, it's complicated, but he's got me by the balls, because soon we're going to open a legal business and he'll be financing all of it.
- What kind of business are going to open?
- We're opening a cell phone store and I need someone to help me organize the business.
I was told that you're smart and I wanted to ask you if you'd be interested in becoming my private secretary?

Murder

\- Oh! For real? you want me for that?

\- Well yes. And if you want to become my girlfriend, by the way, I find you pretty and nice.

I have to tell you that I am very picky when I choose a woman. I haven't had a serious girlfriend because I find all the girls I meet too stupid but you intrigue me and that makes me feel comfortable.

\- Really, I'm not sure if I should take that as a compliment or if I should be worried!

\- It's your call; you can decide how you want to take it.

\- Yes, that's true, but I want to know what you're thinking when you say that.

\- That's the idea. I don't know what to think of you, although it makes me curious and makes me want to discover what it is.

I sort out some of his clothes to be ready for tomorrow. I move his 12-gauge rifle, which is in my way, and I stop. I start daydreaming, wondering if I'm going to die if I stay around him! Can I really trust him with all these guns so readily accessible? I think of his roommate's girlfriend and I wonder if a beautiful model such as her would stay around them if they were dangerous people. I must be too innocent to see that danger really exists, since my dad has some firearms and he never uses them.

As a result, my reasoning is fearless, since I only understand experiences that I have had. My father has fire arms and he's not a dangerous man, so Fly could also be like him. I still have to find trust within me to be able to decide whether to become his girlfriend. My thoughts go further: what if he uses his gun on me? I am definitely going to die. How could I possibly test him in order to be sure that he is sane and not a psychopath? I then have a stupid, spontaneous idea. I tell myself if he intends to murder me, I'll know by his reaction. I take the rifle and go up to him.

\- Fly, can I have total trust in you?

\- What do you mean?

I go into the bathroom and he follows me.

Murder

I take the gun and put it under my throat.
He reaches for the rifle to move it away.
- Don't play with this! It's dangerous.
- No. First you have to tell me if you're ever going to try to use this on me!
I was way too stupid not to think about the danger that existed. My confidence made me excessively sure of myself.
Let me just say that I was lucky, because when someone is bad, they have no heart for any cause except their own and I know this now but didn't know it during those moments in my life.
- No, I never want to harm you, ever. I promise.
He doesn't hesitate; he acts very calmly and has a look in his eye that tells me that my way of reacting was stupid. So I feel relieved, especially when I see how delicately he takes the rifle away from me. After that I feel far more comfortable, so I let him take the gun from me and watch him place it further away from us. I tell him:
- Ok, I give you permission to make love to me. I'm not afraid of you. Make love to me now.
He brings me to his bed and makes love to me. He is kind of gentle and shy and clings to me like a scared little boy, saying:
- I know. I don't know you a lot, but I'm already in love with you.
We fall asleep after smoking a big Jamaican gum joint. The phone rings and awakens me. It's Carina, who is worried and says:
- Christine, are you okay? What's going on?
- I'm fine. Don't worry; I'm sleeping over at Fly's tonight and we made love earlier. By the way, tomorrow, I'll come back only after I've finished cleaning. I'll call you at suppertime and if I'm not finished, I'll come and get you and we'll order pizza or something together.
- Cool. I finish at six in the morning. I'll come home to sleep, but wake me up around four tomorrow.
Good night, and don't do anything I wouldn't do.
- Good night to you, too, Carina.
A couple of months later the cell phone store is almost ready to open.

Murder

It's Halloween weekend. I'm at my apartment with Carina and the phone rings. It's Fly.

- Hello, baby. I know we were supposed to go out tonight but I have to work! But Bill and Fernando told me they're going to Claude's father's bar and if you want to go, you and Carina can go there. It should be a nice party. If I finish early, I'll come meet you there.
- Ok, we'll probably go. Just call us to make sure we're going to be there.

The party is a 45-minute drive away, up north. Carina and I are going there together in her car. On our way there, the air is cool and smells like pine trees. The leaves are almost all gone. The mountains are big and the roads are surrounded with woods. We finally arrive at the bar. Entering the bar, I feel kind of shy. Everyone is dressed up for Halloween except for Carina and me. There's a young woman in front of us, a popular model who is one of Fernando's girlfriend's friends. She comes up to greet me and shows off her cat woman costume. She invites us to dance but Carina motions to me to show that she doesn't want to and says:

- Christine, not right now. I want to go get my cigarettes in the car and you know that I don't know how to dance. But go ahead if you want to.
- Its okay. I'll go order a drink at the table with Fernando until you come back.

I turn to the girl and say:

- We just got here. No, thank you; maybe later.
- Okay. We're at the very back if you change your mind.

The cat woman then disappears.

Fernando is sitting at a table with Alain, Claude's roommate and with Claude's father, so I go and join them. Fernando introduces me, then offers me a chair. Alain suddenly gets up and yells to Carina:

Murder

- You there! Wait! Can I come with you? I want to go out and smoke a cheech!
- Well, come if you want, responds Carina.

I look around at all the nice costumes. Everyone at the table quietly watches the show. 15 minutes pass.

- Fernando, don't you think Carina's been gone too long?
- Yes, I agree. Let's go out and see what's happening.

Walking towards the car, I hear screams.

- Stop! Leave me alone, you jerky pig. Stop! Please, someone! Help me!

Fernando runs toward the car, opens the door and I scream "Jackass, don't touch her!"

Fernando grabs him by the collar, pulling him out of the car and making him fall on the gravel road.

- Stop it, Fernando. I haven't done anything to hurt her.

He grabs him again by the collar and starts punching him in the face. I get in the car and wrap my arms around Carina.

- Are you okay? Did he hurt you? What the hell did he do to you?
- I told him "no", and he ripped my shirt off, saying "Of course you want to; admit it that you like it". He then ripped my bra and tore off my jeans button. He even slapped me in the face.
- Oh, that shit-head.

Fernando looks at him breathless, ready to hit him again, but he stops.

- Don't ever touch her again. Leave this place now and find yourself another lift home, you damn coward.

Alain leaves and we stay there for about an hour more, then go back home, safe and sound. As for Fly, he never came to meet us.

Many days have passed. I'm still going out with Fly and this morning he invites us again to one of his organized parties.

- Christine, my partner Claude has invited you to come up to his chalet, up north. Since you're my new secretary and he's my partner, I

Murder

think it's about time you guys meet. He really wants to see you. Bill is here too, so come join us, and bring Carina with you.
- Give me the address and I'll try to get there, although I'm not guaranteeing that I will.
I hang up the phone.
After asking Carina if she wants to go, we decide we're going. On our way there, we get lost 5 times but we finally make it. As we enter the chalet, we hear the music of the Doors playing very loud. Fly's partner is sitting at the kitchen table, which is covered with beer and all sorts of drugs.
Alain is there, standing next to Claude. All of a sudden, Carina no longer feels good about being there.
- Oh, no! Christine, the pig is here. Fuck, I don't want to stay here. Let's just go back home now.
I can hear Claude talking, asking Fly:
- Why does the girl want to leave? She just got here!
- Ask Fernando. He'll tell you since he's the one who caught Alain doing bad things to the girl.
Meanwhile, Carina and I take a tour of the place, then we decide to sit down for five minutes to smoke a cheech. Looking around, we're surrounded by all the people that are here.
The cat woman girl from the bar is here; she's Claude's cousin's girlfriend. As soon as she sees me, she comes to show me her new white summer dress. I think that this girl really likes to parade around, because she's in front of me again, telling me:
- We have to spoil ourselves before it's too late, don't you think? I paid 300 dollars for this pretty white summer dress.
I look at Carina and say:
- It's a bit expensive for a summer dress.
I then smile at the girl, wondering if she's gay. In the other end of the room, the boys seems to have finished exchanging information and we all listen to Claude, who raises his voice and says:
- Hey! Come here, you girls. I want to talk to you!

Murder

Carina and I hesitate and are a bit worried, but we go over to Claude. Claude is 6 foot 2 and weighs 320 pounds. He has nice green eyes but up close, he's a little scary.

- Girl, you shouldn't be afraid of Alain. Look carefully:
this guy is under my command and I promise that he'll never put his hands on you again. Now look. On your knees, Alain!

Alain doesn't want to get down on his knees, so in front of everyone, Claude squeezes his hand, almost breaking it. Claude doesn't let go of Alain's hand, still crushing it until Alain finally falls on his knees.

- So, are you going to act like a dummy again, huh? Say you're sorry to the nice girl.
- Ouch! Stop it! You're hurting me! I'm sorry!
- Say it again! This time, make me believe that you mean it!

Alain starts crying and repeats "I'm sorry" at least 12 times before Claude lets go of him. In the end, Claude slaps him hard in the face and Alain's lips start bleeding.

- Your name is Carina, girl?
- Yes, my name is Carina.
- Don't worry about him anymore. Stay with us, and if he even tries to just talk to you, he'll have to deal with me.

Carina laughs, feeling relieved.

- I'm better now. There's no need to kill him. I'll stay.

The party unfolds like all other parties and we go back home the next morning.

My first impression of Fly's partner is a good one. He seems to have his ideas focused in the right place, even though he is kind of scary and strong. I am almost convinced that if Fly has a misunderstanding with him, he could negotiate an arrangement. The idea I have of him is very different from the way Fly had described him to be. I could be mistaken because my judgment of people is often innately wrong. Therefore, if Fly says that Claude is mean, it's probably true and no matter what I think of him, I'm still going to have to work with him. The premises they rented for the cell phone store are located on

Murder

St-Denis Street, opposite the theater. The big round window allows me to see the activity going on in the streets. I go with Claude to buy an office desk. I also buy each of them a welcome gift. I buy Fly a crystal ball for his desk and for Claude, a box of expensive cigars. The first week goes by fast. I program customers' files in my computer. Claude has invited me to go parachuting when he gets back from his trip to Jamaica in 2 weeks. One afternoon while Claude is gone, Fly arrives at the office. There are no customers in the store at the time. Fly says angrily:
- I can't take it anymore. I'm going to kill that fucking bastard!
—   - Why are you saying things like that?
- Well, Claude told me that I have to pay him back 40 thousand dollars by the time he gets back, and if I don't come up with the money, he'll kill me, and you too, if I don't leave you.
- Come on, there's no reason he would do that to me. I have nothing to do with your debts to him.
- No, it's just that he's a jealous, crazy guy and I know that he's killed girls before, so I know he's capable of such things.
- You must be joking with me, because from what I saw, he was very nice to me. Are you sure of what you're saying?
- Yes, I'm telling you, he's just a fat homo bitch. I've known this guy since I was a kid and this time he's so serious that he'll end my life for real. Last night he made me play Russian roulette and told me it was a warning that next time he sees me, if I don't give him the money, he'll shoot me.
- Oh, my God; he'll kill you?
Fly looks scared. He's still trembling, but I'm not sure he's telling the truth and whether all of his allegations are real. I believe that he's exaggerating. He asks me to roll his joints while he continues his crazy nervous fit.
- I'll kill him for real this time, I swear to God.
I admit that, since he told me that Claude wanted to kill me too, I was so offended that I said:

Murder

- Well, go ahead and do it, if you really think that he is going to kill us. And stop panicking. Calm down. You're scaring me!

I really don't think Fly is going to kill Claude for real since I would never do that myself. I have an open mind, so I know there is always a logical way of dealing with any conflict. I mostly think that this conversation is just words being blurted out at a frightening moment. These words at this moment are nothing I think I need to worry about. In my mind, they are neither a gesture nor a reality, but a delegation, which we hear all the time when bad arguments happen. These words are just Fly's way of expressing the rage within him. I do wonder about it and am somewhat scared. Therefore, I'll ask for some help in order to pay his debts, but won't mention the threats since I don't know if they are real. The reality is that I wasn't there when Fly and Claude spoke, so I don't know the truth.

Fly and I have been together for only 2 months and he's made lots of progress in terms of getting out of the dangerous environment which he's stuck in, although his major problem is not yet solved. During Claude's vacation, Fly tries to gather money, through bank loans, through his family, or even by selling more drugs, but no luck; he has not been able to accumulate enough money to pay Claude back. As for me, all the people I asked said that they didn't know how to gather such an amount of money so quickly.

Carina has to work this evening and we're at home talking while she gets ready.

- Christine, your boyfriend doesn't seem normal.
- I don't agree. In my opinion, he's just scared. I did think about leaving him but I have a good job through him, plus he's gentle with me and he's working towards turning his life in the right direction.
- You could be right. Just to change the subject, I wanted to tell you that after work, I'll be going to my new boyfriend's place and I'll be staying there for a couple of days.
- Okay, then. Take care on the road and I'll see you in about two days.
- I'll see you soon. I love you. Have a good evening.

Murder

Carina kisses my cheeks and leaves to go to work.
Claude is supposed to come back from his trip tonight and Fly will be staying the night here with me.
In the evening, I am worried but also very tired.
I open the French doors to my room and lie down on the bed next to Fly. I fall asleep right away. Suddenly, in the middle of the night, someone starts shaking me.
- Christine, wake-up!
- What is it?
- My pager is ringing non-stop. I have to go to work and see what's up.
- Can you just pretend as if you don't hear it?
- No, I have no choice. I have to go.
- But why? Can you tell me if you're going out to do what you said you were going to do?
- Don't worry! Go back to sleep. Here, take the keys and tomorrow open the store. I'll come and meet you there sometime later during the day.
- Okay. I'll try to go back to sleep before going to work.
- Bye. See you tomorrow and don't do anything stupid. Again, tell me where you're going.
Fly doesn't answer me.
- Fly, would you answer me? Where are you going?
- I have no time for this. I'm leaving now.
Fly kisses me and leaves without telling me anything else. It's been about 20 minutes since Fly left but I can't sleep because I'm thinking about Claude and I'm wondering if Fly is going to do what he said he'd do, for real! This is making me nervous and
I need to call Claude to tell him that Fly is mad at him and to do something to calm him down before he kills him! I take the phone and dial Claude's number. I let it ring one and an half times, then I hang up. I start thinking that he mustn't have gone to do that for real. Besides, if I call at this time of night he might take me for a nut,

Murder

especially if I tell him something like that. Fly won't do such a thing for real. He's probably gone to deliver drugs as usual. My premonitions probably are wrong and I am worried for nothing.
So I go back to bed and fall asleep until morning. I wake up three hours late, but still feeling very tired, as if I have no energy. I feel weak and dazed, as bad as when someone cheats on me.
I still manage to get ready and reach the office. I'm alone at the office for 3 to 4 hours before Fly finally arrives. I see him coming in and I know right away that something's wrong. I can read in his vacant eyes that something bad has happened. I immediately infer that he did what he said he'd do. He comes slowly into the office, looking at me, not smiling or saying a word, not even hello. He looks like a psychopath and his soul appears to be absent.
- Hello, Fly. Are you all right? What's wrong?
But he doesn't answer me. I'm worried, thinking I could be in danger, so my voice starts to tremble and it shows that I am scared. I have to control myself and react intelligently.
His back faces me but finally he turns towards me, leaning on the display case.
I move close to him, place my hands on his shoulders, then shake him a little bit.
- Talk to me. Tell me, did you kill him? If not, then tell me what's wrong. Please talk to me. I can see something isn't right. Just tell me what's wrong.
Finally some words come out of his mouth.
- It's done!
- What's done?
- You're going to see it in the newspaper tomorrow or in a couple of days.
- What am I going to see? Fly, did you go see Claude last night?
- Yes and he's dead, but don't tell anyone.
- What? Fly, you did this for real?
- Yes but now, I just want to smoke a joint. I was just at my place. I

Murder

told Fernando everything, because he saw me wash my bloody clothes, so he knows.

Fly seems to want to leave. He is very agitated and mumbles things I can't understand.

- Let's go, Christine. Close the office. The store is finished.

I don't know what I'm going to do now because these people are going to find me and murder me, too. I don't know what to do. I need to go talk with someone who will know what I can do to protect myself from Claude's family.

I start to feel guilty that I hadn't believed him and hadn't done something to stop him instead of agreeing with his delegations. I only agreed because every time he spoke to me about it, he always made me out to be one of Claude's next victims. In addition, I had never met someone that commits crimes for real. I've heard people talk about committing crimes; in fact, almost everyone I know has said the words at one time but has never gone through with it. I've always seen this as something that happens elsewhere, somewhere I would never be, or in an old cowboy movie. I no longer understand and have no idea what to do about it. So I'll take the time to analyze the situation, and then I'll be able to make a decision. Fly doesn't seem to be crazy, even if he did something crazy, because he's so nice with me; in fact, he's never even raised his voice to me. Claude's family is well known and even if Fly ends up in prison, someone will end his life in there too. All of this confuses me. I don't want Fly to die, as he is still my boyfriend, but I know his days are counted.

I believe that, as soon as they find out he did it, they'll come for him. Fly starts mumbling again.

- Oh, my God. The neighbours probably heard the 13 shots from my 9-millimeter. Do you know how much I panicked when I saw him still moving after I shot him? So I grabbed the baseball bat and kept hitting him until he stopped moving.

- My God. That's terrible. It must be awful to see that.

Murder

The image that Fly depicted awakes in me and the projected image he sends me is now visible. My sleep of the previous night breaks open like a cloud disappearing to show me what happened. I feel as if I had not slept at all; a weird and bad feeling of consciousness.
- No, it wasn't nice to see but I had no choice; it was him or me.
- You're sure you had no other options?
- No!
- What's going to happen now?
- Let's go get some of your things at home and then get a room at a hotel until I can speak with my Jamaican friend.
- Okay, but can I call Carina?
- Yes, but if you talk to her and she asks you something,
- act as if nothing happened and don't tell her you know who did this if she asks, okay?
- Uh, okay; no problem.

I start thinking that since he's my boyfriend, those men looking for him might torture me. In addition, if I leave him now, he might think I'm against him and could do the same to me just because I know everything. I'm very confused and I have to think about this longer before doing anything. We get to the hotel. Fly rents a suite with a big Jacuzzi built into the floor.
- Christine, one of my Jamaican friends is coming to talk to me. He'll tell me what kind of options I have. I asked for his help because I don't really have a place to hide. So, I'll have to go further away, until Claude's family calms down. I'll have to stay unnoticed until I'm no longer in danger of being a suspect.

Fly orders champagne. Before long, there's a knock at the door but Fly's paranoid about being located.
- Christine, go and ask who it is. If it's the champagne, pay the tab.

I go to answer the door, take the bottle and place it on the table. Fly is walking as if he's trying to get away. I close the door and Fly pours a glass for me.
- I want you to stay here and wait for me while I go talk to my

Murder

Jamaican friend. I should be back within an hour.
- Okay. I'll stay here.
Fly comes back as fast as he left with a solution from his friend.
- We can go and spend some time at a friend's house in Jamaica. For the moment the suspects are members of a biker gang which Claude was supplying.
I guess Fly needs someone to help him overcome his panic of being pursued and discovered. I think that I'm going with him to Jamaica because I'm scared they'll come for me, to extract information from me. Some might say it's a suicidal idea, but I see it differently. As soon as Fly gets settled with his friends, I'll leave, saying that my visa's expired, because it's true. It'll be easier to leave him after I'm back here, knowing he'll be staying there, far away, and knowing that he won't be able to do the same thing to me that he did to Claude. I'm scared to stay here. What if I'm tortured? If I'm far, I'll be safer. I should be able to tell the truth over the phone to my parents and friends, in order to clear my name, before someone has the idea to come after me. That way, I'll no longer be a suspect and they'll leave me alone.
I know that what is happening is neither normal nor legal. Although, when I think about it, if he really did save our lives, I can understand and forgive him. Unfortunately, I'll never know if he was lying or telling the truth. And being uncertain leaves me vulnerable and will lead to no good. We leave the hotel the next day and are in the car on our way to a party before leaving for Jamaica.
- Fly, do you remember I cleaned your room and touched your guns?
- Don't worry about it. I cleaned them before using them. Anyway, I threw the gun in the water, over the Mercier Bridge.
Before we leave to catch the plane in Toronto, Fly decides to take me to a radio studio, C.K.U.T. They're having a party and a D.J. will be playing. The owners have opened their studio in LaSalle near Montreal, but only for a short time, because from what I hear, they move from one place to another all the time. This is where I first saw

Murder

Lesley, the D.J. that night. As I enter the studio, a Spanish girl, who is just starting her musical career, is on her way out. I think she is still going out with one of my step dad's cousins, the one who had a recording studio in Mexico back then. I am somewhat impressed to see her get into a Lamborghini but I wonder why she's accompanied by such a bad-looking guy.

I wonder what she's doing in such a low-class place in Canada. She probably just brought her recordings or something. I look around while Fly talks with his friends. I can see girls dancing to reggae music, so I go and join them to try to learn reggae moves.

It was an interesting stop.

It's towards the end of 1992 and before we leave I have to tell my friends and family that I'm going to Brazil, just in case we're followed by murderers in pursuit of Fly. Fly has involved me in his plot and has told me everything he did, but the truth is that I'm just a witness accompanied by the guilty suspect, and I don't know what to do about this situation. I'm scared that I might be tortured or killed but also scared that Fly might be killed. Arriving at my place, I finish packing and I say good-bye to Carina. I want so badly to tell her what I know and I try to give her hints but it doesn't work. Actually, it's better that she doesn't know. I wouldn't want another person to have the problem of knowing about this and to become scared not to know what to do about it.

We are now starting our 6-hour drive to Toronto in my Rx7. Regardless, I am still happy to be traveling and I know where to get help in another country if I ever need it.

Fly sells his car and keeps the little money he had accumulated; as a result, he's able to pay for our vacation. I turn around and see a suspicious car.

- Fly, look! That car is following us.
- Just ignore him and don't worry.

The road is nice and calm. We listen to my new Whitney Houston CD. We arrive at the airport. The man who was

Murder

following us is still behind us and he keeps looking at me strangely.
- Christine, this will be my first plane trip.
- Oh yeah? Well, just hold my hand if you get scared.
- Wait for me here. I'll get the tickets.

Fly leaves and comes back as fast as he left.
- The flight doesn't leave until tomorrow. Let's get a room. Would you like to go out to see a movie tonight?
- Sure, that's a nice idea.

I wonder why I haven't become disgusted by him after what he did. I say that since I'm still able to have sex with him. It must be because he hasn't really changed his attitude towards me; in fact, he is the same, and maybe even gentler and more afraid, but not meaner. I think the reason I see him as not so bad is that he believes he did it to protect his own life.

No matter what I know, I won't be able to stay with him for very long. We go out and the next morning we take our flight. When we arrive at the airport in Jamaica, Fly realizes that we are 4 hours away from his friend's house by car.
- Christine, I have to find someone to take us there. So tonight we'll stay at a hotel and I'll take care of this in the morning.

In the hotel lobby I see the man who was following us standing at the reception desk, asking questions. He sees me looking at him, then grabs his phone and makes a phone call, staring at me. I'm worried that this person could be a killer sent by Claude's family.
- Fly, look. The man who was following us is here.
- Don't bother with him. He can't even get a firearm here. There's no danger for us. He'll never follow us to my friend's house.
- Okay. If you say so.

I leave to go to the room. I put on my bathing suit and go out by the pool. It's so nice and warm out here. I feel shy because we're the only white people around. It makes my skin sticky and makes me dizzy. The day goes by quickly. Fly comes next to me and whispers in my ear.
- I love you, Christine.

Murder

- But things might get difficult and the worst could be that we'll have to separate. You might have to go back home and I'll stay here. Anyway, we we'll see about that when I run out of money.
- Oh, but are you ever going to come back to Canada and be able to shake off these problems?
- I have no idea, but for the moment let's not think about it.

I wrap myself in my towel and walk back to our room. In the morning we go out looking for a rental car. A little 7-year-old child who is walking behind us on the side of the road suddenly grabs my hand.

- Hey, kid. What you are doing?
- Ma'am, take me with you.
- No, I can't take you with me! Fly, give the boy some money so that he can get himself some food.

Fly gives the child 20 dollars but it doesn't make him leave.

- Please, ma'am! I want to come with you.
- Well no, kid. You can't come with us. Go on, now. You must have a home, so go home.

The boy just continues to follow us.

Fly starts to feel arrogant and starts talking a little too much.

- Hey, kid. Do you want to know what I did before coming here? Well, I killed a big guy. I could be dangerous and if I were you, I'd go home.
- Fly, don't say that to a child. You could scare him.
- Well, I'll say it to the entire world if I want too.

I think Fly has somehow lost his mind. I should tell him he's acting stupid but I'd rather not start a fight. We continue walking on the side of the road and stop to sit on a bench at the entrance to a park. A tall man comes towards us.

Fly starts to tell this man the story of how he murdered Claude. The big man is holding a bottle of whisky in one hand and a big machete in the other. He looks at

moving his machete back and forth under his throat, repeating "I'm going to kill you".

- Fly, hurry. Let's go.

Murder

The young kid takes off running.
Fly looks the man in the eyes and says:
-I've killed a man and I'm not scared of you, drunkard.
I get nervous and push Fly.
- Are you sick in the head? Come on! Let's go now.
I look at the crazy man.
- Hey, you, big guy! You're not going to do this to me. Hey! It's very important that I stay alive to bring someone back to life. Do you even know who you are in your background, big guy?
I get up very quickly, and he thinks about what I just said.
- Fly, hurry! We have time to leave now. Move it. See you later, big guy.
So I leave and Fly follows me. We get to the rental car, which is just a street away. How lucky we are that the drunken man didn't hurt us. The tall man looks like the black man in the movie "Sid and Nancy", at the end, when the black man stabs Sid, saying, "I come on behalf of Sidney and she said never to hurt Nancy. Now you die", after Sid accidentally murders his girlfriend, Nancy. Anyway, he reminds me of this character in the movie.
We finally rent a car but misfortune follows us. A car appears out of nowhere and
crashes head on into our car. Fly is out 2 thousand dollars and we end up taking a taxi, which brings us to our destination, his friend's house. I don't have much to say about the two months spent there, except that I was safe.
It's a 4-storey house, without not a lot of furniture, but big enough to convert into a bed and breakfast.
I meet a girl there who Bill likes. She travels around the world a lot and I'll meet her again later in my life. One time I saw her in a bar, and another time she came to a party in a bar in Mexico with Lesley and others. She even lived near my apartment for a short amount of time.
Also, her sister was one of Flint's lovers. Kirt from Haiti looks exactly

Murder

like the guy sitting in the living room of the house every night. He even has the same limp when walking as Kirt does, but he pretends not to be that person. Two months after arriving, I book a flight to go back home by myself. I consider myself lucky that he's let me leave. The last week before I leave, I lose faith in Fly. One day, he leaves me alone in the house, telling me:

- I'm going out to murder a girl as a favour to help my friend and you can't come.

From that moment on, I no longer believed all the allegations he had told me since the beginning. I knew right away that he doesn't' kill people only to protect his life and that my friend opened my mind to the idea that he was really a murderer.

I often wonder how Fly felt after killing a person and what was he was thinking about. I can make many inferences, but the reality is that a death occurred and as a result, much of the joy of living dies within us after this action.

I know this because Fly replaced my feelings of joy with worries and fear. All my energy for living was sucked out of me after witnessing all he did.

Besides that, while I was alone in the house, one of the Jamaican guys took advantage of me, although he didn't hurt me and did use a condom. But I didn't tell Fly, out of fear that he could hurt me or even kill me.

A couple of days before leaving, I go make a call from a phone booth since there's no phone in the house. Fly follows me, telling me to call my father, which I intend to do. I take the phone and dial the number, hoping Fly won't listen. Unfortunately, he's very close and is listening, so I have to be careful of what I say.

- Hi, Dad. I'm calling you to let you know that I'm okay and that I'm coming home soon.
- Where are you? Tell me! I know that you're not in Brazil because I sent my friend there and you were nowhere to be found. In addition, a guy name Fernando called me to tell me what was happening.

Murder

I also received a phone call from a Claude's father, telling me that if you stay around your boyfriend you might die. I'm telling you: they're not going to let him go because you're there. If they come to capture him, you could get shot. So you better get here fast.
- Yes, Dad. I'm coming home this weekend.
I hang up the phone, not telling Fly that my Dad had spoken with Claude's father, and we go back to the big house. A couple of days before my departure, Fly takes me to a private party and the D.J. and all the same guys from C.K.U.T. are there. I wonder why they're here in Jamaica. Anyway, it's because of this party and the other meeting in Cancun which they broadcast on air, that I know they are an organization that travels and moves around a lot.
I finally get home safe and unharmed, alone and far from Fly. But I wonder about the girl who was at that house, since I met her in so many other places. Did I ever meet her special link for this life, I wonder, or what do I know about her in the past life? She and her sister do look like the girl who was killed by the false Fred in the past. Also, who was the other girl singing with Sidney on the recordings of old music used by Whitney Houston, which were at least 100 years old? I know that Bill likes her a lot, but since he doesn't know his father, she could be his sister. About her seeming
familiar, what I mostly thought was that she might be the link to the boy I met in the Bahamas when I was 4 years old. It doesn't really matter why God had her cross paths with me, because it has nothing to do with me personally, although I could be the intermediary that holds information which she needs to find.

***

After I get home, my childhood friend Paul comes to deliver me from my sexual attachment with Fly. It's sad that our love affair didn't last very long; Paul disappeared from me only a couple of weeks later. I was confused, not knowing which way to go, and I just continued my normal path of life.
So on a nice, sunny afternoon, after picking tomatoes in my small city

Murder

backyard garden, I go visit my mom. As I enter the apartment, my mom is in the kitchen, finishing the lunch dishes and talking on the phone with my dad.

- Frank, give me the number of that guy Claude's father. I'll talk to him. Christine, tell me, were you with him when he did that terrible thing?
- No, Ma. And if the man wants to talk to me, I'll tell him what I know.
- No! no! You're not going to talk with the man. There's nothing to tell him. If you weren't there at the scene of the crime, let your dad handle this

situation. In addition, take the phone and talk to your dad.
- Yes, hello, Dad. How are you?
- I'd be doing better if you could tell me why your wise guy did what he did!
- The real reason? I am not sure, since he told me many things and I don't know if he was lying or not.
- We don't care about that. Just tell me why you went with him to Jamaica!
- I don't know, Dad. It was complicated and I was confused, but see? I'm still alive, so it must have been the right thing for me to do.
- Well, you and your stupidities! God, you're stupid.

My father hangs up the phone.

Many months later, I'm still wondering why my father didn't ask me more questions instead of paying the fees for the authorities to leave us alone. Maybe he could no longer endure the fact that we were receiving death threats or the fact that I had been accused of being an accomplice. The worst thing is that my dad can't find the person who is behind the threats and it could become dangerous. Someone at the bank, with the help of a phantom judge, started to get involved. They used a nonsensical affair involving tax collection from a non-taxable amount from the time and date it was acquired to collect from us for these accusations. I presume that my father went on paying them, thinking that he could get reimbursed as soon

Murder

as he found the person behind the claims and threats.
These problems with threats from these criminals integrated within the system have been going on since I was a kid.
Before, we used to get phone calls from people asking for money, threatening to kidnap me or to kill us if we didn't pay them. This has been going on since the day we got rich. We even had proof that some of them were police officers or people on the inside, although sometimes it's difficult to identify them and with the decoding C.B. we had. We could hear them saying they were police officers, however the C.B.s are not admissible in court. But it could at least help us locate their family and stop them from carrying out their bad illegal plot. The worst in all of this is that my own family, including my dad, is angry with me. He treats me as if I had done something bad, as if I was the one who did these bad, cruel deeds.
Since then he is constantly saying:
- You and your stupidities! Forget about your money. You won't get it anymore.
I find this worse than the end of the world because I'm innocent. I think either he did it to punish me or because he found an excuse to be able to run away from what he owes me. He found a mental way to avoid the truth and steal my share from me. If I had access to the real law, I would ask them to give me back the 500 thousand it cost my father, with interest, for all these illegal taxes that were collected to remove the accomplice accusations from me.
And I was not an accomplice. I should also add interest for all the years I've been suffering, during which I was deprived of too many things, including my children, for too long. In addition, people everywhere accused me of being a bad person for being involved in this murder. I have been insulted, shot at and beaten because of these false accusations. I'm a person being wrongly accused, a victim, and should not be the one paying for Fly's bad deeds. Those people took advantage of a situation involving a lot of lies, but somewhere there is a higher law that says if you get back at someone, it will cost

Murder

you big time and if you get back at an innocent person, it will cost you even more. If you don't want to pay the bill, don't do to others what you don't want them to do to you, and if you take revenge on a bad person, you'll still have to pay someone. A witness is not an accomplice; I am repeating this, in case someone still doesn't know the difference. I feel the need to tell those who had wondered about this. I hope you're no longer wondering, and if the details of all that I know don't quell your suspicions about me, well I'll know you are one of those robbers and that you are the ones who came to attack me, so you should be the ones paying the bill. In all of this, I not only lost money, but I lost my father's love and I heard from friends that other people have a negative image of me.

This made me an accused innocent victim of an organized crime. I didn't accuse Claude's father of being the one who hunted me down since he knew what happened and because he stayed in contact with us when he had questions. The only ones able to continue hunting me down were those who don't talk, but stole, and these are evil people. However, other members of Claude's family could have attempted something if only they had listened to the gossip being spread. I also thought that Fly's family are more likely to have been in on it. I should know about this because I heard it said many times; even once at a bikers' party a man told me that it was the Mc Sween's who did this to Claude. But Fly isn't a Mc Sween.

I did correct the person, but there are many saying this, so may this story be news for them to stop.

*****

Chapter Eight

Separation and war

If I were to make a movie of what follows, it would consist of a quick sequence of short events. Before starting, I should mention that, to date, I still wonder if the attacks were connected my ex, Marc

Separation and war

I'm just back from Jamaica. My father has not yet paid any fees because they'll not be requested for another two years. During these two years after my arrival, my mind is somewhat confused. I am not the person I used to be. Even my physical being has been affected by the stress of being frightened. The one thing different now is that when I hear someone say the word "kill", I take it seriously. I also interrupt anyone who says they want to kill and I tell them not to do so because I know the reality of murder. If I get angry and express the desire to kill someone, I also correct myself by saying "not for real". Many weeks have passed since my return and my friend Paul, who came to help me, has not come back to see me again; he has gone somewhere else, maybe to his other girlfriend's or something.

I am very lonely by myself. Carina still comes to visit but now lives with her boyfriend.

My mother lives not too far from me. She's come back from Mexico to spend some time here after being gone for so many years. I want to see her but I never know what to do with her. I'm home alone and I will start by cleaning my place. I've been thinking a lot about death since my relationship with Fly. I ask myself many questions about where we humans come from. I am in a philosophical-analytical phase about life. I try to imagine the soul-body relationship with the universe and analyze human laws, aware of the dangers and differences between human beings.

All of a sudden, there's a knock at the door. It's Marc, holding an enormous bouquet of gladiolas.

- Oh, my God! What are you doing here? Who are these flowers for?
- They're for you, of course! Christine, you're so pretty! I'm so happy to see you! Can I take you in my arms and hug you?
- Sure you can! Come in! It's been almost a year since I last saw you! Are you still seeing Fly's sister?
- No.

He looked very surprised that I had asked him this question.

- How come you know who I was seeing?

Separation and war

Marc walks towards the kitchen to help me put the beautiful flowers in a vase.

- I was going out with Fly, her brother, at the same time you were going out with her.
- She's looking for her brother and doesn't understand what happened, would you happen to know what's going on?
- Well, if you see her, tell her that her brother is a lost cause and that no one can change what happened. I prefer not to talk about any of this anymore. This isn't my problem and if she wants to know, she can just ask Fly, and he'll call her for sure. He told me he'd call her.

I don't tell Marc anything of what Fly did; actually, I'm trying to avoid thinking about it, especially since I am no longer in Fly's sexual presence.

Marc becomes mellow and starts to stammer.

- I still love you, Christine. Do you remember the times we were happy together? You know I've changed. I've matured and I don't want to hurt you any more, I've learned how to behave like a man.
- I have also changed. I'm not the same as before.

I try to explain to him that I'm aware of death and danger. I believe that everyone unconsciously knows but those who have not yet experienced something that connects them with death cannot really understand. Not having reached life after death makes it impossible to ask these types of questions and makes one tend to avoid these ideas.

Anyway, I don't tell anyone about the details of what went on. I can only think that Fly has become insane because he tells everyone what he did. I have no reason to get involved in his problems.

I also feel guilt due to the fact that I did nothing to stop this from happening.

During this time with Marc, I feel the need to be loved by someone who has emotions and understands other people. Marc could maybe bring me back to the way I was before: innocent and full of enthusiasm. I wonder if the broken pieces can be repaired. I'll ask him

Separation and war

the favour.

- Marc, would you mind staying the night, just to cuddle and keep me warm, but with our clothes on? I really just need to be comforted.
- Yes, I would love to. That's the reason I came to see you.

Marc is a passionate man, especially since we haven't seen each other for a long time. Since Paul hasn't give me any sign of life, it seems that he must have found someone else. I'll make sure of that before making a decision about Marc. The night goes by quickly. Marc leaves in the morning and I don't see him again until I make up my mind about sleeping with him.

I think my cousin helped me make this decision. She came to see me and kept encouraging me to get back together with him.
She said:

- He loves you so much, I saw him the other day and he looked pitiful. You're so lucky. No one has never bought me flowers. If I were you, I wouldn't lose my chance with this guy.
- Yes, maybe. But my decision depends on whether I still feel love towards him and if I still want to have him sexually.

My mother tells me over the phone that Paul is back with his old girlfriend. Concerning Marc and me getting back together, she isn't sure she approves. She says it might not work since our families don't really get along.
She also says:

- Darling, it's your choice. Do what you want and you're the only one who knows what that is. I've given you my advice; now, it's your decision to make.

On the basis of this advice, I conclude that it's really important that the two families get along to be able to form a relationship. But this is a subject I don't know much about, so, I ignore the situation and choose to learn from my mistakes. Tonight Marc will be coming back to see me. I expect that we will make love, so I wear my black garter and purple satin lingerie with lace covering my breasts and buttocks. I then apply some Coco Channel perfume, dabbing it with the tip of

Separation and war

my finger behind my ear and little touches in strategic places. I rush to the kitchen table since I am cooking a nice romantic dinner: sautéed beef and vegetables with a cheese sauce and a strawberry cream cake for dessert. Everything's ready, so I light the candles, impatiently waiting for him to arrive. There's a knock at the door. Oh my God! It must be him. I put a dress on over my lingerie in case it's someone else. I go open the door, all excited to see him again. I look into his eyes. His charm almost makes me faint.
- Hurry! Come in! It's cool outside.
We sit at the table right away since everything is ready.
Noticing my perfume, Marc says:
- Something smells good here.
Wile he brush his nose in my neck.
- Stop! It tickles me.
I'm shivering all over my body.
At the table we have a nice conversation, talking about people we know.
After the main meal, even before having desert, Marc comes close to me, lifts me from my chair and sits me on the table, kissing me and caressing me all over, repeating "I love you so much; don't ever leave me again". He takes me in his arms.
I wrap my legs around his waist, feeling his hardness rubbing against my lingerie and the lips of my vagina. He turns to position me against the wall, so he can more easily enter me. He then carries me to bed, being careful to not slip out of me. He moves in me a little more, then moans in my ear and we fall asleep after we both come. Less than a couple of hours later, we awaken and eat desert.
I wonder if it was a good thing to do to get back together. I don't know, but we have fallen back in love and life appears to be better. In the meantime, I stop smoking drugs, with my mother's help, out of respect for the new body living in me. The next years of my life witness the arrival of love from the little new beings in our lives. They allow me to regain my strength and my will to live. They also chase

Separation and war

away my fear of death. About being a mother, I can either be one of those women who doesn't love her children or one of those that love them too much. I'm in the latter category. I've done everything in my power to spoil them with affection and have taken them on trips so that they wouldn't get bored. I admit it's not easy and to achieve success, it requires help from people that we trust and love. After all, I sometimes still worry about potential dangers because those who had threatened us before are still around somewhere, still to be found.

Nevertheless, I almost never think about Fly and about Claude's family. I've even forgotten about the police threats we sometimes got.

Marc and I, my mother and her husband, my brothers and some friends all moved to the country, all living in separate houses. We now live with the richness of agriculture. I believe that things are better now because my father will soon give me my share of the money and I will buy my first house. I am also thinking about learning more about the field of agriculture. I still want to be able to do more, so maybe I'll study writing or psychology. I think that these areas all go well together and I have chosen them because they will satisfy my desire to learn about different things. I am also curious about the good and bad fortunes of others. I know that I'm good and that that my ideas are also good. Also, I've always wanted to share with others things that I have experienced, knowing that what I have learned might prevent someone from hurting others. I also want to share my knowledge, which has proved to me that eternal life exists for real and to give faith to those who haven't yet experienced anything to offer them proof. Therefore, in addition to being a mother and someone's wife, I decided to take a course in psychology. I took a couple of exams and got marks of 90% and higher.

In spite of all the efforts and happiness in my life, after my second child, misfortune came our way and destroyed everything we had. A robbery took place, which was the beginning of a chapter of my life

Separation and war

that was even worse than I would ever experience in my life. Every possible type of emotional suffering was just about to start for me. However, I wondered why it happened to me, and I never knew why. My phone rings and it's my mother.
- Are you coming? I'm waiting for you to arrive for supper. Tell Marc that the boys want to go rent some movies. Martini will arrive from work in no time.
- Yes, Mom. We're coming real soon.

I dress Beatrice, who is loving towards me, as usual. Her presence fills me with energy and her love makes me happy to be alive. I hope I'll be there to help her at school and with love also, to help keep problems at bay. Up until now, I've helped her learn how to walk and I've spent all my time doing all the good there is to do except for baptizing her. There's no reason why I didn't have her baptized; it's just that when the time came, something very disturbing was taking place, so I had to postpone it.

We arrive at my mother's house and the view of the sunset is spectacular, especially over the fields where it creates a golden reflection.

But it hurts the eyes to look at its splendour for too long.
- Hi, Mom!
- Hi, my daughter! Where is the little dudette? I want to give her a kiss.

Right away, my baby replies:
- Where's Taitos?

Beatrice likes her uncle very much. At 12, he's young to be an uncle. My brother is nice with her, playing with her and throwing her in the air. She likes it because he can spend many hours entertaining her without even getting tired of looking after a 2-year old.

My mom signals to me, indicating that she wants to talk to me.
- Christine, Marc's mother called me. She's telling me weird things, like she wants to adopt children. I don't understand what she's trying to tell me, but I had an argument with her. She tells me things about

Separation and war

your father but she never saw him and never even spoke to him. I'm starting to think that there's something abnormal about her. I'm telling you this because I don't want to talk to her anymore. You'll have to tell Marc to tell her to stop calling me and only to call if she wants to talk to Marc, because I'm not interested in getting into her stories anymore.

- What? His mother called you to make up bad stories? Marc told me that she doesn't like us very much she takes a lot of pills, which make her sick in the head. I don't know if he's telling the truth, but he doesn't want me to disturb or talk to his mother or father. He also tells me not to be concerned when she talks about weird things. So when I see them, I don't talk to them too much and I try to remain polite.

- Anyway, I have no idea, but she's having a nervous breakdown and she also says it's your fault that Marc smokes.

- Well, she's exaggerating there. If he wants to stop smoking, he can look at me as an example; I was able to quit.

- The poor woman wants to call the child protection service on me. She tells me that my husband is beating your brothers and that she'll take them away from me or take yours. She said it could fix her problem with the adoption agency, which has refused her application to adopt.

- What kind of stories was she telling you? Did she threaten you? This makes me mad! Doesn't she have anything else to do? You never did anything to her. Why would she want to hurt you?

- She told me things which I don't understand. Also, your Dad called me to tell me he is being sued for a lot of money. He said they've been calling him on the phone and threatening him to come search his estate, then they'll take all his money and the kids' lives if he doesn't pay. He received tax collection papers from a judge, saying that the accountant didn't pay his taxes and if he pays, they'll hide the murder accomplice charges that they're trying to add to the files. The problem is that your dad doesn't know who's behind the threats.

Separation and war

There's nothing he can do to defend himself, so he'll pay them and when he finds out who's behind these threats he'll sue them with his insurance or do something. Do you happen to know who it could be?
- No, I have no idea, Mom.
- We have to watch our backs since it could be dangerous. -- - Your father is very mad and is having a nervous breakdown. I just hope that he won't have a heart attack.

And if ever it turns out that it's his fault that these stories are causing problems, it will cost him big time, if what I am telling you is the case. He wanted to raise you, well nothing better happened to you, I told him that sufficient times.

My mother looks a little angry and she says nonsensical things when she's afraid that something bad could happen to me. I start to think about Marc and realize he has been lying lately.

I heard him say over the phone that my step dad had given my brother a black eye, when he knew he had gotten it from a fight at school. I will ignore what I just heard for the moment. At my mom's one night, she wants to make me read the Bible because she says that what I had been talking to her about the other day is similar to some passage in the Bible and she wants me to see it. We're all sitting at the table, flipping through the Bible and making drawings of the universe and of how the lightning from the astral universe could be connected to our body in the other dimension. We also speak about business possibilities we could undertake here and in Mexico. Marc and Martini decide to go outside to smoke their joint even if the kids are already upstairs sleeping. After we watch a horror movie, we go home. The stories which Marc is inventing run through my mind. Time is passing by and life seems to be normal, but I'm very tired all the time, perhaps because I've recently given birth. At times, I don't know what to say to change the ordinary into new, entertaining, imaginative images, or, which ideas to choose in order to add some ambience into my daughter's life. Marc doesn't like it. He hates it so much that he becomes paranoid and tries to make people believe

Separation and war

that I'm mentally ill. I don't know what's wrong with him lately. He's become a bit weird, causing trouble any way that he can, and trying to transform everything to its worst. He makes everything seem like craziness and compares me to crazy people. Why is he trying to make me feel guilty or abnormal? Marc has gone on a journey of trying to influence people and call my sanity into question, saying that I am insane and trying to convince people to agree with him. I wonder if it's because of what happened with Fly. It seems impossible, though, since he knew nothing about it. However, it could be a trick to squash my pride. The worst thing is that he always does it when I am feeling bad or when I am in the worst state of mind. I have to say that I do let myself get involved in his stupidities. So it could be my fault since I am somewhat stupid at times. However, I don't understand why he's doing this, since we're in love and we've been friends for more than 5 years. What's going on with him? I really don't understand this. You won't believe how something stupid that I told Marc turned into a tragedy. One time, I wanted to let some imaginative ideas flow, so I told Marc that bugs antennas are acting as a phone for extraterrestrials so they can spy on us and I suggested that it would be a nice idea to make it into a children's movie. He took what I said seriously, without even trying to contest it in order to laugh about it.

He took my idea as evidence of my being deranged. I swear to God he was acting like a real crazy person. Seriously, who does he take me for? Does he really believe that what I said could really harm someone? Anyway, he went on with this and called a psychiatrist, asking him if he could have me locked away for what I said. I told myself there must be something else in his mind, of which I was not aware. In my wounded eyes, his way of reacting is totally illogical and if he is really panicking because of that stupid thing, I wonder why he isn't able to accept this idea for a children's movie scene; it's no worse than the movie E.T. I decide to just forget about it and one day he might tell me the real reason for his bad behaviour.

Separation and war

Meanwhile, my mother has received bad news. She's leaving again for Mexico. Martini's mother is sick and he wants to go spend some time with her in case she dies since she doesn't want to come to Canada. I am soon going to realize that this situation will be disastrous for me since my mother is the only person here to help me with the kids. It's true that Marc's mother wants to help me with the kids, but I can't stand being around her for very long because she makes me feel very uncomfortable. All the girlfriends I have left have moved too far away from me. In addition, Marc keeps saying bad things about them, which also makes it difficult.

As for the situation with my cousins, I wonder how I could ever get into their lives since I haven't been around them. The only option that remains is to ask a stranger and that's out of the question, since I can't endure most people. I have a lot of trouble trusting other people because of the many threats I've received, and because of the nasty reactions of jealous people, which I also have been enduring forever. The mere thought of a person planning a robbery or something bad makes me feel threatened and I want to get away from them as fast as I can before something bad happens to me. Therefore, having a stranger coming here is not an alternative. What am I going to do by myself? I'll never be able to make it on my own. Marc will help me for a while until I can find someone to come and help me, so I should be okay.

In the countryside where we live there's an abandoned apple orchard in our backyard which no one takes care of. We own neither the house nor the land.

It's a Saturday afternoon. The phone rings; its Marc's mother. I try to hear their conversation to understand what they're saying. I hear Marc say:

- What, Mom? You're fighting with Aunty Annette again? Well, stop fighting with her. Mom, I'm scared, her dad's going to kill me. No, Mom, You can't adopt the kids.

What does Dad want me to do? What! Well, no! I'm not going. It's too

Separation and war

far. And stop calling me to argue.
He then hangs up the phone. He walks around the living room, looking stressed out, and says to me:
- I might have to leave for the city for a while.
- Are you serious? But no! You can't do this to me now. You have to help me organize things here first. I am unable to stay here alone with the kids because the starter on the car doesn't work properly. It has to be fixed first. How will I be able to get to someone's house or go to the grocery store if the car doesn't start? There are no busses here and since my mom left there are no other people I can rely on. You can't just leave me like this. First, we have to fix the problems, and then you can leave. Make sure things here are okay for the children and me before you go so far away. Let's look for someone to help me while you're gone or let's find another place to live. At least let's fix the car, but don't leave me like this all alone with the children in the middle of the fields, with a car that doesn't work properly, please!
There's a log burning in the fireplace, the children have had their baths and are sound asleep, so I'll finally sit and quietly, drink an herbal tea and watch a movie next to the small fire. Marc has gone to the pharmacy nearby. I hear the car come up the driveway.
Knowing it's Marc, I wait, expecting to see him come through the door in a second. More than five minutes pass before he opens the door. He comes in with his head down, not looking at me, looking like a walking zombie.
- Oh, my God! Did you see a ghost?
- I have to tell you something. Something just happened and I am really panicking about it. Go outside and look at the car.
I put on my shoes and jacket and open the door, expecting to see the car all smashed and dented. Marc follows me. I look at the car and seen almost nothing different except for a little curved bump in the front.
- Honestly, that's almost nothing. Tell me what happened.
- I hit a tree!

Separation and war

- It doesn't look so bad. I think you're overreacting, baby.
- That's not why I am in a panic. Let me calm down first and then I'll tell you.

I sit down to drink my herbal tea, a bit angry about the accident. I go over to Marc to ask him what happened again. He's hugging his knees, sitting on the floor at the entrance to the kitchen.

- What are you doing sitting on the floor? You're crying.
- I can't take it anymore, I want to die and I'm scared. I have no idea what's going to happen. And your mother is gone.
- Are you crying because my mother's gone? It should be me who's crying about that.
- You have no heart; it doesn't even bother you a bit.
- Hey, don't exaggerate. My mother's not dead. She's only moved further away. We can always go visit them; it's only a 4-hour plane ride.
- Well, I'm scared of airplanes. I also have to tell you what happened earlier, I hit a dog. He was running and he just threw himself in front of the car. The dog's owner came out of his house and started to threaten me with a rifle. He was going to kill me. The man looked very crazy and I got so scared that I ran away. Tomorrow I'm calling my dad and I'll go away for a while in case the guy comes for me.
- But, what! You have another excuse to run away from me before fixing our problems! No, no! You have to face this man because he's not going to kill you. Think about it. He was just mad and sad about his dog. After he takes time to think about it, he'll realize that it's kind of his fault since he's the one who left his dog outside without a leash.

Marc starts to cry, repeating:

- I can't take it anymore. I want to die.
- Stop it! You're exaggerating! The man didn't shoot you and you didn't hit a person.
- No, but you don't seem to understand anything.

A couple of days later, Marc's parents come to the house. When his

Separation and war

mother enters, she makes me feel bad, as if my home isn't good enough. She is already ready to leave, and she ignores me, acting too stressed out to sit and talk to me nicely. When she's here, I feel as if the place is going to be attacked soon and it is very unpleasant.
- Come on, Marc. Go get your things. We're taking you home.
- What about Christine?
- Don't worry about her. She'll stay here and will be just fine. You can bring Beatrice if you want.
I interfered right away.
- What the hell is going on here? Marc, you shouldn't leave today. Just postpone it for a couple of weeks or find something closer. We'll have to move to the city if you take the job. I really don't feel like it at all.
However, Marc just takes his things, preparing to leave, and says:
- Don't worry! I'll help you when I get back.
I have to leave but I'll call you tomorrow.
Marc kisses me and the children good-bye, then disappears. I then realize that my mother's absence is more serious than I had thought because now I need someone and she was the only one I could rely on before she left.
The first night, I'm able to sleep without being too afraid, considering that I'm alone in a house deep in the countryside. In the morning, I get up and in less than 10 minutes, Beatrice has run outside with the dog. She was able to sneak out through the mosquito net that the dog had just broken, while I had gone to pick up my baby boy, who was crying.
It's hell here by myself. I'm not able to do this on my own. Beatrice knows how to unlock and open doors but she doesn't know to stay out of the street. There's no fence between the house and the country road. This house isn't safe for children. We either have to fix it or there'll have to be two of us to supervise the children. So I know what to do today. I won't stay in the house. I'll try to go shopping and visit someone. I just need to start the car and everything will be just

Separation and war

fine. I put the baby in his crib and go outside to get Beatrice. I'm able to catch her before she runs into the street, pulling her by the hand and forcing her to follow me back inside.

- How many times do I have to tell you not to open the door and not to go outside alone? You have to listen to me when I tell you something. We're going to eat, get dressed and go to the market.

In the meantime, stay close where I can see you. Before leaving, I'll ask the neighbour if he'll be able to come and get the kids and me if ever the car decides to quit on me. Now everything is in order, the dog is tied up outside and I've arranged for a ride in case of an emergency. I'll try to start the car; if it starts, I'll be fine.

I grab snacks, the baby's bottle, Beatrice's glass, toys, diapers, a change of clothes, and I'm ready to go. Both children are buckled into their seats. I kiss and hug them before leaving. I turn the key twice in the ignition and the car starts. Hurray! I turn around to look at the kids, smiling, eyes shining, happy to go for a ride. I don't leave right away, but I stop and wonder where else could I go. Maybe I'll stop at my dad's to ask him to help me fix the car or stop by to see Marc. He's at his aunt's house, which is closer to the location of the job he is seeking and which he's taking exams for. I'm driving slowly, coming into a curve on the bridge, just at the place where Fly had thrown away his gun. My car switches off and everything is in slow motion. It's as if a cloud engulfs the car, giving me time to stabilize, in order to be able to turn the key and put the car into neutral with the steering wheel blocked. There's enough time for the steering wheel to unblock, although I'm going 80 kilometers in a curve, which is a miracle and scientifically impossible.

I then turn on the emergency flashers and let the car roll all the way off the bridge. The car stops right in front of a pharmacy. How lucky I am! I'm almost sure that angels came and stopped time, allowing me to do all the necessary manoeuvring in order to be able to control my stress. I stayed calm considering the circumstances of not ever having planned what to do if something like this happened. In a fraction of a

Separation and war

second, which felt like 3 minutes, I reacted appropriately and avoided any collision. I was happy to find out that I was skilful enough to handle this crisis, especially when I had just exercised bad judgement with respect to the condition of the car. There will be no more excuses or delays in having the car fixed. I walk inside the pharmacy. The clerk seems unfriendly.
- Hello, ma'am. My car broke down and I am alone with my two children. Can I please use your phone?
- We don't let people use our phone here!
Did she really say no? What a cow!
- Well, ma'am, could you just call a tow truck for me?
- I have no time for that! Go ask elsewhere!
Is she serious? Oh my God, where am I? Do I really look like a weird, crazy or dangerous person with my baby in my arms?
Beside me stands a couple, listening to the conversation.
The man comes over to me and says:
- Poor thing! Don't worry! There are many bitches in this world! I'll call a towing service for you.
- Thank you very much, sir. I'm so grateful.
My nerves just explode and I start to cry, thinking about the worst thing that could have happened. The tow truck finally arrives and the man brings us to the garage. From there we take a taxi and go to Marc's aunt's house, which is close to the garage. A taxi ride back home would have been too expensive. I have to find a place to stay until the car is repaired, which should take about two days. I also have family here. Someone must have space for me. When we were young, there used to be 14 of them in a 2-bedroom apartment, sometimes even more when boyfriends were staying over. So I can't believe that no one will find a bit of space for us for two days.
As I arrive at Marc's aunt's house, Marc looks at me angrily, and says:
- Why did you come here?
- I couldn't stand it staying alone anymore without help and an adult to talk to, so I decided to come see you and stop at my dad's store to

Separation and war

ask him to help me pay for the car repairs. In addition, we're going to find a place to live in the city if you get the job, even if I'm not thrilled by the idea. Marc doesn't seem very happy. His aunt is there, whispering something to him but I can hear what she says:

- Marc, do you remember your friend, the blond girl next door? She came to help her grandmother last week and gave me her number to give to you.

With his bad mood and the crazy story I just heard, I lose my temper, especially since he had just left me alone. I can't take it any more.

- What the fuck are these stories? Did you come here instead of staying at your parents so you could see your ex? That's the girl you always run to see when we're at the mall, right? I know it's her; you'd told me that she has a grandmother who lives here.

I feel so angry that my mind is overrun with bad ideas. In spite of the argument, I am able to spend the night there that night. The next morning comes and it's not much easier to be there with people because Beatrice is not behaving.

She starts running everywhere and I try to punish her to make her stop. I put her in a room but I hadn't been told about a mirror behind the door which wasn't properly attached to the wall. The mirror falls, but it doesn't break into pieces, and Beatrice is unhurt. Misfortune seems to be following me, trying to warn me of something, but I don't know what.

The day had just started and Marc is still trying to start an argument. He, too, must be possessed by that thing wanting to do me harm.

- Marc, let me try to find Francine. I could go spend some time with her if the car isn't ready soon.
- You're not going to call your bitch of a whore.
- Aren't you tired of saying mean things about my friend?
- Well, it's true that she's only a whore. I should know since I fucked her.
- Now you're starting to get on my nerves. I already know that and it doesn't matter to me. She's still my friend. Anyway, that was before

Separation and war

the children and we weren't even together.
Since we're at it, there's something I've been meaning to tell you. When we first broke up, I slept with your friend Carl.
- You did what? And with whom? No, don't tell me you did that. Carl told me it was with J.F.
- No, I never did that with J.F. I told you a million times that it was Francine who had slept with J.F.
All of a sudden, there's a knock on the door and it's his mother.
- I'm coming to get Beatrice. We'll go shopping while you settle your problems.
- It's your son that started it. I hope you'll be coming back early.
- Well, my son can say whatever he wants. I'll always take his side and I'll come back when I'm finished. As for your permission, I'll take her whether you like it or not.
Marc's mother leaves and now his aunt decides to add more hatred.
- Your girlfriend has to leave.
- Don't worry. I'll leave.
Frustrated, Marc continues to say bad things.
- Its finished, you and me. Over! I can't believe you slept with Carl.
- For Christ's sake, we broke up and you do love him. Wait a minute. I know! You just want an excuse to go see the girl next door.
The phone rings. It's Marc's mom, calling to say that she's not coming back with Beatrice, but that she's taking her home for the night and that if we don't settle our problems, she's going to keep her forever.
- Okay. This is way too much for me to handle. I'm going to try and get some help and don't tell me that your mother is going to keep my daughter for good if we split up. We're not back in the '40s. People are allowed to get separated nowadays.
Having no alternative, I call a taxi, take the baby and leave for one of my aunt's who I haven't seen for a couple of years.
That is the first time I've been separated from my daughter. I'm nervous and find it difficult and my mind is not at ease since I consider this as though she has gone to a babysitter's, but is going to

Separation and war

be taken away from me forever. This is what his mother said to him on the phone many times and also to my mom. Meanwhile, I leave. Marc calls my father to tell him a bunch of lies, which no one shares with me and which makes my father worried.

At my aunt's I receive no help whatsoever with my problems, so I end up visiting two more aunts with no luck, as they're all doing their little routines and have no ideas to help me start doing something about my problems. I think I am about to have a nervous breakdown. The first night I'm not able to get any sleep at all. The next morning, at the first aunt's house, she tells me:

- I really don't know how to help you, Christine. You should ask your father.

I decide to try my father's sister, even though it's been more than 24 hours since I was able to sleep.

In the evening, my aunt gives me a bed to sleep in and Marc shows up, giving excuses.

My aunt and her boyfriend spend the whole night in the kitchen, drinking beer, while Marc and I talk in the bedroom. Marc tells me:

- I swear I'll be nice with you, Christine. Please forgive me.

- For now, Marc, I don't want to talk about it. I just want to get some sleep because I'm so exhausted. If you want to stay with me, tonight, it's okay; we can talk about this in the morning.

Many hours later, I'm still unable to fall asleep, even though I'm very tired. Marc stays to sleep with me and the baby, all in the same bed. Morning comes fast. I didn't get a wink of sleep and stress has frazzled my nerves. I'm also worried about my daughter.

Marc wakes-up, with a hypocritical, suspicious look. He must be up to some scheme.

- Christine, I spoke with your dad yesterday and we agreed that you should go see a psychiatrist.

- What in hell are you telling me? You spoke with my father? What kind of lies did you tell him? Tell me what you're up to.

- Nothing. I only told him that you were sick!

Separation and war

Get out of here! How dare you call my father to tell him stupid things and tell him God-knows-what kind of lies. I knew you were trying to get my daughter for your mother, you asshole! Leave me alone.
I get up and leave to go to the restaurant at the corner of the street to call my dad, because here my aunt and Marc are yelling at me about everything. I'm at my wit's end, feeling very hyperactive from fatigue and from arguing. On the street, I quiver as I walk, trying to get away from the discussion. I can't take it anymore. It's been more than 48 hours since I last slept. My heart is beating too fast and I'm shivering and scared. If someone looks at me right now, they will definitely think that I'm a druggie, in need of my fix. I finally enter the restaurant and look around. Everything seems murky, but luckily, the man who works there has known me since I was young.
- Hey! Hi! Long time no see. You don't look well. Are you ok?
- No, I'm not feeling well. I haven't slept for 2 days.
Why did I just tell him that? Now he'll think that I am on cocaine or something.
- Sir, I came to use your phone.
- Sure; for you, anytime.
I take the phone and dial my father's number. Lucky for me, he answers.
- Papa, it's me, Christine. You have to come pick me up right away at your sister's. I need to go somewhere for at least a week. I can't fix anything here. I'm not even able to sleep. You have to help me, please.
- No, no. You're not coming here.
- But why? You have the chalet, the upstairs part of the garage. All you wife's family sleeps there. What the fuck, Daddy.
- It's because of the stupid things you did in Jamaica.
- What the hell are you talking about? That has nothing to do with now! This makes no sense. There, I've done nothing wrong.
- Well, yeah. I just paid 500 grand with interest and I'm not very

Separation and war

happy about that, so you can forget about your money and your house. I still don't know who's behind the collection agents, but if it's your fault, I'll find out.
- Daddy, please stop this nonsense! I need your help. For Christ's sake. Help me!
- Okay, I'll come over to see you later at aunty's. Stay there.

I turn around and see Marc and my aunt coming into the restaurant.
- No, but are you ever going to leave me alone? I can't take this anymore. Stop following me.
- Christine, come home or I'm calling the cops.
- Marc, are you crazy? Go home! Leave me alone, I said.

Unfortunately, he had already called the police and the patrol car pulls up out front. Marc goes to speak with the officers then they signal to me to come closer.

They ask me questions such as "What's going on here?" and "Did you take any drugs". I tell them that his mother threatened to take away my kids. Then they let me go and tell me that Marc called them saying that I was dancing in the middle of the street.

I have no idea what this means nor does it have anything to do with what's happening. Marc probably lied to get their attention so they would come. I've never understood Marc's tactics nor his intentions, but they often work to get him what he wants. Maybe he tried to make me look like a crazy person, knowing that's how I looked after not sleeping for 2 days. He might need to hold something against me to get custody for his mother. Marc finally leaves and I go back to my aunt's house. My aunt keeps telling me that there's something wrong with me but she doesn't want to tell me what it is. I wonder what Marc told her. I lie down on the blue leather sofa, trying to get some sleep.
- Aunty, would you mind rocking the baby while I rest?
- No. I'll gladly do it, as long as you're here, because I won't baby-sit him, if you're not here. I never had any children and when they start crying, I don't know what to do; it makes me nervous.

Separation and war

- I understand, aunty. I'll talk to you later.

She leaves me alone, but I'm still not able to rest. My stress makes my heart beat way too fast.

A couple of hours later, my father arrives. He comes over even though he had hurt my feelings earlier on the phone, when he told me I couldn't go to his home, which is also my home. In fact, it was because of me and his ex-girlfriend that he was able to buy himself the small mansion. In my mind, right now robbers are manipulating him. He has no notions of thankfulness or justice in his way of living. My father stands in the living room and we greet him with hugs and kisses. He says:

- Well, well! What's going on here? Your Marc called me. He told me that you're not doing well. Well, did you see what you look like? You look like you've come back from a war. Ha! HA!

My father thinks it's funny when someone around him is feeling bad.

- Daddy, I need help. Marc and I got into an argument, and my life is all upside down. Things are really going bad. I don't even know where to start to fix things, nor do I know what to do. I have to find a new place to live and someone who can come baby-sit and help me. I really have to settle my problems. In addition, it's about time that you give me my share of the money we won, for I, too, have to get myself a house and land where I can be safe.

- No, I told you that I won't help you. I have a new wife and new kids. There's no place for you and your share is all gone because of those stupid things you did in Jamaica.

- What the hell are you saying? Are you going out of your mind with your nonsense stories? Do you think I would have brought children into this world if I didn't have some money set aside? I want you to understand something: I won't let you give my share of money to your new family, who made me live through hell, who almost put me on the street and who have treated me badly all these years.

- You're so stupid. Try to call your mother's sister or cousin. Someone can probably help you. This situation could all be your mother's fault,

Separation and war

since she left you alone.

Not having any choice, I take the phone and call my godmother.

- Yes, darling. Just come over and we'll discuss the matter.

My father smiles at me. He doesn't look like he's feeling guilty about having refused to provide hospitality to his own daughter. My father gets up, holding his keys in his hands.

- Come on. I'll give you a ride to your aunt's and I'll come in with you to talk to her.

It's obvious that I'm unable to properly think about any matter, the way I'm feeling now.

My aunt stands there looking guilty.

- Christine, forgive me. I do love you and I would help you if I could, but my boyfriend is hypoglycaemic. I can't risk having a child around if he has a crisis, because an accident could happen.

- Don't worry, Aunty. I understand. I know that if you were able to, you'd help me.

My father and I leave to go to my godmother's. On the way, he starts to talk in weird coded words which I don't understand.

- You're going to get treated. Hey, tell me you are not fine. Marc told me what was wrong with you and I know you're sad. Tell me what's wrong.

- But what are you talking about? I already told you what's wrong, My car broke down, then I had an argument with Marc. I haven't slept in almost 3 days, and on top of it all, Marc's mother wants to take my baby girl away from me.

- Hey! You have to tell me what's really going on. There's no need to lie to me.

- What the hell are you talking about? Are you going out of your mind? What lies did Marc tell you?

- Hey, there. Don't start. I know you're not doing well.

What's going on with my dad? He doesn't understand me. We arrive at my aunt's house. I'm starting to feel very dizzy and I let everyone know before I faint.

Separation and war

- Frank, that's enough. Let's bring Christine to the hospital, Look at her. Are you sure you didn't take drugs?
- Of course not! Since Beatrice went to Marc's parents' house, I haven't been able to sleep. And I'm going to lose my mind because they told me that they wanted to keep her forever and never bring her back to me.
- Don't you think you're exaggerating a little?
- No! Ask my mom. She'll tell you. Marc's mother
told her about her intention to make up stories so that she could take the children, because the adoption agency has rejected her application.
- Would you stop lying!
- I'm telling the truth. Please stop taking me for a crazy person. It's not me who's lying here. I only want some help from you, please.
- Well, we're going to start by taking you to the hospital, They'll give you something to help you sleep and tell us what's wrong with you.

Before leaving, I look at my cousin. She's wearing a baseball cap and looks pretty holding my baby on her lap. I tell myself that he's in good hands. I walk outside, get in the truck and go to the hospital. We arrive at the Montreal General. In the doctor's office, I have to explain what happened but I'm feeling so tired and on the verge of a nervous breakdown, that I talk too fast and the doctor doesn't understand what I'm saying. He sends me to lie down in a dark room. Very soon after, a nurse comes in
with a syringe in her hand and tells me:
- Turn on your side. I'm going to give you a shot.
- No. What do you want to inject me with? Tell me what it is first.
- Just turn around; it's just something to help you sleep.

I hesitate many times and finally I let her give me a shot in my rear. Time passes by but I have no idea what happens because I'm fast asleep.

When I finally wake up, I'm somewhere else, but I don't know where. An ambulance technician is next to me.

Separation and war

- Where am I?
- You're at the Douglas psychiatric hospital, I can tell you that you weren't waking up and I think you've been sleeping for a long time.
- Why have I been brought here?
- I'm not sure. I heard the doc say you were going to a place closer to your family so that they could visit you.

I'm in a panic to be waking up here because since ever since I was young, I've heard that only very sick and crazy people get sent here. I also have a cousin, the only abnormal sick one in the family, who died a couple of months ago in this hospital.

She no longer wanted to live and after getting strong enough medication, she died and they gave her organs away. She was only 30 years old.

When I was young, we used to call this hospital the human slaughterhouse. There's even a gas chamber somewhere in there. So I wonder why they've brought me here. This must be a mistake and I'll ask to talk to the doctor.

A male nurse comes up to me.

- Sir, could you ask the doctor to come see me? I've slept enough and now I'm well enough to go.
- No, you can't go. The doctor should be coming tomorrow. I have to give you a room and you can then ask the nurse when you'll be able to see the doctor. I can't give you any answers because I have no information about you. I'm not allowed to let anyone leave because I know nothing about the patients.
- Are you telling me that I'm stuck in this place, that I can't leave, and that I can't find out why they're keeping me?
- I'm very sorry, miss, but I can't help you with this.

They bring me into a room and it takes 2 weeks before the doctor comes in to see me.

One of my childhood friend's fathers, a psychiatrist, works at this hospital. I always thought of this friend as being from a good family, which I admired and liked.

Separation and war

When I was young, I was the only one of her friends to whom her father would say:

- You could be a psychiatrist. You're the only one of all the children here who likes to talk about morals. Your ideas are very much in line with the principles of psychiatry.

My girlfriend used to tell me that I was the only one of her friends who didn't laugh at her father's dictating and she didn't understand why. Nevertheless, it made her feel good.

I think the doctor I saw in the hospital might have been him, although I'm not sure, since the last time I saw him, I was 8 years old. I could be mistaken but the probability it was him is 70% and if it was, he didn't recognized me.

Anyway, at my first meeting, I sit down in his office and wait for 30 minutes before he comes in.

- Hello, young girl. Tell me why you're here.
- I don't know why. Can you tell me? All I know is that I went to a hospital because I couldn't sleep, they gave me a shot, and here I am, being told that I cannot leave. You must know that I don't want to stay here. Just give me my leave please, sir. I have to go meet with my kids because I think that the mother of the father of my children wants to take them away from me.
- Whoa, girl! Before you leave, I have to make some calls, do my investigation and try to understand what's going on here. Until then you have to stay here.
- But no, I don't want to stay here, sir. I want to go home. I need to move and I need to see my children. In addition, I'm not mentally sick. I was even studying psychology a month ago and my lowest mark was 90%.
- I don't necessarily think that you're sick. You could just be depressed and I can't let you go until I find out what's wrong. If you get bored, you can take one of the books on my bookshelves and read it. You look intelligent enough to read one! I'll come back to see you next week.

Separation and war

- What, next week? No, I can't stand to be here another week. You can't keep me here if I don't want to be here.
- You'll have to control yourself. Good-bye for now. Give me time to check with the others to find out what's going on with you and why you were brought here.

I have to be patient and wait for many days before being able to see him again. I have no one to speak to; I only listen to music, read and cry at times. The days pass slowly but finally I see the doctor again.

- Hello again, young girl. How are you doing today? I finally spoke with your Marc. He told me he loves you and that you want to leave him. He also told me that you want to commit suicide. This is what he told your father, who is worried about you.

It finally clicks in my head; I now understand why everyone's telling me that they want to take me to see a psychiatrist.

- Sir, what you just told me makes me angry because it's a lie. In fact, he's the one who had a crisis. I can only presume that he's saying this to get custody of our children, to make his mother happy. She's crying about wanting to adopt. You can verify this information at the adoption agency.
- Christine, listen! I have to do more research before releasing you.
- Well, no. I don't accept that. I worry too much here and it's a scary place. I don't trust this place. I want to be released now or I'll leave by myself.
- Christine, you can't do that or your stay could be longer. Now you can leave the office and close the door on your way out. Stop worrying. You'll get better soon.

I go back to my room. I don't like it here and I'm becoming somewhat paranoid. I think about the fact that they helped my cousin die here and that Marc told them I wanted to die, and these things make me wonder if they're going to drug me to death in order to sell my organs.

It's a terrible feeling to be trapped in such a place without any love to support me.

Separation and war

So I have to run away because I'm in danger. My mind is in a panic; I'm almost sure that I believe in these ideas.

I'll wait until I'm able to go outside, then I'll run away.

The door opens for someone coming in, so I go close to hold the door open and just walk out.

Outside, there's a taxi in the parking lot. I walk over and get in. The driver doesn't ask me too many questions, even though I'm still wearing my hospital gown.

- Where are you going?
- Well, let's make a stop at a clothing store, and then I want to go to the Canadian National.
- No problem, ma'am.

We arrive at the C.N. after stopping at a store to buy a shirt and pants. At the entrance, I ask the guard if he can go get Marc for me. He takes the phone, then tells me where I can find him. I walk towards his workstation, but before I can reach him, Marc appears in front of me. I start talking to him but can't keep myself from arguing.

- Would you stop lying? It's not a game. You have to stop. Please, this isn't a game. My life could be in danger, and you should know, or is that your goal? Don't do this to me. Do you know that they don't want to let me go because you told them I wanted to kill myself?
- You shouldn't run away from the hospital. I'm calling the police.
- Are you out of your mind? Can you just answer me? Tell me why you told them that I wanted to kill myself.

But he doesn't respond. I think to myself it's terrible what he's making me suffer through. Does he want them to euthanize me or what? He's not human. What he's doing isn't normal. I never was allowed to lie; he, on the other hand, permits himself to do that. How was I able to stay with him for so long and never see what he was? My mother once told me that Marc's family were not the same kind of people as us and that she didn't trust Marc. I should have listened to her and I wouldn't be in such a mess. Unfortunately, it's too late for that, so I have to find a solution.

Separation and war

The police car arrives. I again lose my temper with Marc.
- I don't believe it. How can you do this to me? You're just an asshole. I'll find a way for them to know that you're the one with all these mental thoughts. You'll see; you won't get away with this so easily.
The officers took my arm and pulled me towards the car.
- Come on, ma'am. We've got to bring you back to the hospital.
All I can say is if I wasn't depressed before arriving at the hospital, I am definitely going to be depressed now. What gets to me the most is that he doesn't admit he lied and it's not good for my heart to lose my temper.

During my stay at the hospital, the doctor asks my mother to come back from Mexico for a short stay.

She comes alone by plane and stays 3 weeks. My mother and I have a session with the doctor. My mother is disturbed about not knowing why I'm being kept there, so she decides to bring up another subject to discuss.
- Sir, my daughter went on a trip to Jamaica a couple of years ago and apparently over there the man she was with murdered a girl.
As the doctor takes notes for his report, I see him write that her mother finds her pretty. I never understand the connection between the pretty part and what my mother said.

During the rest of my stay at the hospital, I am visited by my cousin, I try to run away again and I go shopping to buy clothes with my father for the first time. I also think I see Fly on the floor below me when I go for a walk. However, sitting in the hospital thinking for so long, I finally come up with an idea and act on it. I call a lawyer in hopes that he'll have the answer to my problem and that he'll believe me.

Believe it or not, he arranges a court date for me in no less time than it takes to hang up the phone.

At the court hearing, I stand before the judge and it's my turn to plead my case to someone who finally takes my side.
- Sir, they are holding me against my will and I haven't committed a crime.

Separation and war

My doctor is also present and states:
- In my opinion, this girl presents no danger to others or to herself. Therefore, based on my professional expertise, having been informed that she wanted to commit suicide, my diagnosis of her condition is that she has had a slight case of depression, something which women may experience after giving birth.

These accusations are false, which I mention to the judge.
- These suicide attempts are not true.

The judge then asks the doctor:
- Do you have any objection to her release?
- No, I have no objections to her release!

I then explain the whole situation from the beginning to the end to the judge, adding the part where my father was rich and did not want to help me.

The judge gives his verdict:
- I therefore order that Christine be released from the hospital and that her father give her an apartment, and that he help her pay for the move. Concerning the children, you will have to go to juvenile court, because it is not my field of work.

Good-bye and be good, everyone.

I should have asked for an indemnity for the suffering they made me endure, such as my being frightened the entire time I was held against my will.

In fact, every day of my confinement, I had to think about the fact that I might end up dead if I didn't escape.

After this incident, I lose confidence in many people who I thought I was safe with before.

I know that the reason I thought they wanted me dead was that my cousin had died after wanting to die and because of Fly the murderer.

After this incident, I finally go home, pack my things and move into this apartment here, which I am still stuck in. I will be stuck in this place until I can get my stolen money back, and until then, I won't be able to do anything useful nor will I be safe. My mother has gone

Separation and war

back to Mexico. As for Marc and I, we arranged to stay together and did not need to go to court.

The worst thing about the confinement is the mean gossip that spread among people who know me. My friends went from admiring me to having a bad image of me. Since my confinement in the psychiatric hospital, I am no longer the nice rich person who comes to help them, but the sick person who they should no longer talk to. If I had to identify the guilty people to sue, apart from the hospital, it would be Marc and his family, since they are the first to have terrorized me, with their threats to keep the children and with the lies which they told everyone about me.

I know that in their own world, they are probably good people but in a conflict with someone, they know how to lie and be mean to the person they choose to target.

Unfortunately, this is only the beginning of the living hell and doesn't compare to what will come next.

***

In the apartment where we live, on the third floor, the floors need refinishing. When we moved in, I didn't see this as a problem since Marc often worked doing this kind of job; I even went with him to help him work. But I wouldn't be able to do it by myself since I'm not sure I'd remember how. Tonight, I'm in the living room talking with Marc about it.

- Marc! You're going to help me refinish the floor, because we really can't afford to move right now. We have to put our money aside to buy a car, save for a down payment on a house and get all the money needed before starting to pay a mortgage.
- Christine, I'm not your nigger, so do the math. I won't do your floors for nothing.
- What? It's surely not for nothing. Our daughter gets splinters in her feet every time she takes off her slippers or shoes and you know how much trouble I have to get her to keep them on. In addition, you don't even pay rent.

Separation and war

- The floors aren't my problem. You never should have moved here!
- In case you hadn't noticed, it wasn't as if I had a lot of alternatives, so please stop saying stupid things.

Marc has been difficult to live with since our last fight. I know that he's looking for a pretext to pick a fight and he still talks to his mom about the adoption thing.

On top of that, he's smoking too much dope lately.

I have no problem with him smoking lightly because it dispels his aggressive moods but now that he smokes too much, when he's running out, he becomes even more aggressive.

For weeks, he's been staying awake all night, alert for danger; then he goes to bed in the morning. He gets up to go to work or to hang around elsewhere. Around the home it is I who takes care of all the chores and the children; he, on the other hand, arrives when they're ready to go to bed. We don't go out much anymore and the zoo is probably the last place we went in 2 years. However, I still haven't found anyone to help me, although I am trying to, asking here and there, and I definitely am still way too messed up from giving birth to go to work.

A year later, our love affair is still going well, but money problems begin to plague us when Marc runs out of money to pay for his dope. I find it hard to continue being nice after he comes and empties my purse behind my back.

I don't hate him, nor do I judge him, but he seriously needs to go into treatment and he definitely needs help. We have to have a discussion about the matter.

As usual, I'm unable to come up with a cost-free idea, so I know that I'll be the one to blame again for someone else's mistakes.

Today I'm in the kitchen preparing lunch for the children. My purse is on the washing machine and Marc enters the room.

- Christine, I need money! Give me what you have. I need it, right now!
- No, I can't give you any. This is all I have left and I need it to buy

Separation and war

diapers and more food. I'm sorry but this week I'm very low on money, so ask someone else.

- I'm going to call my mother. She'll come and give it back to you tomorrow. So come on, give me the money!
- No, I can't. Wait for your mother to come. Why don't you call her first?

He gives me a push. It makes me angry but I try to control myself since it's not the first time that he's gotten this way over money. Things aren't going very well between us because of his problem and I told him the other day that I wouldn't tolerate being with him anymore if he didn't change his aggressive behavior, acting like an irresponsible thief.

He takes the phone and calls his mother.

- Mom, Christine is out of money to buy diapers and food. Can you help?

I listen to him lying, making me pass for an irresponsible person, so I interrupt angrily:

- Marc, no! Don't tell lies about me to your mother, you damn hypocrite! Don't you dare use me to get what you want from your mother.
- I'll call you back tomorrow, Mom.

Then he hangs up the phone.

- Shut up.

He goes to the washing machine to get my purse and grabs my wallet, saying:

- My mother is bringing you food and diapers tomorrow.
- Well, Marc. I say no. You've gone too far; I can't take any more. Furthermore, I need to get some things today. And I don't want your mother here, telling me how irresponsible I am.

I see him going through my purse.

- No, don't touch my purse. Fix your problem with your mother so that she gives you money. This problem of yours isn't any of my business! Besides, you should go spend some time at your mother's...

Separation and war

and get detoxed.
I snatch my wallet out of his hands.
- Let go of the little money that I have!
The fight begins. Marc shoves the table over, then jumps on me.
- Are you going to give me the money?
- Stop it. Let go of me. Help me, someone!
I scream.
He raises his fist and punches me on the leg, then slaps my face so hard that my lip starts to bleed. I'm lying on the floor with Marc on top of me and hear a knock at the back door.
- Open the door! It's the police!
The door is unlocked, so the officers come in, rushing right away to grab Marc and handcuff him.
It must be my uncle Oscar who called the police. He must have heard us fighting since he lives next door. Our daughter stands in the kitchen, watching the officer take Marc away. I can still see the terrified look in her eyes. This reminds me how scared I was of never seeing my father again, especially since I had imagined that someone was going to kill him and I was always terrified of officers when I saw one. Anyway, it breaks my heart to see her so emotionally hurt. As for the other officer sitting at the table writing his report, he leaves soon after and I have to wait for the court date. Meanwhile, there's a restraining order against Marc until a judgment is handed down. Also, even if I decide not to press charges, the law has an obligation to protect me.
Many days go by and I find it difficult by myself.
It's wintertime, it's the middle of the day and there's a knock at the door but I'm not expecting anyone.
I go downstairs and open the door to find Marc's oldest sister there, looking furious. I ask her:
- Yes, what do you want? Why did you come here?
- I've come to warn you that if you don't drop charges against my brother, you'll have to deal with me and you won't like that.

Separation and war

... - Hey, you! Don't come here to threaten me. I have enough of your brother for that! Also, if you're here just to be mean, then you have no business here. Please go away.

I then close the door, moving Beatrice away from the cold draft coming in through the open door.

About a week goes by. Marc calls me every day from his mother's house where he is being detoxed while awaiting his court date.

I'm happy that my wish has been granted, because there is hope for us if he gets better. About two weeks later, I'm trying to reach Marc on the phone and his mother tells me that he has gone out for the night. So I try calling some friends of ours who live nearby.

- Hey Luce, would Marc happen to be there?
- No, he went to see Caroline.
- Okay. Then I'll try calling him back sometime later.

Caroline is a girl I've known since I first started to play outside when I was 4 years old.

I haven't seen her since I was 7 except for one time, a couple of months ago at Luce's, where she came to deliver some marijuana to Marc. Anyhow, I start having some suspicions after many hours pass and he still hasn't come back from her place. Is he having an affair on top of his bad behavior?

I've had enough of him. I want to take a vacation far, far away, before I lose my mind. I'm unable to deal with all that is going on right now. So I get myself together and go straight away to the travel agency. I buy tickets for me and the children. We're all going to visit my mother for 3 weeks while waiting for the court date. This way, my mind will have a break from all my worries.

The next morning I finally reach Marc on the phone.

- Marc, I need something from you. I need for you to stop at the notary's office and sign an authorization for me to take the children on a trip to my mother's for 3 weeks.
- Well, no! If I do that, you won't come back!
- Listen to me, you. Don't start acting stupid. I've been visiting my

Separation and war

mother since I was 11 and never have I stayed longer than I was supposed to. And with children, there are even fewer chances that I would. To stay there, I would need to be much richer, plus it's a tourist area and there are a lot of army personnel there, too. There's no way I'd be able to stay there without being deported after 6 months. Marc, don't be stupid, I only want to take the children on a vacation and put my mind at ease. You at least owe me that after all you've made me suffer. It would give me a chance to go think about us and about our relationship. And, by the way, can you tell me where you were yesterday?

- Ok, I'll sign the authorization form for you. You know that I love you. I hope you'll forgive me.

Also, drop the charges against me.

- For now I'm not sure what I'm going to do. But I'm going to go think about it somewhere where I can think clearly.

I hang up the phone and am so excited about my trip that I start packing my things. Our plane will be leaving on the weekend.

I guess I was at a period of my life where I was young and ignorant and somewhat stupid, which often leads to making mistakes.

Marc's at my door the night before our departure, in spite of the restraining order against him. He's standing on the porch, holding a bottle of wine, so I let him in. He goes to sit on the sofa, my authorization forms in hand.

After drinking the whole bottle, we start to feel drunk and we end up spending the night together, talking about the good times we had had together. At sunrise, Marc leaves.

Last night I could have sworn that Caroline's soul was present with Marc, and this is why I am almost sure that he had sex with her. What a relief it is to know that I am going on vacation. Once I'm there, I'll be able to ask my mom for advice. Evening comes, and in a blink of an eye, we're aboard the plane and arriving at the airport, where my mom is waiting. Exhausted from the trip, I'm glad to see someone that loves me and to finally be far away from my problems.

Separation and war

Right away, my mother wants me to feel like I'm on vacation.
- Christine, tomorrow we'll find you a nice hotel where you'll be able to rest, enjoy the beach and be waited on. The kids and I will come to visit you at the hotel.
- That's a great idea, Mom.

A couple of days later, I'm settled in a nice place. I take the time to call Marc every two days so that he doesn't worry about the kids. I do this so that he won't start saying that I've run away to hide and will never come back. I'm not stupid enough not to know that there is nowhere to hide and that putting ourselves in a safe place has a high cost. The hotel where we end up staying is right on the beach. There's also a pool and a restaurant on the other side where we go to eat every day. It's the good life, and I only wish I could live like this every day or almost every day. Not too far is a big bar named Christine which opened right after my brother was born. The owner is a friend of my step-dad's or a member of his family. I remember once the man came to tell me that he named the bar after me to make me feel at home in case one day I got lost, but I'm not sure he was being truthful. He also told me that he felt guilty for losing my mother to them, but I wonder if he just said these things to be nice. I remember when I was 14 years old, when they first opened, my step-dad took me and introduced me to the owner and his son. The bar is beautiful, with mirrors everywhere. Many well-known stars have made videos inside it. However, during my stay, being with the children, I won't be going there.

I'm walking outside, listening to the sound of the sea, feeling the warm breeze caressing my skin and sweetening me with its salty smell. I walk inside the restaurant to have lunch, but wonder why, every time I come in, the waiter is laughing, pointing me out to his friends. I hear him say.
- Es ella, es ella!

It makes me laugh, but I can't seem to recognize him. He is particularly attentive with me, unlike Marc, since we started to fight.

Separation and war

I do want to stay faithful to Marc, but when I start thinking about Caroline and about the bruises I still have, it makes me want to try and be with someone else to see if life could be better elsewhere. At night, I make my usual call to Marc. From what Luce tells me, he has gone out with Caroline again.

I'm unable to contain my rage any longer. It makes me so mad. I've been gone for nearly three weeks and I'm trying not to cross the fence, but he has gone out again with Caroline, the nude dancer who sells marijuana. Well, no way, I say to myself. My daughter sits there, smiling at me and looking so pretty, but she doesn't understand what I'm saying. I need to talk to an adult, so, without giving it much thought, I decide that I am also going to enjoy myself, just like Marc. Maybe there's something better for me in life. Clearly there must me better things in life than being abused and cheated on. I'm only 23 years old, so it's not too late for me. And these days, women are liberated and have the same rights as men. So I'm going to ask the waiter if he wants to come with me for a walk on the beach and then for a drink and a chat with the sound of the sea in the background.

I gather my courage and nervously go over to ask him. I stand before him, trembling, but I persevere and ask him.

- Do you want to go out and take a walk on the beach with me tonight?
- Are you sure you want to go out with me?
- Well, yes I am, if I'm asking.
- Yes, then. I finish at seven. Come back this way then and we'll go somewhere.

Night arrives and we're walking towards the beach together. I wonder why he asked me if I was sure I wanted to go out; after all, it's not as if I had asked him to have sex. I realize that my idea to ask him out in order to get his opinion about my situation might not be appropriate. We are close to the hotel where I am staying. The beach is deserted and I can see the people in the lobby since there are floor-to-ceiling windows all around. On the beach, the wind is chilly and the brilliant

Separation and war

moon is reflecting its beauty on the surface of the water.
The young man beside me looks very tall.
- Come! Let's go sit somewhere further.
- Sure.
While walking, I talk to him, asking him for his point of view.
- What do you think of a woman being treated badly? Should she endure it or should she just leave the man who's mistreating her?
I continue telling him my story, hoping to find a solution that satisfies me.
- You should go back home and take him back. It would be the least complicated solution, although he shouldn't lay a hand on you. He certainly deserves to be punished for that.
His answer doesn't really help me.
I'm shivering from the cold, so he gives me his shirt and rubs my arms to warm me up.
It's the first man that's touched me in about 5 years other than Marc. It makes me feel weird and I became hypnotized enough that I just let him continue. His face then moves close to mine and he kisses me softly, lays me down on the sand, then slips his hand under my skirt to move my panties to the side and thrusts his penis inside me. I feel the heat of his body. I look at his muscled chest and I see the shiny chain and cross hanging from his neck. Why do I have the impression that it's not the first time I've been intimate with him? As soon as he comes, I sit up. Everything happens so fast that I don't even have enough time to think about whether I want him to do it to me or not. It just happens. Everything goes silent and we get up to walk back towards the hotel elevator, where he wishes me goodnight and seems to be in a big rush to leave.
I smile at him and wish him goodnight as well. I want to ask him more questions about himself but I fall into a trance.
At the same time, I realize that all inside communications with Marc are gone. I go up to my room, go to bed and all I can see are the images of that man I can't recognize.

Separation and war

It's my last night at the hotel and I'm going to stay at my mother's until the departure of my plane in 2 days. I totally forget to ask the man on the beach for his phone number, name and address. All I know is that he's here with his sister to work.

The next day, before leaving and since I'm staying at my mother's, I decide to take a taxi and go to the restaurant to ask him more questions about himself. I'm disappointed to see that the restaurant is closed. I end up leaving that night, taking the plane back home without any information about the man I had gone to the beach with.

I have committed the sin of infidelity but Marc did too. One thing that I'll never understand about Marc's stories is that he always denies everything he's done wrong. Even today, Marc says that he never met Caroline and has no idea who she is, even after she called Marc by his name when entering the room at Luce's place right in front of me. Yet he still denies ever having seen her. He's basically a pathetic liar; that's the only logical explanation, unless he has Alzheimer's disease. It's Easter. I've just spent the evening at my dad's small mansion with the children.

The court date is in about a month. At suppertime my father decides that he'll accompany me.

The weeks fly by. I have time to visit my doctor for a physical exam. I'm fine except that I'm pregnant again. Then the court date arrives at last.

My father tells me to wait, so I don't even go inside the courtroom. He signs a paper which I am not able to see, exonerating Marc, and I conclude that the punishment of not seeing each other for such a long time is sufficient enough. That night after court, Marc comes back to live with me. I tell myself that since Marc is now afraid of being incarcerated, he'll take better care of me. Marc and I stay together and everything goes well between us, except for the fact that we need to move. Time passes and it's finally time for me to give birth. On that important day of my life, I am left alone at the hospital

Separation and war

and Marc doesn't even come see me while I'm there. He just tells me on the phone:
- I can't get the children ready to come and can't find a baby sitter.
I find it very difficult to be alone during these painful moments. My father comes the next day to visit me but that's all. Something even worse comes my way to change the path of my life on the day I return home. I'm walking towards the taxi and suddenly I see a ghost.
He's standing there frozen in the middle of the parking lot, looking at me with a murderous look. It's Fly. He's back from Jamaica. I haven't seen or spoken to him in about 4 years and to see him like this gives me the chills. I hurry into the taxi, pretending that I don't see Fly and ask the driver to start driving and get me home as fast as he can.
When I get home, with the children jumping around everywhere and with all I have to do, I forget that I'd seen him.
Several months later, Marc and I decide that we're going to get married but he's acting unstable and I'm not sure what's made him become so nervous and aggressive.
It could have something to do with our mistakes, although this isn't what made him crazy enough to try to run away.
His strategy to escape starts one morning.
This particular morning, as usual, after Marc gets up, he goes downstairs to the store to get the Montreal paper.
I'm finishing cleaning up after lunch when I hear the door slam. I guess it must be Marc, and I'm right; he comes bursting into the kitchen all upset, and then abruptly throws the newspaper on the table.
- Here! Look at what happened to your stupid asshole!
- Which stupid asshole? What are you talking about?
I take a look at the newspaper, which shows a photograph of Fly. The article says that Fly died after being shot in the middle of the street near the hospital. It says that some black men were seen running away from the crime scene.
- By the way, Fly's not my asshole. I was only with him for a couple of

Separation and war

months and that was 4 years ago. What's your problem with me about this? Let me remind you that you were with his sister at the time.

Marc becomes hysterical and yells:

- I'm leaving. Fix your problems by yourself.
- What problems are you talking about? If you're referring to Fly, he's not my problem. But I must say that it's sad, don't you think so?

Marc becomes weird. It's as though he's no longer with me and is no longer my friend and he looks at me suspiciously. He seems less bent on causing a fight. He's got an idea in his mind and I wish I knew what it is. Marc decides to leave and doesn't tell me where he's going. He goes to see the child protection service. He plans to leave me and will use a story that doesn't concern me, or he'll use lies.

Alone with the children, I pause for a moment and remember back to that night a week ago when I was alone with them and heard a knock at the door. I didn't open the door and became very quiet when I saw Fly's shadow through the window.

Don't ask me how he found my address but as soon as I saw him, I was scared to the core. I'm thinking and trying to understand why Fly came to see me when he knew I had children and a new life. Well it's useless to try to understand, because I'll never find out anyway what he wanted from me and it's probably better that way.

Two weeks later, it's the middle of the night. Marc arrived late that night and I'm already in bed when I hear a big boom.

- Marc, please go see what that is. And, by the way, Oscar came by earlier and asked me to tell you to go see him about an important issue as soon as you arrived.
- I'll go see him later. Don't worry; it's probably just a door that slammed.
- Promise me that you'll go see what it was; I'm very tired and I'm going back to bed. If you think that you don't want to do it, tell me now and I'll make an effort to go check it out.
- Don't worry. I said I'd do it as soon as I finish what I'm doing here.

Separation and war

- Okay, then. Goodnight.

I go back to bed and fall right back into a deep sleep.

As for Marc, he never goes to see my uncle and he falls asleep on the sofa almost right away.

The children usually get up very early in the morning, around six, but this morning they're not waking up.

It's almost noon and everyone is still asleep. Suddenly, my soul starts to travel in the in-between world and into a red dark light. Not knowing what to do, I try walking forward but I have trouble because the atmosphere is very heavy. I'm trying to get to my father's store, thinking that he'll know what to do. On my way, I can't see the road well but all of a sudden I can hear their voices. I'm half-blind and scared and can only see their shadows. My father and his friend are there, laughing and smoking their joint, and I try speaking to them, shouting so they can hear me.

- Help me! I'm here! Can you see me? Please, I need your help.

They can't hear me so I tug on their shirts so that they can see that I'm there but nothing happens. They don't respond. I feel as though I'm dead and my soul is trapped in this dark alley in between the two worlds. Then suddenly, in a dizzy whirlwind I awaken in my bed. I must have had a bad dream. But the children are also not awake. They're probably trapped in their sleep just like me, so I go wake them up, though it takes some time to rouse them. What's happening here? I've never felt so bad. I intuitively go to my uncle's door to see if he's ok and he doesn't answer, so I take a peek through the window. He's lying dead on the floor, his face white as a ghost, his body soaking in a pool of blood. The fact that no one woke this morning was unusual and something I don't understand, but I know that after death the soul goes through another dimension. We were brought into the other world as part of a paranormal experience, and we were trapped in a waking dream, our soul awake and being carried around in a place that I couldn't clearly see. I don't know why this happened since I am not aware of all the laws that keep us

Separation and war

connected to each other in this human world.

The next day Marc acts paranoid. I think the death scared him and for some reason he's wanting to cause problems for me again. I hear him talking on the phone with his mother, saying more stupid things such as:

- Mom, why didn't you tell me it was aunty? Do you know that her father will kill me if he catches me? Mom, I have to leave this place. I'm scared that I'm going to die.

He even starts to shout over the phone:

- It's the mafia, Mom. You'll never understand all the things I heard inside.

I see that he's traumatized, although I don't hear everything he's saying and whether he's referring to my dad when he makes all his crazy accusations.

Well, I'm sure that he doesn't know the difference between the echoes and visions coming from the memories of Fly and the telepathic echoes of my silent, living father.

For a long time, I haven't been able to understand why Marc's scared of my father but today I deduced that he must be confusing my father with Fly and other people.

He hangs up the phone and acts as if nothing happened.

- What were you talking about on the phone with your mother? It sounded serious.

- It's nothing important. Just some family argument issues with my aunt and mom.

I set my curiosity aside, but keep my guard up, because I know he's preparing something to do me wrong.

A couple of days later, in the early afternoon, I'm doing some laundry in this non-kid-safe washing machine. So, in order to avoid accidents, I always stay in the kitchen next to the machine while it's running. I often end up punishing the kids because they just keep pushing the chair towards the machine to be able to see and feel it shaking. The problem is that they open the machine, which doesn't lock.

Separation and war

This afternoon, Marc is home with me and it's time to give the baby his bottle, so I take advantage of Marc's presence and ask him to watch the kids around the machine.

- Marc, will you stay in the kitchen and watch that the children don't climb on top of the dryer? Tell me if you can't and I'll just turn it off.
- Don't worry, I'm here. Go in the room and give the baby his bottle.
- You're sure I don't need to worry? Promise me you'll stay here because I warn you, they always climb.
- Yes, I'm telling you that I'm here.
- Okay, then. I trust you.

I give the baby his bottle in the warmth and tranquility of his room, sitting in the rocking chair. Five minutes later I suddenly hear a hell of a scream coming from the kitchen. Carrying the baby, I run into the kitchen and see my little girl inside the machine and my little boy on the dryer, holding her hand.

I yell very loud:
- Marc, you stupid fuck, what the hell are you doing?

He's in a cloud of smoke, opening the bathroom door, and he's looking at the same thing I'm looking at. I reach into the machine, still holding the baby in one arm, and try to grab hold of Beatrice with the other. I have to keep her head from going under the water, because the machine's still shaking from side to side. I can feel how frightened she is. She's still screaming, but with only one hand holding her, I can't do miracles, so her leg ends up a bit bruised.

Marc arrives shortly after me and turns off the machine. He then takes her out, telling me that I'm stupid. Anyhow, I think I had been clear enough when I asked him to watch them carefully. It was his mistake for sure and he knew. I become so angry with him that we end up arguing for the rest of the day. The fight intensifies in the evening and we finally split up. Once again I am savagely wounded by him but this time, I'm afraid of dying and can no longer forgive him. During this episode of abuse, I have nothing left to lose, so it's the perfect time to talk to him about what happened when I was on

Separation and war

vacation, since it's possible that the guy on the beach is the biological father of the baby. On the porch, Marc pushes me, trying to make me fall three floors to the ground, so I scream:
- Marc, stop it! Please, let me go! And what do you think of this: the baby might not be yours!
As soon as I say this, Marc freezes and goes quiet. I consider myself lucky because he stops manhandling me and goes off to think about it.
I might have made a mistake, but our separation had nothing to do with the baby's paternity. Even before I left for vacation, we were having some problems that were probably unfixable.
I can only think that destiny might have brought us together, to let us make our mistakes so that we'd know what not to do if we ever were to restart our lives separately and elsewhere with other people. I did have some difficulties with the problem of the baby's paternity. From the start, I tried to avoid thinking that it was possible. What made me explore this possibility, even though I knew it would destroy my image, was that the baby seemed to have some developmental issues. I only pursued this path in order to help my child live a better and more normal life. I know that the law of nature follows its own course, but sometimes it can be influenced. I wanted to find that person to tell him so and see if my child could improve. Meanwhile, Marc insists upon taking a paternity test. The test results show that he's the biological father but I have my doubts, not because it isn't the best thing to be, but because the child seems to understand Spanish and Italian better. Also, when he's in my arms, I see the man I walked with on the beach. The much bigger issue is that the child has physical problems which are difficult to explain. I know that the biological father has a role to play which helps some stages of the child's growth. Therefore, I don't care about what the results show. I'll do whatever it takes to make him better and if I'm wrong, well, I'm only wasting a bit of my time.
As for our relationship, even if I feel guilty about our break-up, I know

Separation and war

that it's due to Marc's aggressiveness with me because the detail about the paternity didn't exist when our problems first started. On the day after our fight, Marc goes back to the child protection services office to report me, telling them lies.

Because Marc is scared of what might happen because of what he did, he has his sister, a head nurse, call them. She influences them in their decision, as they probably see her as one of their superiors. I also think that Marc spoke to the judge and everyone else about Fly, trying to implicate me, which explains why no lawyers wanted to take my case or help me after they had spoken to his lawyer.

It's a shame that I'm not able to find help anywhere. I presume that they get scared when they hear the names of the people involved in what Marc is talking about, considering these people are known to be in with the mob. The worst part of all this matter is that I'm unable to find out what's being said between the lawyers and the judge since no one tells me what's going on. It's impossible for me to defend myself when I don't even know what I'm defending myself against. They decide to come take the children from me, after accusing me of lies behind my back. According to the lies, I had put my child in the washing machine, I had wanted to kill Marc and I had wanted to send a killer to his home. In the end, I lost everything and had people trying hunting me down. One odd thing is that every time I was arrested, Claude's uncle or someone connected to the crime was either on the phone or present at the courthouse.

It must have all been arranged by corrupt members of the law, because they were asking the lawyer representing me for five thousand dollars' bail under the table for my release. This lawyer didn't talk to me very much and wouldn't tell me what was really going on. Since I had not committed any crimes, I was scared, especially when they kept me in prison. Inside the prison some women wanted to beat me up and the place was disease-ridden and disgusting. I want to sue them for mental anguish and for putting my life in danger. Now, if I had committed any crime whatsoever, I would

Separation and war

have accepted and paid the price which was to be around these people in such a place, but that was not the case. I blame them for the heart problems that I started to have after being frightened from all they did to me. The only rights I was entitled to was to visit my children at Marc's place. That didn't work out, since every time I visited, his mother or sister called the police, making up stories against me and they weren't even there. His mother and Marc kept threatening me, telling me they'd have me locked up somewhere, so that I'd never see my children again.

The police just keep knocking at my door. They're after me non-stop. They're definitely up to no good. I really don't know what to do about it and no one can or will help me. I watch the news and see so many weird murders involving couples with children that the conclusion of death isn't logical to me. It makes me stop and wonder if the police or other people around were really the ones who committed the crime in order to steal the insurance money. The only thing I know is that I am in danger and that they've chosen me to be their next victim but I won't let them win. So I need to find help or a place to hide where they have no rights. I decide to leave for Mexico again, and at the same time I'll try to find that guy to tell him he could be the father, even though I don't really need his direct help, just some of his inner time to see that the boy exists, or whatever spiritual connection is needed to make my child better. I'm not asking him to become my boyfriend, nor do I want his money; my only goal is to try this awakening to see if it makes my boy better. It happened that I was right, because as soon as the person had heard about the child from his friend, the boy became engulfed in a cloud which gave him the time needed for him to get his balance and his eyes finally secreted tears of water. In my opinion, it made him regain control over his body. I knew that the animal laws of the human body have special characteristics that make it work properly. This is why I've always said that the reality of traditional medicine, which perceives the human race as lacking any connections whatsoever, isn't always

Separation and war

able to cure and fix problems. The important thing is that he now is normal and fine. Meanwhile, while on my trip, I'm trying to forgive Marc for his behavior. However, even though I try, I remember that he had put my life in danger with his lies. I really try to recapture the love but it dies inside every time I remember being beaten and locked up in disgusting places or could of even being killed because of the lies he told. On my trip, I meet rich and popular people from California and Europe who are on their spring break. I also realize that very rich and smart people own shares in the hotels in this area. I feel lucky and privileged to be approached by these good people, although I miss some seemingly good opportunities. I remember during one of my first trips, I met an 83-year-old man who asked me to go to lunch with him. This was back when I was learning to sell time shares in hotels. This man had over 100 million dollars' worth of time shares. My mother had been trying to get my father to engage in this type of investment for a long time but he was never interested. Briefly, we were in the employees' break room and the man introduced me to a young man working for him who was popular, well known, rich and handsome and lived both in Europe and the U.S. What a disappointment it was that I had to miss my date with the guy because I had to return to Canada for a court date. Life in Mexico was paradise but it was way too expensive for me to live there. Also, I have a phobia of dangerous reptiles, which makes it impossible for me to stay in the affordable places for very long.

I make many trips to Mexico in order to get away from the corrupt authorities but still, every time I arrive at my apartment in Canada, the police don't miss the opportunity to come and get me. This is how it happens: upon returning after a three months' absence from the country, I'm at my home for 6 hours and the police are already at my door. It's impossible that I've done anything wrong but they keep coming, ordering me to open my door.

I don't understand why I'm the unprotected prey, the defenseless innocent person. I wish I knew what I could do to be protected from

Separation and war

them. I survive that particular arrest, and I manage to travel many more times after that and once more I come back full of hope after talking to Marc on the phone. I'm so sure he'll finally come clean and be honest. This means that I'll have normal time with my children, which I miss so much. I believe that if he loves them, he won't deprive them of their mother. He knows the truth; therefore, he knows that I never hurt them. Anyway, I'm wrong. Marc only has an instinct for revenge or he's under the control of his family. I can understand that he has a broken heart but his sadness makes him very mean, in my opinion. If I can get my money back I'll be able to pay for a good lawyer, move and work, but that's not going to happen for a while because they took my entire share. I also am being deprived of the precious moments of watching my children grow up, which I can never get back. I am so disappointed and angry about the injustices done to me by corrupt people who took my fortune and made me suffer.

The police are at my door once again, saying:
- Open the door or we'll break it down.
- Why are you coming to get me again?
- We don't really know, you must have missed your court date or some such thing. Regardless, we have to take you and bring you in. Tomorrow, you can ask the judge.
- What kind of stupid things are you telling me? This isn't legal. I have my rights!
- Just open the door if you don't want anything bad to happen to you.
- I've done nothing wrong; I'm telling you, your illegal stupidities are gonad cost you.

I have to let them take me once again since I don't know what else to do. This time, I go to court in the morning and they tell me that I have to wait for the judge to come back from his vacation before I can be released from prison. I can't stand being in prison. It makes me feel sick the way they mistreat me and the beds could be infested with all kinds of diseases. Thinking hard about what to do to get help, I

Separation and war

remember my mother talking about the U.N., which gives me an idea. I take the public phone installed in the cell and dial the embassy number and the woman gives me the number for the human rights organization, which I call:
- Hello. Is there someone who can help me? I'm being held in prison but I haven't committed a crime. My father's a millionaire and says he doesn't care if they kill me; he's not paying anything.
- Yes, we can help you. Tell me where you are.
- I'm at the St-Jerome women's prison.
- Wait patiently; we'll be there in no time.

In under a couple of minutes, two policewomen arrive at my cell. They enter, come over to me, grab my arm very hard and start to pull me forcibly.
- Okay, you foolish girl. Come on and hurry up! Let's go. We have no right to keep you here. Why did you call those people? You shouldn't have called the embassy, you trouble-maker! Come on, now. We're taking you somewhere else before they get here.

One of them restrains my hands and feet with chained handcuffs. They take me to a small cell inside a station for the night and refuse to allow me to make any calls.
- Tomorrow, you'll go before the judge; meanwhile, stay quiet, do what we say and don't cause any problems.

I remain quiet, trying to stay calm, knowing I'm being treated illegally as part of a scam. I'm afraid for my life.

The next day, they take me before a judge. I think I recognize the lawyer who is pressing charges against me. She looks like one of Marc's cousins. During the trial, I don't understand the language they are using. I've watched many legal shows in English, which I might understand better. In addition, my French is rusty; since I've been to Mexico, I haven't spoken or heard French for at least three months. So I'm very confused about what's being said. I have to stop them since my lawyer isn't doing or saying anything to help me. I have to act fast before the charges against me get worse.

Separation and war

- Your honor, may I please interrupt to say? Please take your time speaking because I don't understand what you're saying or try to say it in English.
- Clause number…

I interrupt him.

- Clause what, your honor? I don't know any clause, so tell me this in another way, please, because, as I said, I don't understand.
- All right, then. You're not allowed out because you're charged with death threats. Do you understand that?
- Are you fucking kidding me? I've never made any threats with any object nor have I done this to anyone. No, I refuse to accept these accusations. You have no right to do this to me. Get me out of here. I want to see another judge immediately because I don't understand you and I believe that you are corrupt. Damn rotten system! Get me out of here! I've been treated like an animal and I am not one.
- I can't let you leave if you don't plead guilty.
- No, I'm not guilty of anything. I refuse to have a criminal record when I've done nothing wrong. I might have let some bad words slip out in a panic but I took them back right away. Also, you have no proof of any of this, as I haven't made any real threats.
- I can't help you. You'll have to go back to prison.
- I have rights; I demand to see another judge and to be transferred to a hospital until then. I might have a heart attack if you put me back in prison. My heart isn't very strong and I'm innocent.
- No problem. If you insist, you'll be placed in a psychiatric ward until your next hearing.
- You have no right to treat me like this. You have no proof to accuse me like this. I'll get back at you.
- Be quiet, or you'll be kept here longer.

I am finally transferred to a hospital. Meanwhile, some agents from the human rights protection organization are still trying to find me. They go to the prison but the officer pretends not to know where I am. I have great hopes that the hospital is going to be a better

Separation and war

environment, but they treat me like an animal. They keep me in handcuffs and put chains on my feet for more than 2 weeks. One of the nurses seems to hate me and acts and talks mean to me. Once, when she sees that I'm not taking the pills they're giving me, she becomes hysterical, trying to force me to take them even after I say to her:

- Ma'am, please understand that I'm allergic to lots of medications and I won't take these pills.
- I don't care what you say. Take them!

This woman must be an accomplice to that judge who wants to harm me.

The next day, she arrives unexpectedly in my room, lifting me up by force and squeezing me so hard that she leaves bruises on my arm. She drags me into a room where she puts me in a strait jacket then attaches me to a bed. She has this crazy look, as though she needs to win a fight but one that she's in alone.

- Take your pills, I said.

She takes out a needle and shows it to me.

- If you don't take your pills, I'll inject you with this.
- You have to tell me what's in that needle first.
- No, I don't have to tell you anything. To me, you're a criminal who shouldn't be cared for.

I just start screaming very loudly.

- Help! Someone, help! I'm allergic. She wants to kill me.

I scream so loud that a male nurse from the floor below hears me screaming and in less than a minute, he's standing at the door.

- Let her go or I'll call the director to file a complaint about you. What the hell are you doing to this girl?

The young man recognizes me and comes over to me. He was the one there the last time they arrested me, when I was sent to hospital after my complaining.

- Are you all right? I see that they brought you here again.
- Yes. I'm so happy to see you. This woman is nuts. You saved my life,

Separation and war

I think. Thank you very much.
- Don't worry about her anymore. I'll take care of her. Is there anything else I can do for you?
- Yes, I want to make a phone call and she won't let me.
- Yes, I'll also tell her to let you make phone calls.

The mad female nurse gives me a dirty look but finally leaves me alone and lets me use the phone.
I take advantage of the situation to call the human rights protection organization again.
- Hello. I called two days ago.

I have trouble talking. I'm on the verge of bursting into tears. I can't hold my tears back any longer and I start to cry.
- Calm down. Yes, I remember you. I'm also happy you called because we weren't able to find you anywhere. Just tell me where you are and I'll send someone right away.

In under an hour, a woman dressed in army gear and holding an M16 walks into the hospital, looking for me. She and two others stay with me 24 hours a day until finally they send me to court. I don't know if I'd still be alive if I hadn't had this protection. I remember during my hospitalization that there was a New Year's Eve party on TV and I heard my name being called in the crowd. A few days later, the news broadcast the image of the judge in front of my stepfather's rich aunt, asking for money for my release.

They broadcast this event for a couple of seconds with the voice of my aunt yelling:
- Take whatever you want, but get the hell out of my house!

I find it so weird that the judge was going to Mexico on vacation to ask my step-dad's aunt for money. That doesn't have much to do with my life. This propaganda is a little too suspicious to my taste and I'm starting to understand that fraud and robbery are occurring around me.

Finally my court date arrives. I'm so exhausted from being scared that I'm not able to think straight. While waiting for my turn to go before

Separation and war

the judge, I'm held in a cell downstairs from the courtroom. In there I hear some of what's going on in the courtroom and I become very confused when I hear the name Claude as a witness.
That's it! It all makes sense now! I think I know what's really going on: it's the stories about Fly. That's why they keep coming to arrest me. They used Marc as an excuse to come for me, when in fact they were trying to put me away for other reasons. I shout loud enough for everyone on the floor above to hear:
- Claude's father, if you can hear me, I want to know what your problem with me is. Is it because your son's murderer, is dead, so now you have not the guilty one alive to blame, and you want to use me in order to vent your anger?
I stop shouting since I don't really know what's happening up there. The officer doesn't waste any time in arriving and takes me to the chamber to appear before the judge. It's a new judge, who addresses me in a friendly manner:
- You're free to go and I don't want to see you in here again. Good-bye.
The nightmare is suddenly and finally over and I go back home by myself.
Even after I get home, I'm still feeling terrorized about everything I had endured. Sleeping in my bed, I feel like I'm going to have a heart attack. My chest hurts so much that I start to vomit and I stay sick for at least a month. Two day after getting out of prison, I'm waiting for Mustafa to arrive. I've been seeing Mustafa on and off for about two years. Our relationship isn't very sane but he comes to see me and I need it. While waiting, I watch the news. The news item concerns a military investigation that's taking place, and I listen attentively when I hear that it's happening at the hospital where I had just been. The reporter says:
- Hypodermic needles have been found containing a substance that causes death six months after injection. Any person who received this injection should contact us at...

Separation and war

...These injections were given at the psychiatric ward of the St-Jerome hospital and could have been given elsewhere. We are reopening 50 fatality cases which we believe are related to this medication. All those concerned are asked to call and all cases will be dealt with individually.

I'm sitting in my living room and can't believe what I'm hearing. Now certain that they really wanted to kill me, I get sick to my stomach again.

I fall into a meditative state, thinking about how to defend myself and realizing that no one loves me anymore. I almost lose my will to live. Nevertheless, I consider myself lucky to have avoided getting that injection!

Mustafa finally arrives. I'm going to be comforted.

- Please come in! I'm so happy to see you.
- Well, this is no time to be happy. I'm not feeling good.

He then jumps on me and, pinning me down on the floor, tries to slap me in the face.

- Stop it, for Christ's sake! What's wrong with you? Please stop! I love you; don't hurt me! I haven't done anything to you. I was held by the police for over a month and they even tried to kill me.

Mustafa finally lets go of me, puts his bag down on the table and sits on a kitchen chair.

- My daughter's dead. She was just seven months old.
- Oh, my God. That's terrible! What happened?
- She had internal hemorrhaging in the brain. They gave her anesthesia but the medication appeared to be too strong for her age and she died.
- They're crazy! I'm sure that giving general anesthesia before the age of two is illegal!

Mustafa looks at me with tears in his eyes, thinking about what I just said, then reaches in his bag and takes out a piece of paper.

- I swear! Look, I have her death certificate.
- I believe you, Mustafa. That's not what I'm telling you.

Separation and war

Mustafa stops talking and lowers his head.

- I'm going to look into this later. Let's just go rest together for a while.

Mustafa hasn't been very lucky with his loved ones. When he was eight, his dad was killed in the army and now his daughter has died. His daughter passed away while I was incarcerated. I wonder if our sexual connection could have affected his daughter. Could she have felt my emotions while these corrupt people were terrorizing and trying to harm me? When the connection is unbroken, I can see and sometimes hear them, so Mustafa and his daughter might have also heard and felt me. That reminds me again that these corrupt people always find a way to cause misfortune when they act for illegal purposes.

Mustafa doesn't stay very long but he says many stupid things, such as:

- I'm going to blow up the White House.

He also starts talking about his ex.

- My ex's family is Russian. She and I broke up before our daughter was born but now she and her family have plans to seize my rich uncle's hotel in Morocco. I'm going to blow up everything around me. I can't take it anymore.

- Please, Mustafa! Calm down. Stop being so aggravated.

We end the evening having sex, after which he goes to his mother's house nearby.

These days I've been arguing a lot with my dad and I've been blaming him for many things. I feel it's his fault that I'm not able to spend time with my children since he's not helping me by giving me money for a better place to live and for a good lawyer. He still owes me my share. I've given up trying to understand why I'm always the one left aside everywhere with everyone. Anyhow, I've decided to try to live near my mother for good. At least over there the police and their killer accomplices will no longer be able to hunt me down like an animal. I pack my bags, buy a cheap airplane ticket and I'm ready to start my

Separation and war

life elsewhere.
There's no place to hide but there are places that are safer. When I arrive, I don't have lots of money, nor do I have any furniture.
When I get to my mother's place with my luggage, she makes a scene because she doesn't agree with my decision.
She's at the kitchen table, correcting her students' papers. Anyhow, when I came in the door, she greets me with harsh words:
- What are you doing here? You can't stay here! You have to find another place to live!
- But Mom, what can I do now?
- I don't know. I think my husband can try to find you a job. But you'll have to go live elsewhere. This is the best I can do for you. And are you aware that you won't be able to live in this country indefinitely if you're not married to a Mexican? And please don't tell me that you want to marry a Mexican. It's truly not a good idea. You should go back home. It's the best thing for you to do.
- I could go back to Canada every six months to have my visa renewed.
- Sure, but you need a special visa from the Mexican government to be allowed to work here.
Tell me, what will you do for money? I can't afford to support you!
- I have no idea. Let me think about it, I'm too tired now, so let me get some rest.
- Okay, just use your brother's bed for now.
The next morning Martini finds me a job selling tours and renting cars for travelers.
My mother serves the usual spicy eggs and sausage to Martini.
Martini is happy to tell me of his plan to keep me here. He's heard my mom cry many times because she missed me, so he wants to help me in order to make my mother happy.
- Christina, your job will involve going on tours to Chichen Itza in the company of a guide, and you'll be translating what he says to the tourists into French.

Separation and war

My mother adds:
- You have to work six months before the boss can ask for legal papers for you to work.
- But that doesn't make sense, having to be illegal to become legal! That's stupid.

My mom finishes getting ready to go to her teaching job.
- I'm leaving for work now. Come see me if you want.
- Okay, I'll try to.

She kisses me goodbye and leaves with Martini.

The next day, I go to work and Martini tries to find me a hotel to live in since there's no room for me at their place other than a hammock in the middle of the living room. After a week at work, it's payday at the office. I wait patiently for my turn to be paid but the boss runs out of money before getting to me.

One of the employees behind the counter looks at me oddly and says:
- Christina, don't worry. You'll get your pay next week.

At work, I get sexually harassed by the men who only talk to me to ask me to go out to fuck. The bottom line at this job is that they never pay me, and they tell me it's because I refuse to have sex with any of them.

I start to notice that life isn't that easy here, but I don't let myself get discouraged too easily. I decide to go see a friend I'd met here since I first started traveling back and forth.

He's a police officer who patrols the area around Fifth Avenue in Playa Del Carmen.

My stepdad isn't able to do anything about my not getting paid, plus he has a fight about it with the owner and he even removes his tour business listing from the hotel list where he works, but it still doesn't make them pay me. When I explain my situation to my police officer friend, he decides to go with me to the tour operator's office. We are in the middle of the street in front of the tour operator's office and my friend suddenly starts talking loudly.
- What's going on here? Where's Christina's pay?

Separation and war

Two of the men I worked with are outside, running away as fast as they can, screaming:
- Her friends are killers! Help!

Inside, the boss hears what's happening and signals to me to come inside. He then hands me some money and says:
- You no longer work here.

Getting paid is a good thing but what am I going to do now? I wonder how people manage to live here. It's not working out for me, so I'll have to leave Mexico, even though I don't want to. I'll never be able to live here if I don't have enough money to support myself and it's expensive. On top of it all, it's dangerous here, even though the beach seems like paradise, with all the vacationers walking by, greeting me and smiling at me nicely.

One day, I'm walking down the street, with lots of people around, when suddenly a man grabs me by the arm and forces me to go with him to his room nearby. I scream for help but no one comes to help me. Weakened from trying to fight him off, I decide to stop resisting before he kills me. Luckily I have a condom in my purse, which will at least prevent me from getting an STD. I beg him to put it on, trying to scare him into it.
- I might have a disease, so please stop it.

I don't manage to scare him enough to stop raping me, but he does put the condom on. I keep my eyes closed until he's finished and as soon as I get the chance to escape, I run outside.

He doesn't follow me and I'm able to reach the place where my police friend is posted to tell him what just happened. When the police officer and I arrive at the scene of the crime, the man is nowhere to be found. The landlady doesn't have any information about him. These are hard times for me. My mother is angry with me. She refuses to see me, thinking that this tactic will make me go back home, which is what she wants. Jobless and penniless, I'm forced to live in the streets for at least a week, with the beach and the canopy of stars my bedroom at night, but unable to sleep because of the

Separation and war

constant fear of danger. I beg for change or food. I've never felt so bad or poor and I pity those that lead lives like this, unfit for human beings. All my pride and strength is being stripped from me and if I ever thought of myself as being special, well I now know that some people treat and see other people as less than nothing, because that's how I'm being treated.

There's a saying that says that the lower a person falls, the higher that person will be when he wakes up.

I'm waiting to receive a little money from my father to either buy my plane ticket and come back home, or pay for another month's stay in a hotel, so that I can stay far away from the bad officers who are after me in Canada. In addition, during the whole time I've been here, I haven't seen the guy from the beach, even though I know he got the message from one of his friends. Anyhow, that doesn't matter anymore since my child is fine now. While waiting for my money, I look for my friends but, as it happens so often when we need our friends, they are nowhere to be found. During my time living here, I've met some European girls whose lives resemble mine. I talk to them when I have time to chill or party with them. Like me, they also live in hotels. One of them got pregnant then had her baby and stayed here for about two years until her dad came to get her. She was friendly with the popular guys who were with the rich old man but they were long gone and not helping her. For sure, if I had the money from my father, I'd invest in a small, quiet hotel surrounded by fruit trees, and I'd leave a couple of rooms available for people in situations such as the one I am in.

I've now been here for a long time; in fact, it's the longest I've ever stayed here. I can't take it anymore and feel like a useless good-for-nothing. Actually, I haven't felt good anywhere since my money was stolen from me. Finally, I get a bit of relief when some friends from Canada decide to come and get me. This is the first time in many years that someone has decided to help me. It's also the first time in this lifetime that I've met Arnold, the one I saw die with my father in

Separation and war

the sequences of the weird movie.

Arnold is here in Playa and I had been told that he went into the Daddy Rock bar in Cancun to ask to see and talk to the boss. In the bar he supposedly shouted out "I offer ten thousand dollars to anyone who finds my friend Christine". The Spanish guy started to laugh and one of them left and then returned with another young man, who brought along his tiger on a leash. I heard that the young man was the son of the owner of the bar "Christine". He looked mad, afraid tourists would be disturbed by all this, so he went over to Arnold with his tiger and said:

- Why are you looking for Christina? I can find her, but I'm warning you that I don't want any noise or problems about this or you'll have to deal with my tiger. You have to understand that there are important people here.

So these people are here to tell me to come back. They tell me that they're ready to take my side and that it's my turn. I will now be under the protection of the members of the embassy. When I realize who had financed this search, I feel flattered impressed and special. In the evening, as I walk down Fifth Avenue, I see a limousine pass by. I wave, even though I don't know who's inside since I'm feeling strange. About an hour later, walking by a small café on the Quinta, I see Alain, deceased Claude's ex-roommate, sitting with the husband of the Queen singer from Canada.

As soon as he sees me, he waves to me, asking me to come and join them.

- Come here, you! I'll buy you a coffee.

I slowly walk over and pull up a chair, a little surprised to see these people, but my mind is still somewhere else.

- Yes, thank you; I'd be delighted to have a coffee.

I sit down, proud to be with this influential person.

- What are you doing here? Shouldn't you be at home in Canada already?

- Well, I'm still looking for someone here and besides, in Canada, I'm

Separation and war

constantly being hunted down and it scares me that corrupt people can do whatever they want with me, even though I'm innocent.
As I turn around, I'm surprised to see the Queen singer herself waving at me from the balcony of a small hotel right beside us. I'm unaware of the luck and opportunity within my reach. It's not the first time I've met a well-known rich person and my step-dad has warned me not to disturb them if I want to work in the hotel industry. So I finish my coffee, forgetting who Alain is. I know that I know him, but who is he? I then get up, not taking advantage of this nice opportunity.
- I have to go change. It's getting cool. Thank you for the coffee. It was nice meeting you.
When I get up, the two men shake my hand good-bye and I go back to my hotel room. It's strange that I only remember who Alain is once I get home to Canada. When I remember who he is, I think that maybe he needs my testimony so that he can stop being considered a suspect in Claude's murder, as he was the one who found him dead in his bed. I change my clothes and go to the opening of a bar in Playa. As I stand outside beside the doorman, I see Arnold doing karate with Pep, the one who inspired me to compose most of my songs. I wonder why he inspires me. I know that every time I get close to him, my heart gets warm and filled with love and I wonder why, when I'm around him, I'm able to see memories of myself when I was younger. I know he's not for me but who is he? I can't remember him from all my trips. After much reflection and after getting knocked by the cloud, I become aware that he has the same sound as the guy who popped my cherry here when I was younger. This guy must be him, older now, because even his friends are the same people. All of these events occurred before I was hit by the lightning cloud, through which I received my memories that allowed me to recognize people; that's why I recognized Pep. Pep is gifted in this life and was in his past life, too. I heard people say that he was a saint in his community and that he was someone like me, who believes in honesty and respect and was going to warn me of something. He was my imaginary lover

Separation and war

when I wasn't feeling good and I also heard him cry to me every time his heart was broken. I received his cry to offer support. He was one of those who appeared in my memories when I was eight and Charles's father spoke to me at the table playing cards. In my ancestral life I can see him, an old man coming to meet me. His marriage is over. He had been totally devoted to his wife, a small, blond Italian woman with whom he had a child who was asked by the family to be reborn. His wife left him for another woman and his mind his probably still blinded affected by this, because he always ask women's if they're gay.

In my vision, my husband had passed away not too long before. At that moment, I had just passed away myself, and my soul is traveling through the air, visiting all those I loved, before passing into the other world and that's when I saw Pep leaving the airport, coming to see me. He's telling his friend that he's curious to see me again. Kurt had told me he had also passed away and that was a lie. I have to admit that sometimes these memories of the past mixed with images of the present create an amazing effect.

Now I am watching Pep and Arnold doing karate on a balcony in front of me. In the street, people are mentioning my name, telling others that I am important.

It feels and looks like a recreation of an event from the year 0 or 1400, with that Spaniard with his tiger and company, but updated and set in modern surroundings. It's like a déjà vu to see the same events taking place with the same taste of blood, and the same people assembling, although instead of the action being held in an arena, it's happening on balconies and in the street.

Walking towards my police officer friend to speak with him, I see Mustafa standing at the other end of the street. He seems to be afraid of the officer and he stays far away, waving and shouting to me.

- Christine! Come back home.

Then he disappears, running away.

Separation and war

I do get confused seeing all these people who came here for me who I usually see in Canada. I feel a warm, comforting feeling coming to fill up that hole that was empty from not being loved by anyone for so long.

This is when I decide that next week I am going back. Anyway, I have to leave before I get arrested for staying here longer than I'm legally allowed to. This is how my trip ends.

When I get home, I wait for Mustafa to come see me. I hear that war has broken out between Mustafa's family and the Russian family of his deceased daughter, although it's just a rumor.

This week, Mustafa goes from being loving and nice to having a vengeful mindset. I wake up in the middle of the day in my room in Verdun. There is total silence everywhere and time is standing still, as if the earth had stopped turning. I feel adrenaline coursing through me, making the blood rush to my brain from my heart like when I'm on a roller coaster. It's a feeling of agony. Meanwhile, Mustafa arrives at my place, looking very agitated.

- Its war. They've murdered my uncle and kidnapped my only girl cousin, the heiress of the family hotel in Morocco. My cousin ran and took an army jet to follow the kidnappers. They're Russian or German, but I don't know exactly who's piloting the airplane that my cousin is in. Wait a minute. My phone is ringing. What, Mohamed?

Mustafa looks at me, his eyes as big as saucers, then he becomes delirious.

- They hit the tower during their chase! Not for real?!

He starts talking in Arabic and I don't understand a word he's saying. He hangs up the phone, looks at me, trembling, eyes red, and says:

- They're all dead.

He starts crying and leaves, almost running down the stairs. His will to live is gone. The ones he loved and relied on are dead.

This story isn't mine and I don't know the details but if it is ever written as a book, this is a bit of advertising for it. If what Mustafa just told me is true, then I know the September 2001 attack

Separation and war

in New York City wasn't an attack, but an accident caused by a robbery committed against Mustafa's family.

Several months later, Mustafa arrives at my door one evening with his luggage. He leaves his belongings with me then leaves right away with some of his friends.

Mustafa comes back at around six in the morning, smelling of smoke.

- Christine, you'll never guess where I went last night.
- Well how could I know?
- You remember what happened to my daughter? Well, I did some research and found out that about 100 such deaths occurred this year in two different Jewish hospitals. I was supposed to receive insurance money from the embassy. I've been told that the insurance money will come from the White House. Well, they're way past the due date for payment, so I'm going over there to blow up the White House.
- Have you lost your mind? You want to solve the problem with bombs! Just be patient and everything will get settled.
- No, you don't understand. Last night I went to the hospital, asking them for the name of the doctor responsible for the injections and no one wanted to tell me who it was. I then gave them a warning and they still wouldn't tell me who it was, so I made sure they would never give illegal injections again. I went to both hospitals and, without killing anyone there, I fired shots with an M16 to scare those hypocrites. I also went to the hospital where your ex-sister-in-law works and she won't be making any more false accusations to get you arrested. She got the message and understands.
- Are you crazy?
- That's nothing, I had orders from the Israeli army to shoot clandestine Jews who had received a one-year warning to leave the country and who were still here in hiding, so I shot close to 200 Jews in an apartment building in Côte-des-Neiges.

My heart starts beating fast and I feel that I'm going to die from hearing these stories.

Mustafa leaves again after I tell him that the police wired me.

Separation and war

I've never let him in since. I had my doubts about his truthfulness for a while, thinking he might have invented these stories to scare me, but the newspaper had an article about the massacre of the Jews in which it was said that the Canadian authorities weren't concerned by the event because the people killed were clandestine immigrants. I have to say that it scared me quite a bit.

Two years later, he comes and knocks on my door once again, but, fearing for my life, I don't let him in. I tell him:

- Mustafa, you have to leave now! The police are coming. You have the choice to leave or deal with them.
- Christine, you must know that I'd never hurt you.

He goes down the stairs to leave. The officers are there and Mustafa tells them he hasn't seen or spoken to me in two years. The officers let him leave, just telling him to cross the street and does nothing to him.

Even though I don't totally agree with what Mustafa said he did, I know that if he hadn't, the corrupt people in the legal system would have kept coming to arrest me and the outlaw doctors would still be putting children to death. I don't understand why it takes an extreme act to bring an end to deadly violence by those who think they have power over all.

I personally wouldn't be able to defend myself this way if it were the only way of being protected.

A couple of years later, I hear on the news that an army from another country captured Mustafa's boss Mohamed and threw him out of a helicopter. Also, one of Mustafa's friend told me that Mustafa was also dead, which I doubt.

Since all these events took place while I had a sexual connection, I have reason to believe that all the blood of these murders have poisoned the ideas of the pure angel. The soul of the angel who hit me lives with God's laws and she will defend all innocent people, following God's rule of "do unto others as you would have them do unto you". But unfortunately, the angels from up there don't see

Separation and war

everyone, which sometimes can cause monstrous disasters. However, stories such as the one about Mustafa are many times good enough to make a good movie for them to get insurance money and that is what stops the defending wars from happening. For example, with the insurance money, he could have gone to hide at his uncle's hotel and the insurance money would have given him more time to live, but the robbers left him with no other choice than war to protect himself. If there were no swindlers stirring up war, many innocent people would be saved. Mustafa could no longer bear to be the next victim after watching those dear to him being attacked and there's nothing else to say but that it's the swindlers' fault.

***

CHAPTER NINE
Hopes of a waking dream destroyed

I wonder how I was able to maintain the will to stay alive after being attacked and after experiencing extreme deception in life. What kind of hope gave me faith and gave me a reason to continue, after knowing that I'll always be living only to die and relive and that I'll have to continually confront the attackers again! Even though negative situations make me understand why God sometimes wants to destroy all human beings, I know I can live the life I dream of because I've lived it before. This is why I'm able to hide within the dreams of possibilities, which I can experience. Let me tell you how I came to believe that I had the right to live on higher, different grounds than many of the people around me.

I'm eleven years old. My mother just left to live in Mexico. My father sits on the couch, crying because she's gone, but in just a couple of weeks later, his new girlfriend Estelle moves in with us. Estelle impresses me because she's young and everyone makes comments about her big boobs. This young woman is passionate about horses and she teaches me to become interested in them. She's nice with me

Hopes of a waking dream destroyed
and takes me out all the time.

One calm evening, sitting by myself on a high bench that separates the dining room from the kitchen, I'm dreaming about one of Charles's kids and, I'm trying to find out telepathically how others live. In my dream, the boy seems to be in a castle far away and he's named Prince. My dream is interrupted when Estelle comes in the back door and walks through the kitchen.

- Hello, Christine! What are you doing? I have a favor to ask you. Are you busy?
- No, I was just dreaming. What do you want?
- Look, I have these papers here and I want you to choose six numbers on each. Can you do that? It's for us.
- Sure, no problem!
- I'm going upstairs to get ready. Just call to me when you're done and I'll go validate them.
- Ok, I will.
- Just don't tell your father.

Sitting on the bench, I look at the papers and wonder what it would be like if we were to win. Would she even give me my share? I'm not sure I can trust her, but I believe any person would be grateful towards a person who helps them win. Leaning on the counter, I'm thinking and listening to the prince, who just came back into my mind. I wonder if it's Charles's son or could it be my brother on the way since my mom is pregnant. As I meditate about this, I ask the voice in the echo to help me choose numbers and I choose four or five different combinations for the lottery papers, then the echo suddenly vanishes. Estelle comes down the stairs.

- So, are you finished yet?
- Yes, I was about to call you. Here, take them.
- Good, I'm going to the store right away before it gets too late. Promise me that you won't tell your father. I swear we're going to win! You know it would be nice if we could become good friends.
- I hope so and it would be super-cool to win. Hurry!

Hopes of a waking dream destroyed

Estelle leaves for the store. Meanwhile, my father comes downstairs and comes towards me.
- Are you doing your homework?
- Yes, I'm doing a drawing for art class.
- Tell me what Estelle told you just now.
- Nothing special; why?

Suddenly, a breeze brushes against my cheek as Estelle comes in the door. She's out of breath, but smiling.
- I have them.

My dad looks at her with a naughty smile.
- Where's the milk? Did you get my tickets?

Estelle lowers her head, looking discouraged.
- There's five minutes left. Let me go back.

Estelle returns to the store and soon comes back with the same discouraged look on her face, as if she just saw a dead person.
- Frank, I'm so sorry. I was too late. I wasn't able to validate your ticket on time.

My father becomes angry.
- It's all your fault. Don't take me for an idiot. I don't believe that you went to the store earlier, because you came back empty-handed. Tell me. Did you go out to get some drugs? I'm warning you if you don't tell me where you went earlier, you'll have to leave because I won't tolerate a cokehead here.

Estelle becomes mad and pushes Frank.
- How dare you judge me like that? Yes, I went to the store. You're not being fair.

She looks at me with a sigh, disappointed with my dad, as he gets even angrier with her.
- What kind of secret are you hiding with my daughter?

She looks at him, unsure of what he'll do next after just squeezing her hand very hard.
- Frank, I just went to buy my own tickets and forgot to get all the rest.

Hopes of a waking dream destroyed

She holds the tickets out to my father.
- Here! Take these! They're our tickets. I give them to you, but if you win, you have to give us our share. By the way, these tickets are winners; I'm sure.

My dad looks at me with a pitiful face.
- I'm not nice sometimes, I know. Please forgive me for frightening you.
- No, Dad. You aren't nice. You should apologize to Estelle and admit that you've been mean to her.
- Yes, for you I will apologize. Estelle, I'm sorry. Do you forgive me for accusing you for no good reason?
- Let me think about it. Yes, I do forgive you, but don't ever do that to me again.

The two lovebirds leave and go upstairs, leaving me alone with my drawing. If my father wins, I'll get my share for sure and Estelle will tell him that I was the one who chose the numbers.

Many days pass by and I forget about the tickets. As for my father, he had not yet verified to see if we won. The news broadcaster makes an exciting announcement: someone won 14 million dollars in the lottery draw and someone else won a million something, almost 2 million dollars, but they have not yet claimed their prize. And the winning ticket was bought at the store on the corner of our the street. Many more days go by. I'm at Francine's place and there's a phone call for me. My father is calling and he sounds worried:
- Come home quickly. And listen; it's very important that you be careful crossing the street.
- What are you saying? At my age, I know how to cross the street.
- Yes, I know you do, but you'll have to look around you and if you see someone coming at you, run! Do you understand me?
- Sure, Dad. Can you tell me what's going on?
- I'll tell you as soon as you get home.
- Okay, I'm leaving right away.

I hurry to put on my shoes, anxious to know what the paranoia is all

Hopes of a waking dream destroyed

about. Francine also seems curious to know, but I ignore her many questions. When I get outside, I cross the street and there's nothing abnormal in sight. I reach my door, walk inside and hear my father making monkey sounds, something resembling hoo, hoo, hoo! Estelle is there also. I can hear her talking to my dad:
- I am telling you it's because of Christine.
- Daddy, I'm here! What did you want that's so important?
Worried, my voice starts trembling. I wonder if I've done something wrong.
- I have to tell you something. Come upstairs, but make sure the door is locked.
- Yes, Daddy, but why are you so scared?
- Hurry up! I have something important to tell you.
I start climbing the stairs one by one, very slowly, afraid that I'm going to be punished. I finally reach the threshold of his bedroom door. My heart pounding, I shout:
- What's going on?
- Shh, be quiet! Talk low; someone could hear you.
- But who? There's nobody else here!
- The police can hear us. We're under surveillance. We've been hacked. Christine, listen to me. We won the lottery.
My father smiles at me with tears in his eyes and with his arms open wide.
- Come here and give me a great big hug. But you have to promise me not to tell anyone. It's very important.
- But are you telling me that I can't even tell Francine?
- That's right. For now, you can't even tell her. I'll let you know when it's okay to tell. It's just because if dangerous people hear about it, they might come and try to kidnap you. You may tell her when I say that it's safe to.
- Okay, then. But it will be difficult. But I'll do my best.
- Hey what did I tell you!
- Alright, alright.

Hopes of a waking dream destroyed

I leave their room and walk back down the stairs, listening to Estelle talking to my dad, saying:
- Frank, promise me to put Christine's share aside for when she's older and promise me that she'll never have to go work for those pigs.

Estelle watches me go down the stairs and smiles at me and says:
- Tomorrow you won't be going to school.

So this is how it was.

Time passes by slowly and I forget that I chose those numbers. Winning makes all the burdens of life disappear, giving me a fresh outlook on life and letting me see that my life is now in my hands because I can decide to do almost anything I want to. The strangest thing about luck is the coincidences which are connected to it.

I'm watching T.V. in my father's private living room when he comes in to tell me a secret.
- Do you know who won the first prize?
- No, I have no idea.
- It was Charles and his dad.

This coincidences make me start asking myself questions which have no logical answers.
- That's very odd, Daddy!
- Yes, but promise me that you'll continue to be nice.
- For Christ's sake, Dad, why are you asking me such a question? Aren't I always nice?
- Never mind you better listen.

The minute my father leaves, I have a flashback of the prince, making me wonder if the prince, who was telepathically present with me when I chose the numbers, could be one of them. I will never know, but this situation is one of the coincidences that prove to me that telepathy is a true human capacity.

The rest of the school, year my father has someone pick me up at school every day with a limousine, which brings me a certain amount of popularity. My life is changing but it's passing by slowly.

Hopes of a waking dream destroyed

Estelle and my father buy me a horse and we buy a small mansion that my dad has renovated from top to bottom. Luck continues to follow us. Hidden behind the walls of the house are a big safe and an underground passage that leads to the lake. In the past, the passage had been used by gangsters to escape. We also find papers bearing Al Capone's name, which increase the value of the property. Living in a house which contains such intriguing vestiges of the past can give a person pause. Although this person lived in this house for a short time, I heard that another person named Al Capone existed and the stories change from one place to the next. The American gangster named Al Capone was not the first one; there was also the Irish man who they nicknamed after two slaves. the father Al and his son Capone. There was an Irish man who refused to bring in or to kill slaves who were accused of rape. After hearing the names repeated so many times, saying he was a coward, they named him after them. Although this story is much older than the one about the Italian American, it serves as a reference point of where from was coming the clones they sent to Ireland. Anyhow, life is better for us now that we've won the lottery, because everything changes wile the hope for an awaking dream comes to life.

***

My mother still lives in Mexico and I visit her there every summer and at Christmas. This is at the end of one summer, I get back from my vacation at my mother's and Estelle is gone. Soon after, as I enter the kitchen one morning, I find my father leaning forward with his head on the counter, crying.
- What am I going to do all alone?
- Daddy, don't cry! She'll come back and if not, you'll find someone else.
- No she won't come back because a friend of mine called here and told her that she also has a baby who might be mine and I don't know what to do.
- Are you telling me that you have another woman? Who is she?

Hopes of a waking dream destroyed

- She is not my woman yet but I can introduce you to her if you want.

I find it odd that my father tells me that this other woman has a baby when, in my mind, it was Estelle who just had a baby. Plus I just had a baby half-sister, whom I saw come to life and now I won't be able to see her anymore.

This is the start of troubles in my life. It almost becomes a living hell because the new woman in my father's life has come to destroy everything I had going for me.

In fact, I'm very disappointed with how this relationship turns out. Regardless of the mistakes Estelle may have made, she always made sure she told my father about what he needed to get me. We did quality activities together and all of my friends liked her. But these are not things I can say about the new woman, although appearances seem otherwise.

Sitting on the wooden elephant chair in the big room surrounded with windows, I am admiring the jungle engraving on the wooden table, a piece of art which my father brought back from his vacation to India.

My father seems different since coming back from his trip. Estelle also accused him of not being the same person. During an argument they had when he came back, she said:

- Where's the birthmark you used to have? What's happened to the Frank that I knew?

My dad laughed and they both ran outside. Estelle ended up punching the windshield of my father's truck as he tried to get away from her. Thinking back to that day, there's something about it that makes me feel suspicious.

My father finally arrives with food from McDonald's.

- It's about time; I'm starving.

Since winning the lottery, we've had takeout food from McDonald's for lunch every day, as my father doesn't cook.

- Christine, I want you to meet Aline before I bring her here to live. I need your advice and approval.

Hopes of a waking dream destroyed

- Sure, no problem. I'll meet her.

I meet Aline and find her to be nice. She's delicate in stature, just like my mother, and her baby girl is very cute.

- Daddy, are you the father of that child?
- No, I'm not. Her father was put in prison and he died.

He immediately retracts his words, saying:

- Well, she doesn't really know. I could be the father. Christine, what would you say if this weekend she comes over and takes you out shopping? It will give you the opportunity to get to know her. So, what do you say?
- Okay. Yes, that would be fun.

The weekend comes fast and, as planned, she comes over and brings me out shopping.

We go to the pharmacy since I need some cosmetics. Aline has a soft voice which makes her seem nice, although her replies sometimes seem strange. Underneath her sweet way of talking are some vicious ideas.

She acts like a snob to the clerk behind the counter, waving her hair in the air, looking wicked and answering sharply but she finally smiles and says:

- It's excessive for such a young girl.

I immediately start thinking that maybe she's poor and would like some cosmetics herself, so I say:

- Aline, you have to buy something for yourself! My father gave you more than enough for both of us.
- No, nothing for me.
- I insist! You must choose something for yourself.
- No, I don't want anything. Let's hurry. I want to leave.

I was unable to detect that below her sweet surface lay hidden bad intentions.

Back at the mansion, I reflect a while before telling my father what I think of Aline. Finally, believing that she will be like Estelle, taking me out for activities and being friendly with me, I tell my dad that I find

Hopes of a waking dream destroyed

her nice.

She moves in soon after. It turns out that the time she brought me shopping for cosmetics was the one and only time she ever brought me out. Once she starts living with us, she keeps herself locked in her room and only comes out to complain about me and insult me. On the other hand, she is submissive and nice towards my father. She seems to have chosen me to be the person she will destroy. With me, she acts like a hypocrite, just waiting for me to be gone.

I can't figure her out, since all women I have met up until now have been nice to me and have behaved normally. But I give her the benefit of the doubt because my father is also acting differently, which makes me suspect he could be another person, just as Estelle had insinuated.

It makes me sad to say this about my father since I love him very much and don't wish him any harm. As for Aline, I believe that she is unable to live with anyone who doesn't have a blood relation to her. However, I live in the same household as her and I'm even able to hear her think telepathically since she lives and has physical contact with a blood relative of mine, my father. In spite of this, she ignores me and manages to make my father believe that I shouldn't be with them in order to be free of all responsibilities and obligation towards me. Believing in Aline's crazy ideas, my father is becoming illogical and insane.

I come to the conclusion that if Frank, my father, is in fact another person pretending to be Frank, I am definitely in danger. He has become so cheap and ungrateful towards me that he seems to have forgotten that it was thanks to Estelle and me that he got his fortune. He refuses to pay for decent clothes for me to wear to school. He also refuses to allow me to go to a private school where my friends and cousins go.

This is unfair, as he helped Aline pay for her sister to go to the private school, where I want to go. They're treating me like a target, which they are trying to destroy and put aside others. I don't understand

Hopes of a waking dream destroyed

her jealousy towards me; its' not as if I am sleeping with my dad. I'll never understand why they are acting this way towards me. Nevertheless, I see that my opportunity to make something of myself is ruined. Even though my grade average is 90%, I decide to stop trying, now that I'm perceived as less important than those imposters. I revolt by shaving off my hair, tearing up my jeans and taking drugs.

Aline tells me:

- You don't even need to go to school, since you won't need to go to work later in life because you're Frank's daughter. Anyway, the only job you'd be able to do would be as a streetwalker.

Tears still run down my soul when, I remember this. I feel so stupid to have lacked the strength to be able to ignore the nasty words of a woman who hates me. During the whole the time I live in the same house with her, she never cooks for me. She prepares food only for her people and she always says that she'll never be able to make anything good enough for me even though I insist that I am not a picky eater.

Now that I am older, when I look back at that time, I wonder if the fact that I was at a difficult age may have colored my interpretation of everything she said to me.

I want to forgive her and act as though nothing bad was done to me, but she doesn't want me to be in her life. I guess she doesn't accept the fact that I exist, although she knew of my existence before she even agreed to get into a relationship with my father, so she must know that it's illegal to try to make me disappear, as well as being abnormal. Unfortunately, she's just waiting for me to be gone, and let me say that nowadays people with Joan of Arc ideas are everywhere. It seems she only has nasty things to say, but that's because she never hangs around me to say nice things. One day I ask her:

- Would you be with my father if he were poor?

She crosses her arms and replies:

- Of course not. I wish he'd marry me but I'm disappointed that he

Hopes of a waking dream destroyed

refuses for the moment. I only want to give him another child, a boy, who would become the heir. In addition, if he doesn't marry me, I won't get anything.

What she says breaks my heart, so I tell people, but they have a hard time believing me and think that I might be lying out of jealousy. However I always accept someone who cares for me. I'm not jealous of my father's girlfriend; I'm just intrigued about her motivations. It seems that instead of finding a place of her own among the people in my father's life, she wants instead to push me out of this circle of people. In my life, I've been able to accept Estelle and others, and I'm sure I could accept Aline if she treated me normally. However, if my father's been cloned, I would understand why things have turned out this way. It's just like my adopted cousin, who I thought was among his brothers, when in fact I just found out that he was with someone else who has the same first and last names and the same life, including being married to an Asian woman, and who lives in the same city. Life can be very confusing at times.

***

I try to forget about all the negative things and try to continue to love my father's girlfriend until one day I realize that she will ignore me all my life and will make my life become a part of her dangerous game. Even though Aline acts normally with my father, that doesn't make her a normal person towards the other people in his life.

I lose all hope and desire to be any part of Aline's life after the year 2000.

I won't reveal the identity of the person I am with because I don't think that he deserves to die and he's already been punished for what he's done.

Anyway, this is just in case someone gets the idea to avenge me. This particular night my boyfriend is later than usual and things are not going very well for me, as I have no money and am still in bed with a high fever caused by the radiation from the cloud touching me. I get up to look out the back-door window to see if he's coming.

Hopes of a waking dream destroyed

I see a truck parked right in front of my window with its lights still on. I can't believe my eyes: it's Aline and she's had her hair cut. I'm sure it's her; there's no one else with a nose like hers that would be driving a truck like my father's. It's odd to see her here since I haven't seen her in about 4 years; the last time was at the mansion. In addition, she's never come to visit me nor has she ever called me. I wonder what she's doing here. Is she coming up to talk to me? I see my boyfriend crossing the street. As he gets near the window of the truck, Aline calls to him. They talk for 2 minutes, then she closes the window and slowly leaves. It's strange because I've never introduce her to him, and I don't think he knows her neither. I close the curtains, thankful that they didn't see me looking at them.

Before my boyfriend enters the house, I go back to lie down because, with my fever still running high, I'm not able to stay up for very long. He comes in furious, slamming the door.

He enters my bedroom, leans over on the bureau, still he's wearing his steel-toe boots, and asks:

- Christine, did my boss come here today?

I hesitate a moment, wondering if a clone of him came here over in the past few days.

- Your boss? No. Why would he come here?

He pushes himself upright and turns his back on me. As fast a lightning, he turns again to face me, swings his leg up to kick me in the head with his boot, and yells:

- Yes, he was here! He told me so! Did you sleep with him?

He kicks me again about two more times. I wrap my arms around my head to avoid being hit with his steel-toe boots.

- Stop it, you stupid idiot! Your boss never came here! You're a crazy sicko!

I'm scared and fear for my life, but I'm able to slide off the side of the bed and I run to the neighbor's house. Unfortunately for me the stupid neighbors don't want to help me nor do they let me use their

Hopes of a waking dream destroyed

phone. Not knowing what to do, I return to my apartment to get my cell phone. My boyfriend, standing at the top of the stairs, says:
- I'm so sorry. I thought you had fucked my boss, I swear that I'll never do that to you again. I have to tell you something else.
Disturbed, I look at him, not knowing how to react.
He takes off his boots then shows that he has no weapons with him. I suddenly decide to go up to get my phone, so I grab the banister, holding it tight.
- I told the neighbor what you did. They're armed and if they hear me scream one time, they'll come right away.
It's a lie but it works.
- No, Christine. I won't try to harm you again, I'll go out to get some food and then I'll come back, to tell you why. And please, you have nothing to worry about. I swear that I didn't intend to hurt you, really! Someone came to ask me to do it.
- But what the fuck? Don't lie to me! And tell me right now who did this!
- To tell you the truth I don't really know the person. Please forgive me! I'll try to help you instead.
I hesitate, although my curiosity takes over and I want to know who could want me dead, because I've never hurt anyone in my life. Most of the time, I've tried to help everyone I know.
After my boyfriend leaves to get something to eat, I sit at home waiting, unsure if I want to stay here to see him come back. I feel sad thinking that I will have to leave him because he's too dangerous. I also know that he had done some time in jail as a juvenile for causing the death of two black girls by hitting them on the head.
Maybe I won't let him in when he gets back.
He knocks on the door and through the window he shows me that he's not armed, even showing me under his shirt and pants. I decide to let him in just to find out who asked him to do this to me. I go to the kitchen to make sandwiches, then I ask him:
- I want you to tell me who asked you to do this to me. You have to

Hopes of a waking dream destroyed

tell me who it is.
- I don't really know the person but I was receiving a ten-thousand-dollar bike for it.
- Don't pretend to be stupid; you have to know who it is. Could it be someone from Claude's family?
- Maybe.
- Was it a woman with a crooked nose?
- Yes, maybe.
- Ok, stop it! You'll have to decide which one it is and tell the truth.
- I don't know what else to tell you.

The evening ends in silence and my boyfriend doesn't end up staying with me much longer. I pack all of his belongings and ask 3 male friends to stay with me until he moves out completely, to avoid any bad situations. I'll never know who the person was who supposedly asked him to kill me, if there ever was someone, but I do find it odd that Aline was there talking to him and never came to talk to me.

I imagine she could have tried to end my life since she and my father are not paying me what they owe me.

The bike story reminds me of the Harley my father once bought me but never gave to me.

It was a nice fall day; I'm outside walking around the grounds of the mansion, breathing in the healthy, fresh air when I hear my father call my name.

- Christine, come see! I want you to try something. Come here. I'm in the garage.

I go to the garage right away and see a super-nice woman's Harley.
- Wow! What a nice bike! Who's it for?
- Try to sit on it to see if it fits. You reach the floor.
- Oh, yay! The bike's for me!
- Well, I did by it for you, but I'm not sure when I'll give it to you.

Aline enters the garage and starts to squeal with delight, putting her hands up to her face and saying:
- I can't believe you bought me a bike! Wow! Isn't it gorgeous?

Hopes of a waking dream destroyed

She then just walks out, closing the door behind her.
My father looks at me with a big smile, and tells me:
- Well, it isn't going to be your bike.
This really pisses me off since he had promised me one.
My father had brought me with him on rides since I was two years old. The most awful part is that he had just bought Aline a new B.M.W. and then he had to give her my bike!
This makes me realize that everything she says influences my father's decision, just like when she is supposed to tell him that I need clothes for school but instead tells him that she don't need any. I know someone is robbing me; all the little things make me aware that my father isn't the same person he was before.
In my heart and mind it isn't normal for him to act so inconsistently. For example, he lends his vehicles to Aline's sister and brother but won't let me drive them. Absurdly, Aline never uses the Harley and arranges to let her sister drive it once in a while. My father has even forbidden me to come to the mansion since I moved out. For all of these reasons and more, I believe he could be someone else. The most intriguing situation is when he refuses to have his fingerprints taken one time when my uncle asks him to come to the station to do so, and I catch him burning the ends of his fingers. Nevertheless, I have to say that he was not all that bad, as he came to help when I was attacked and he helped me many other times. He might be following someone else's orders, and somewhere hidden behind his meanness, there's a human being with good intentions, which doesn't seem to be the case of his new girlfriend Aline. I think this about Aline only because I suspect her of trying to have me killed. Anyhow, I was not able to continue living the good rich life I had won since it was all taken by some people who didn't take share in my life but instead acted as crooks and took it all. I suspect that Aline lived her life with my father or with the person pretending to be Frank, dreaming of another man, Charles, the one who had refused to leave his wife for her, the one whose father is the grandchild of my

Hopes of a waking dream destroyed
ancestor. However, maybe it's her way of getting revenge for not being chosen to be loved by the one she wanted.

***

Chapter 10
Pursuit

During the time I've spent here in this apartment looking for the right person, I've dealt with many difficult situations that have exceeded my ability to cope. Nowadays, a movie that will interest audiences will often show people suffering, just as the people in the audience have suffered. This is my motivation for relating the event in this chapter, even if I don't think it has any importance in my life.
One afternoon, Kurt arrives at my door, acting like a crazy person. He knocks at my back door and shouts:
- Hurry, Christine! Open the door, please.
I recognize his voice so I hurry to open the door. He bursts in, pushing me aside. With him is a 15-year-old Italian boy.
- For Christ's sake, Kurt! Why are you panicking?
- Christine, hurry! Lock the door, now!
Unfortunately, I'm not able to turn the key to lock the door before three men shove the door open, pushing me over again.
- Who the hell are you? I never gave you the authorization to come in here. Get out of here!
The two younger men start arguing with Kurt's teenage friend and the older man is looking at me with a big smile on his face and seems to want to get close to me. He must be in his thirties.
- Please, sir, would you at least sit down? We can discuss this matter. I'd like to know what's going on here in my home.
The man sits down and starts to act agitated.
- That young boy is mine; he owes me money.
- Good lord! He's just a kid! How can he possibly owe you money? By the way, how much are we talking about, for you to be so angry?
- He took a hundred dollars.

Pursuit

- What if I give you the money? Will you leave him in peace?
- No, he also owes me drugs! I just arrived from Africa with a kilo of cocaine and the stupid kid lost some of the drugs I gave him to sell.

All of a sudden, they all run into the living room, leaving me alone with the man.

I hear them arguing again.

- Stay here, you idiot! You're not leaving until everything is settled, you fuck.

I hear Kurt yell:

- Leave him alone.
- Shut up, nigger, or I'll blow your brains out.

The guy starts laughing as he says to Kurt:

- Now you have nothing more to say, fucker.

The man with me gets more agitated and stands up, yelling:

- Okay, calm down over there! Leave him alone for a while. I'm going to try to make an arrangement with the pretty girl. I'll let you know what to do with them after I'm finished with her.

The man comes up to me and starts touching me all over. I push him away, disgusted by him, but he grabs me and holds me very tightly.

- Leave me alone! The police is coming! The neighbor surely heard something.

I start shouting again.

- Leave me alone! Please, someone, help! Don't you understand? I don't want to! Don't you know what the word "No" means?

He lifts me up in the air.

- Yes, you're coming with me. Show me where your room is.

I yell:

- Kurt, please do something!
- I can't do anything! I'm so sorry.

The man is hurting me, holding me too tightly. I'm scared that he could kill me. I decide to stop resisting him because I know he's 100 times stronger than me. I know how to play the game, so I decide to change my tact before I end up getting cut into pieces.

Pursuit

- Listen, don't hurt me. I have some condoms in my purse. Let me get them and I'll be nice and let you do it to me,
but please stop hurting me.
- Well, if you're going to be nice with me, I won't hurt you; yes, I can be a very gentle and sweet man, if you want.

I roll the condom around his penis, shedding a few tears at the same time. I'm disgusted but I put my mind on something else while the pig takes advantage of me.
As soon as he's finished I ask him:
- Do you intend to stay here longer?
- I don't know. Can I offer you some coke or some money?
- No, thank you. I don't use drugs and you can keep your money. Just leave the kid alone and don't hurt him anymore.
- Ok, it's a deal, since you've been a good girl.

It's a couple of hours later and the young Africans are still here, looking around the house, trying to find something but all they've found is some jewelry. I go to the front porch and see Flint's father coming towards me.
- Hi there! Do you need some help?
- Not for the moment, but...

I'm about to whisper to him to but Kurt yells:
- The guys are leaving out back.

I look at Flint's father with relief.
- Thanks, anyway; it's very kind of you to ask.

Beside, the harm has already been done.
I'm feeling better and relieved that someone came to help me, even if he got here a little too late. I go back upstairs. The older man is still in the kitchen, about to go out the back door. Minutes later, the younger ones come back, catch the Italian boy and drag him down the front staircase. I hurry behind them.
- Leave him alone right now! My friend already called the cops; they're coming.

The African or Jamaican guys are hitting the Italian boy's head against

Pursuit

the brick wall, but let him go as soon as they hear that the police are on their way. They leave the boy alone and run away. The boy has a large lump on his head that seems to be growing bigger by the minute. A couple of hours later, I decide to let him stay in my spare room for a couple of days. I can't keep him here for long since I can't afford to feed him and he's way to young to be anything other than a visitor to me.

The next day I have to tell him to start organizing his life, so I knock on the door of his room to talk to him.

- Come in.
- I hope I'm not disturbing you. I just want to talk to you.
- No, you're not bothering me at all. I was just admiring the ring I bought for my girlfriend. Come look at it.
- You're so kind. Wow it's beautiful. I am sure that she is going to love it.

He smiles at me.

- Listen, young man, you have to find a solution to your problem. Now tell me, why don't you go back home to your family?
- My mother threw me out because I fought with my step-dad. In addition, the African will come to see me there and try to force me to sell his drugs. You know, before I came here, I ran away from him because he had put a gun to my head.
- Ok, this is too much. Do you know where he lives?
- Yes, I have his address.
- Is it true that he has a kilo of coke in his home?
- Yes, it's true.
- I'm going to the police station and file a report even if I have something against some of those cops. For sure it will make them happy; they'll be able to get drugs free, those corrupt idiots.

I hate causing problems, but this is too much. If that African thinks that he can come here to rape me, give drugs to our young people, and kill them if they disobey, well, he needs to be punished.

- Yes, that's a good idea, Let's go there.

Pursuit

- Wait, I think we should call your mother first, if that's okay with you.
- Sure, but I'm telling you that she wants nothing to do with me.

I give him the phone so he can dial his mother's number. As soon as she answers, I hear her yelling:

- No, I told you I don't want to see you here anymore.
- Give me the phone. I want to talk to her.

Despairing, he hands over the phone.

- My name is Christine. I need you to listen carefully to what I have to say. Your boy is nice; he doesn't even use drugs. I've allowed him to stay at my place for 3 days now, but I can't afford to keep him here.
- Yes, okay, but here he doesn't respect us and because of that, I no longer want to see him in this house.
- May I ask you if you love your son? Because if you don't take him back, he'll get killed! I swear this is what will probably happen. He almost got killed by some Africans and I was the one who made them go away. Ma'am, this is not a joke. Life on the streets without a home and a family is very dangerous for youngsters!
- Ma'am, I didn't think of that. I wanted him to learn a lesson. Of course I love my son! Let me talk to him. And thank you for being there to help him.

I turn to Italian boy and gave him the phone. He listens to his mother, then hangs up and has a surprised look on his face.

- My mother just told me that she loves me and I that can go back home!
- Fantastic! I'm happy for you.
- I have no idea what you did to her, but I haven't heard her talk to me like this for a long time.
- Good, let's go to the station now. It's just on the corner of the street. Then I'll give you enough money to get home.

We went file a report about the attack and give them the whereabouts of the man and his drugs but I don't talk about the rape, as I feel too ashamed. Anyway, I don't feel like going to court just to see that rapist get a little more time in jail. Besides, the judge

Pursuit

hasn't been nice to me lately and he should get enough time for possession of a kilo of cocaine.

The young boy leaves and I never see him again.

Two days later, there's a knock on my door. It's that African man again. I'll never be able to get rid of him. He'll always come to bother me or abuse me if he gets the chance. I have to do something to scare him off so that he won't want to come disturb me ever again, because I don't want to have to hide. I have an idea. I'm going to ask my friend Steven to help me. I look, find his number, and call him. What a coincidence! He's visiting my neighbour downstairs, so I shout to the African guy:

- Wait, I'm coming down to open; just wait!

I take my phone and talk to Steven, who's on the line.

- Steven, do you remember the story I told you about the African? Well, he's here at my door right now. Can you help me? He has to understand that he can't disturb me ever again! I'm a little scared of him because the police have already arrested him because of me and he's awaiting his court date and sentencing.

- Yes, I'll be with you in a minute.

I hang up the phone and go to open the door for the African man.

- Go sit in the living room. I just have to finish in the bathroom. Stay there and wait for me for a couple of minutes.

- No problem. I came to tell you that I have a family.

What a stupid fuck! Couldn't he have thought about it before doing all these bad things? He has such a nerve to come and ask for my pity! "No" means "no". We don't hurt people and that's that.

The stupid guy takes out a bag full of cocaine rocks.

- This is for you. If you need money, just sell this.

- No, I told you before that I don't want any of your shit.

At the same time, the back door opens and Steven enters.

- Christine, are you okay?

- Yes, I'm okay.

- Okay, let me talk to this idiot.

Pursuit

Steven takes a couple of steps towards the strong African man who is standing near the staircase.
- Hey! What are you doing here? Didn't the girl tell you that she wants nothing to do with you and with your shit?
- So what? I'm the one who's with her.
Hearing him say that made me so mad that I had to interrupt:
- I want you to leave and understand never to come bother me again.
The man starts to laugh, which angers Steven.
- We told you to leave! Anyway, what do you really want from her? You smart-ass, listen to me carefully. If you don't leave or if you ever come back here again, I'll go downstairs, get my piece, hunt you down and shoot you in the head. Is that what you want? Because I can go down right now.
The man looks at Steven, thinking seriously.
- No, man! Calm down, I just wanted to help her.
Steven continues to move towards him while the man tries to go down the stairs. Steven takes out a big pile of cash and throws it towards the African, shouting:
- Do you understand what I am telling you? Is it money you wanted?
The man quickly goes down the rest of the stairs, his head lowered.
- Its okay, man! I won't disturb her again. I'm leaving! I have a family to provide for and I want no problems with you.
The African man leaves, never to be seen again. I have to thank Steven for getting rid of him in all possible ways. I like Steven, even though I can never stay around him very long because of his hyperactive nature. But I can work with him in matters such as this. I could have caught him and turned him in to the police but I prefer he doesn't know I'm the one who filed a report against him.
A couple of months later, near where I live, I see a black woman moving a big chopper, about 5 feet tall. I've never seen such a big chopper. I wonder if it's the same gang, because a young teenage boy I see there is the same one that had been with the African rapist and the same one who I also had seen coming out of the apartment with

Pursuit

Lesley where the woman and her 4-year-old boy disappeared. That's when I start fearing these gangs. I even wonder if they could be cannibals. And drugs are a bigger problem.

It's sad because I do have black friends. After this, it's difficult for me to know which ones are dangerous, unless I know them personally and even if I do know them, many are traitors. So the bottom line is that venturing into their territory is risky business. However, I never would have thought that my sexual weapon would one day save my life and that of a young boy.

***

I do believe that one day I will finally be paid and reimbursed the money that I'm legally entitled to. I wait for that day, to be able to give a hand to those I know and to be able to live normally. By normal, I mean living close to those I love and before it's too late. I don't have much time left to live since life is short. I've spent more than enough time waiting for my turn, while others have taken their turn on my behalf.

Meanwhile, at the store downstairs, the Chinese doctor from a laboratory in California will soon be leaving because after 3 years, she's sold her shares in the store to another Chinese family. Before leaving, she brings almost all the associates from the stores in Montreal to come see me. She tells them about the cloud event and about the music I've created and invites them to see if they want to play with the lottery papers I had completed. This occurs before the lottery decides to change the machine and papers. She's even kind enough to ask important rich people to come and see who I am; a well-known actor-director-filmmaker comes to see me and a well-known talk-show host comes and waves to me. This all happens while they're in Montreal shooting a movie. This goes to show that the big guys are quick to see the truth. That's why I wonder why thieves don't understand that they can't take another person's copyrights. Why can't they see that those who are paying, the big guys, are the first to know the truth? Anyhow, I say this only because it makes me

Pursuit

sad when some innocent thieves end up dead. But the nice Chinese woman reassures me before leaving, telling me:
- Before I go, I'll give you my diagnosis about your being hit by the cloud. You're cured and are of no danger to others. You can also have more children if ever you want to.
She gives me a big hug before leaving. And that was that: the woman who had come from the California research laboratory had given her diagnosis.
My name has become known and every time I go through the U.S. border, they take my fingerprints to make sure it's me, as there's a person with my name but taller and with different prints, who is wanted for murder. Sometimes it's complicated to travel but the good thing about it is that when they hold me hostage, they pay for a luxurious hotel room and meals for me.
I am well aware of cloning, but I trust that there still are good people in this world, even if it's filled with too many crazy people.

***

I will now tell of a coincidental event that occurred, involving paranormal phenomena.
One year after the street wars, I spend 5 months in the sexual presence of a Hindu person, following a one-night stand. I'm coming back home the morning after and I start wondering if I should do something to have the female officer captured because she might still be murdering children. If so, she's definitely a threat for society.
I often have visions of that little girl from the clouds. She keeps crying, and saying "Why me? Doesn't someone love me? No one is doing anything to stop her, aren't I important to someone?"
I can see her soul feeling worthless, which makes her feel vengeful. She thinks "Since no one cares about me, then I don't care if they die too".
In my office, I take the phone and call the police department's professional ethics office. They tell me to write a letter with all the details. So I sit at my desk, pen in hand, and I have to think back to

Pursuit

that awful day, but I freeze when I see the image of the little girl with the tear-filled eyes and many questions pop into my head.

Why doesn't my ex tell me where he's moved? Why was that little girl, who looks so much like my little daughter, there? Why doesn't my ex don't even let me hear my daughter's voice on the phone, so that I can know she's okay, as I keep asking him? I sit there for 4 hours, crying like a baby. This is the first time I realize this could be my daughter; it's the first time in my life that I've cried so much. I think back to this morning, before I started writing. I had seen a report on travel and I think I saw the female officer on a beach in India where they were reporting from. I'm not sure it was her but it's what triggers my nerves. It made me open a pathway to get there and capture her somehow or do her wrong. Anyhow, I finally begin to write the letter at around 10 o'clock.

The next morning is the day of the famous tsunami of December 26, 2004, and this is the day that I develop a theory about natural disasters. The idea comes to me only because I'm feeling guilty, because, at the time of the disaster, I'm with someone whose family is at the location of the tsunami. I wonder if the attachment could open the path to there for the angel who thinks her murderer is there. The phenomenon is coincidental, but what makes me consider this is that all of the big disasters since the death of that child, happen at the location where the parents of the person I'm sexually in contact with are at the moment of the disaster. Perhaps someone else had planned it, but all I know is that I see the image of that little girl, continually asking me "why me" and I really feel her pain.

***

Time passes. I still feel guilt about the tsunami and I'm still looking for a way to stop the progress of natural disaster. I'm still depressed. I've stopped eating and sleep a lot. No one comes to see me; I'm just a lost cause. Weakened, I fall into a deep sleep and don't wake for about 2 days. If no one shows up, I'll probably die because I'm unable to rouse myself. I open my eyes once every 6 hours for a couple of

Pursuit

seconds; then the pressure bearing down on my body puts me right back to sleep. If I make a move to get up, my heart starts pounding quickly and I freeze like a stiff corpse. In the dream where I awaken, I'm on another planet. It may be hell, but it's a dream, not an astral voyage. I'm not at all sure where I am. In my dream I find myself among deformed black people who look like big mice. Here I am, stuck on this planet where the sun never shines, wondering how long I'm going to be here. All of a sudden, the creatures of the planet start talking to me.

- We have a bed for you here if you want; here you can make anything appear but only to look at, not to use. If you're hungry, you can conjure up food, but you can't eat it because you don't need food to keep yourself alive. You're going to be staying here with us now.

- No, I don't want to stay here! I have to wake-up. I never wanted for anyone to get hurt or for a disaster to happen.

Suddenly I hear the sound of thunder and see a very beautiful woman, glowing with fire, next to us. She calls out to me:

- My daughter, I come from a family of emperors, I am your spiritual mother and I'm considered the majesty here.

She looks at the creatures, raises her voice and points towards them.

- Release her right now! She's innocent! This is an order!

I started to tremble. My eyes close and I find myself back home in bed. I still hear the flickering of the fire and think there's a fire in my home but it's only a little mice running around. I am still somewhat paralyzed but I'm wide awake and relieved, for I no longer feel guilty. In less than 2 minutes, I hear someone knocking on my upstairs front door. It's Hector and his friend who have come to rescue me from my long, deep sleep.

To help me, when the holidays are over, Hector gives me the job of taking Josephine to school.

I just want to forget what the female officer did in front of my eyes, but something had to come and remind me that she could come back again.

Pursuit

I'm in the metro one day, on my way back home with Josephine. Josephine is worried and she talks to me about her day at school.
- You know what, Christine? I no longer like police officers.
- Why?
- Well today, an officer used me for a demonstration and I didn't like what he did to me at all.
- What did he do to you?
- He grabbed me and put me on the ground, then put his gun to my head and said "this is how we proceed when arresting people".

I instinctively start to panic as I listen to Josephine telling me her story, especially after what I had witnessed.
- I see. Tell me everything he said. Did something else happen?
- They are coming back the day after tomorrow for another demonstration! They said it will be a game and that they'll make someone disappear and then re-appear.
- Don't worry. I'll talk to your father and arrange it so that you don't attend school on that day.

When I get home, the news announcer on the radio says:
- In two days, at a province-wide meeting, a decision will be reached concerning a salary raise for teachers.

I wonder if it's not a coincidence that the police will be in every Montreal school on the same day that politicians announce their final decision on the raise.

The worst part of it is that not even one person had complained or even acknowledged that there could be a plot in all this. I don't want to insinuate that it's a threat against the children, but there's something fishy about it. What if it is a threat by the teachers to force the administrators to give them a raise? This could turn into another disaster! So I don't hesitate to call the principal at Josephine's school.
- Hello, is this the principal?
- Yes, what can I do for you?
- Could you explain to me the game of making someone disappear and reappear? What kind of game are the police officers going to play

Pursuit

with the children? And can you tell me if their weapons are loaded around the children? I shouldn't have to remind you that accidents happen fast.
- I haven't specifically asked, but I think that they are always loaded.
- Really? You let people with loaded guns play games around children! I have to tell you that I once saw a child get shot by an officer.
- I'm very sorry to hear that. Let me verify this. I'll look into the situation.

The principal ends up closing the school for the day.
I then call the R.C.M.P. to tell them I'm concerned about the situation. Many other schools close because of my phone call, except for one in Laval.
As suspected at the Laval school, the police holds the students hostage until about 6 p.m.
During negotiations, the R.C.M.P. asks the police to send the female officer with the name of that I had seen next door.
The police agree to send her to the address but they still refuse to release the children. Meanwhile, in the apartment where the R.C.M.P. officer is waiting, he ends up shooting the female police officer to death in self defense.
Unfortunately, the female officer who died is not the one who had killed the child and who was running the army of corrupt officers.
I believe that the child killer had been using a stolen police officer's badge and her soul was the reincarnation of Jeanne of Arc from the year 0.
In corrupt societies, these situations and questions are disturbing, especially when we know that a child killer is running still on the loose.
Fortunately, Josephine and her friends are in a safe place when all these events occur.
After the death of the female police officer, many of the police employees were changed.

Pursuit

As for me, they had me hacked. I'm sure of this because I tested them by crying wolf. That's when I knew, as they came right away.

***

I wonder if someone will sue the criminals who inflicted all these injustices on me. On the other hand, will they all just hide and hope they'll be safe?

But life goes on and I'm still waiting to either become involved or for someone to show me what to do to fix my problems, because up until now, everyone has told me to give up.

Downstairs, a new Chinese family is running the store and the woman wants me to translate the papers she receives from her daughter's school.

Sitting behind the counter, I've just finished explaining to her the meaning of a letter concerning a parents' meeting. A man enters. He looks like the man I'd seen getting out of the train in the scene in the movie, the one who was related to Janice Kennedy Maxwell in the past. I leave at the same time he does, and as I reach my staircase, he stops me to say hello.

Standing there, smiling broadly, he remains paralyzed for many seconds, just looking at me, and then says:

- I wonder if I you'd care to join me for a coffee or something.
- Sure, I'd like to have a coffee with you! Do you want to come upstairs? But if you come upstairs, you have to promise me to be nice and to keep it to conversation only. I'm telling you this in case you think that I'm one of those prostitutes.
- No need to worry. I'm a good guy.
- In that case, come up. But I'm telling you that my apartment isn't very beautiful!
- That doesn't matter. I just want to have a conversation.
- Come in. Don't bother to take your shoes off.

He's still smiling and continues to look at me as he stands in the hallway.

- Well, come sit in the kitchen.

Pursuit

On my ugly table is a cake dome containing an unappetizing cake and a lot of crumbs, which I feel embarrassed about. He's staring at it, so I offer him a piece but he declines.
- So, tell me, do you live around here?
- No, I'm here to visit my adoptive grandparents; I'm adopted and I lived with them for most of my life.
- Okay, but where do you live now?
- Actually, I'm moving to New York to work on a contract. I'm a contractor and have a two-year contract.
- That's interesting. And is there a wife who'll be coming with you?
I put the cups on the table and sit down.
- No, I've been separated for almost a year and I haven't been with a woman since. It's time for me to get involved with someone else.
- Yes, I understand your point of view; I agree that we do become lonely after a while. I haven't been with anyone for about 10 months. I do see this guy Flint, who lives across the street. He tells me all sorts of lies every time he decides he wants to fuck me. He tells me things like that he came to live here just for me, and then once he's had me, he just leaves me alone and doesn't want to see me.
The man laughs and something suspicious comes to my mind.
- I'm sorry, but I have to ask you a question. I've had something on my mind since the minute I saw you.
- Go ahead, ask me.
- Many months ago, a man came to knock on my door. This happened not long after I filed a report with the police department's professional ethics division about a child's murder. The man who came to my door was with an orthodox Jewish guy who was wearing the hat and dreadlocks. I didn't answer the door, as I was frightened. When I looked out the window to see who it was, I saw them standing in the middle of the street, looking at me and the man looked exactly like you. I wonder if it was you.
- No, it wasn't me!
- It's crazy how much that guy I'm telling you about looked like you.

Pursuit

It doesn't matter, but that man I'm telling you about went on and did something about this whole thing because I saw him on the news not long after he came to my door.

He went to China. I saw him on the news getting out of a government truck, then he went inside a house and came out with a handcuffed Chinese woman, the sister of the Chinese guy who ran the store for 2 years, the one involved in the kidnapping of the young girl before she was shot.

I recognized her because she had worked there too. I can't say for sure that it was them or which look-alike kidnapped the girl, because there were two of them, but whoever it was, the man who looked like that man coming out of train was trying to do something about this situation by trying to capture the people involved in this organized crime.

For all I know, the man could be the father of that deceased child, because my daughter is still alive, so I have been told.

How odd would it be if the man I'm looking for is that man and if he's the father of the child I saw get killed. I bore his pain, thinking she was my daughter, for so many years.

- That wasn't me, the person who went to China.
- I should have opened the door that day. You and that man look like a person from an ancestral life, who had an attachment, through having kids or something like that, with my ancestor.
- Yeah, life is sometimes bizarre.
- I'm still trying to find my real parents. I just met a woman who is supposedly my mother.
- Really? I've met many adopted people and it can be difficult to know which one goes where when their age and other information is the same.
- My mother told me that she has an old aunt that lives in New York. She must have old pictures that show my aunt's sister, who is supposedly me, and her husband, since she appears to be the daughter of my aunt's sister's daughter.

Pursuit

- I have to go to New York. If I'm able to, I'll look into this for you. I'm leaving for a 2-year contract but I'll be back this Christmas to visit my grandparents and I'll try to stop by to see you.
- I'll be here if they haven't killed me before then.

He gets up, ready to leave, but keeps talking.

- I'm going to the beach next weekend before leaving. Would you like to come with me?
- No, I'll pass this time, but maybe next time.

Heading towards the door, he stops and wraps his arms around me to give me a friendly hug. Then he goes out the door.

I don't know if he was the person that Charles's father had spoken to me about, but he had something to do with me here. God had put him on my path for something but I'm not ready to say he was the one. His blood and my memories were not there when he was present with me, although he does look like that person. If he is not could he be the person who should be with the person, who is with the person I am looking for?

The corrupt police officers were listening to the two of us talking. I know this because they followed my new friend all the way to New York. I also know it because, in the meantime, a reporter who most have been on to them, followed them.

During their visit, they broadcast the officers on the news, showing them leaving a bank and running down into a New York subway station, dressed in their Montreal police uniforms. I'm suspicious of the images.

From all I know, my great-aunt died around that time.

I have my doubts about the officers' visit to New York because lots of money went missing after their visit. God or an angel came to show me the location of the money, which was dedicated to me.

In New York there were 3 officers: the woman child murderer; her partner, the woman singing a remake of a Celina Gomez song; and a man who I saw at the court house acting as a lawyer and who was present at a store robbery one Christmas eve many years before.

Pursuit

A couple of weeks later, the apartment building next door, which had been owned by a member of my cousin's father's family, got sold, and the new owners are rebuilding it and changing it in to condos.
I suddenly see the male officer who was in New York going into the construction site, dressed in a suit and carrying a briefcase. He's talking as if he he's in charge of some of the operations. It seems kind of suspicious, but I don't stop to dwell on it.
Today I'm doing some home repairs so I take a walk to the Canadian Tire store to get a couple of things. When I get to the store, I see one of the workers from the construction site next door to me talking on the phone. Curious, I walk near him to listen to what he's saying.
- Tell me how much is left in ... account.
He says the name of my deceased aunt from New York.
I suddenly understand why all these bad activities have been happening and why they went to New York. We were robbed by members of an organized crime group.
I'm not sure how much was taken or why they were after me, but I got my answer later that year, on a T.V. report about donations. In the news report, they said that my aunt had donated 2.5 million dollars to the foundation in the name of the police killer's partner. That is when I understood that we were victims of a big robbery.
The money inheritance, which was place by Charles father with his half sister's for me, was stolen, by the women murderer who used my identity for the transfer.
Many years later, the head office in England, by order of the embassy, receives the authorization to pay me an amount for the loss and for damages suffered but the corrupt system is still trying to stop and take the funds intended for me.
Even if many other things have occurred in my life, my story ends here for now, but if my story becomes a movie, this is how I want it to end.
After Nicky's father, the one who could be the father of the deceased girl I saw get murdered, catches the Chinese woman, he gets

Pursuit

information about the identity and whereabouts of the rapist and murderer and puts them in prison.

He comes to my house to give me my share of the insurance money. As he stands at my door, I open an envelope with the picture of our ancestors together, so we can bring back to life those asking me to.

The End

If the insurance company pays me back, I'll do what I have to do to provide my share for humanity and I'll be able to spend safe time with my children, who I haven't seen in more than 10 years. I will appreciate that, even if they can't give me back all the precious time I missed when they were growing up, which organized criminals have taken away from me. Unfortunately, in real life, things don't always happen justly. I've met many jealous people in my life who want me to be like them, but I will keep ignoring the voices of those malevolent people and will keep the faith that justice still exists in this world.

….The End….

www.ingramcontent.com/pod-product-compliance
Lightning Source LLC
Chambersburg PA
CBHW071652090426
42738CB00009B/1496